Joseph Conrad

Twayne's English Authors Series

Kinley E. Roby, Editor

Northeastern University

TEAS 333

JOSEPH CONRAD
(1857–1924)
Photograph of a painting
by David Wainapel

Joseph Conrad

By Adam Gillon

State University of New York at New Paltz
University of Haifa, Israel

Twayne Publishers • Boston

Joseph Conrad

Adam Gillon

Copyright © 1982
Twayne Publishers
A Division of G. K. Hall & Company
70 Lincoln Street
Boston, Massachusetts 02111

Book production by Marne B. Sultz

Book design by Barbara Anderson

Printed on permanent/durable acid-free
paper and bound in the United States of
America.

**Library of Congress Cataloging in
Publication Data**

Gillon, Adam, 1921–
   Joseph Conrad.

   (Twayne's English authors series : TEAS
333)
   Bibliography: pp. 191–202
   Includes index.
   1. Conrad, Joseph, 1857–1924
—Criticism and interpretation.
I. Title. II. Series.
PR6005.04Z7263 823'.912 81-13301
ISBN 0-8057-6820-3   AACR2

Contents

About the Author

A native of Poland, Dr. Adam Gillon is professor Emeritus of English and Comparative Literature at the State University of New York at New Paltz, and professor of English Literature at the University of Haifa, Israel. He received the M.A. degree from the Hebrew University of Jerusalem and the Ph.D. degree from Columbia University. He taught at the University of Kansas and was Head of the English Department at Acadia University in Canada.

He is the author of *The Eternal Solitary: A Study of Joseph Conrad*; *Selected Poems and Translations*; *Cup of Fury*, a novel; *Introduction to Modern Polish Literature* (with L. Krzyżanowski); *Contemporary Israeli Literature*; *The Dancing Socrates and Other Poems of Julian Tuwim*; *Poems of the Ghetto: A Testament of Lost Men*; *In the Manner of Haiku: Seven Aspects of Man*; *Daily New and Old: Poems in the Manner of Haiku*; *Strange Mutations: In the Manner of Haiku*; *Summer Morn . . . Winter Weather: Poems 'Twixt Haiku and Senryu*; *Joseph Conrad: Commemorative Essays* (co-editor with L. Krzyżanowski); *Conrad and Shakespeare and Other Essays*; *The Withered Leaf: A Medley of Haiku and Senryu*.

Dr. Gillon has written numerous articles, reviews, short stories, and several plays. He received the 1967 Alfred Jurzykowski Foundation Award for his translations of Polish literature and awards from the Joseph Fels Foundation, the New York State University Research Foundation, Fulbright, the British Council, and the Canada Council. He has read papers at several national and international conferences (MLA, ICLA) and has lectured at a number of major universities.

He is president of the Joseph Conrad Society of America and the editor of its newsletter, *Joseph Conrad Today*.

Preface

The March 1925 issue of the American journal the *Mentor* featured a major article entitled "Joseph Conrad. Master Seaman and Master Writer," preceded by a full-page ad from Doubleday, Page & Co., which began thus: " 'I'm not a literary man,' he said—yet at an auction before his death, his original manuscripts sold for $110,998. Such was the judgment of contemporaries of Joseph Conrad being counted among the immortals. The leading writers of the world themselves had united in acclaiming him 'the greatest master of fiction.' " This ad is perhaps one of the best examples of the many ironies of Conrad's life. Until 1913, when his *Chance* appeared, Conrad had known little if any financial success or popularity though some great minds of his age at once perceived his talent. When success did come finally, it was *after* he had done his greatest work. Ironically, then, he became popular on the basis of his inferior writings, and his reputation sank quickly after his death in 1924.

Most of the literary critics in the United States hardly read Conrad in the late 1940s, yet, strangely enough, in his native Poland, where some of his compatriots had once branded him as a "traitor," Conrad enjoyed a certain reputation even in the darkest years of Nazi occupation. Two decades later, however, Conrad's star began to rise. In 1964, for example, *Modern Fiction Studies* devoted an issue to Conrad, listing some ninety items about *Heart of Darkness* alone. And today we are witnessing a veritable explosion of critical studies, new editions, film adaptations, and sundry activities, learned and not so learned, dedicated to the life and works of this amazing son of a Polish patriot. The truly global publication of his novels and stories suggests a measure of universality and a particularly contemporary appeal to our generation.

A thriving Conrad industry has come into being. In the United States we have a Joseph Conrad Society with subscribers to its quarterly newsletter *Joseph Conrad Today* hailing from twenty-six countries. Similar societies have been founded in England, France, Italy, and Poland, each with its own newsletter or journal. A major international journal "devoted to all aspects, periods and phases of the life and work of Joseph Conrad," *Conradiana,* is published three times a year at the Texas Tech University, edited by Leon D. Higdon. Recent books on Conrad include two major new biographies, ten concordances to novels (*Heart of Darkness, Almayer's Folly, Lord Jim, The Secret Agent, Victory, The Shadow-Line* and *Youth, The Nigger of the "Narcissus," The Arrow of Gold,* and *A Set of Six,*[2] two new bibliographies, a definitive edition of his work (in progress)[3] and a multi-volume collection of his letters (also in progress) to be edited by F. R. Karl. So many books and articles about Conrad have appeared during the last decade that one is tempted to apply to this novelist the dictum used by Goethe about the Bard of Avon: "Shakespeare *und kein Ende.*" Indeed, there is no end in sight to the proliferation of critical exegesis and the publication of Conrad's works. Moreover, national and international meetings dealing exclusively with discussions of Conrad's fiction have been held regularly since 1974. Conrad is being taught at universities, colleges, and high schools throughout the world. Film adaptations of his stories and novels are beginning to appear with increased frequency, as are stage adaptations. There is little doubt, thus, that Conrad has arrived.

This study attempts to explain why Conrad has arrived and what makes him our contemporary. It is intended for the general public rather than for the specialist who has no trouble navigating the high seas of critical literature raging about us. I have tried to examine Conrad's entire output, proceeding in chronological manner but departing therefrom when thematic treatment was deemed necessary. In my introductions to each work I have emphasized some of these themes, e.g., betrayal and fidelity, crime and punishment, existential choice, isolation, human solidarity, and the destructive dream. My assessment of Conrad's achievement as a novelist is related, whenever possible, to his cosmopolitanism, his Polish heritage, and his affinities with English, Polish, Russian, French, and German writers.

I have stressed the psychological and intellectual dilemmas of the Conradian protagonist, while also delving into the technical aspects of Conrad's art, suggesting, among other things, its painterly qualities. The major thrust of my appraisal has been an attempt to reveal the nature of his contemporaneity and the reasons he is considered to be a great novelist.

Note

Unless otherwise indicated, the page numbers referring to the works of Joseph Conrad are from *Complete Works* (Garden City, N.Y.: Doubleday, Page, 1924).

All italics are mine unless otherwise indicated.

Adam Gillon

State University of New York at New Paltz
and *University of Haifa, Israel*

Acknowledgments

This book was completed with the help of a research grant from the Research Foundation of the State University of New York.

The author gratefully acknowledges use of copyrighted material from the following publishers and publications: J. M. Dent & Sons, Ltd. (London), *Joseph Conrad, Edition of the Complete Works*; G. Jean-Aubry, *Joseph Conrad: Life and Letters* (published in the United States by Doubleday & Co.).

Short sections of this book appeared in a somewhat different version in articles published during the period 1968–1979 in the *Slavic and East European Journal, Conradiana,* and the *Polish Review.*

To Professor Kinley E. Roby my special thanks are due for his analytical and conscientious editorial guidance.

To Bill Riley for his thorough copyediting.

Chronology

1857   Józef Teodor Konrad Korzeniowski born December 3 in Berdichev (or vicinity) to Apollo Nałęcz Korzeniowski and Evelina (Ewa) Bobrowska.

1862   May 8, Apollo Korzeniowski exiled to Vologda, Russia, accompanied by his wife and son.

1865   June 6, Conrad's mother dies. Conrad in care of maternal uncle, Tadeusz Bobrowski.

1869   Apollo Korzeniowski and son return to Cracow in February. Apollo dies on May 23. Conrad attends (sporadically) school in Cracow.

1873   In May leaves for a three-month-long stay in Switzerland and northern Italy. First view of the sea.

1874   On October 14 leaves Cracow for Marseilles.

1875   Apprentice on the *Mont-Blanc,* bound for Martinique.

1876–1877   From January to July in Marseilles; from July to February 1877 on schooner *Saint-Antoine* to West Indies.

1877   Acquires (with three other men) the *tartane,* the *Tremolino* which carries arms illegally to the supporters of Don Carlos, the Spanish pretender.

1878–1879   In February attempts suicide by shooting himself through the chest. On April 24 leaves Marseilles on British steamer *Mavis.* On June 18 sets foot in England at Lowestoft. Serves as ordinary seaman on coaster *The Skimmer of the Sea.*

1883   Passes mate's examination on July 4. Meets uncle Bobrowski at Marienbad. Mate on the sailing ship *Riversdale.*

1884   Second mate on the *Narcissus,* bound from Bombay to Dunkirk.

1885–1886	Second mate on the *Tilkhurst*; August 19, receives British certificate of naturalization. November 11, passes examination, receives his "Certificate of Competency as Master"; first story, "The Black Mate," submitted to *Tit-Bits*.
1887	First mate on *Highland Forest*. Hurt by a falling spar, hospitalized in Singapore (experience recalled in *Lord Jim*). Second mate on steamship *Vidar* (Singapore –Borneo).
1888	On *Melita* (bound for Bangkok), then his first command on the barque the *Otago* (Bangkok–Sydney–Mauritius–Port Adelaide). Experiences described in *The Shadow-Line, Victory*, "The Secret Sharer," "A Smile of Fortune," and other works.
1889	Summer in London; begins writing *Almayer's Folly*.
1890	First trip to Poland since he left in 1874. In May he leaves for the Congo. Second in command, then in command of S. S. *Roi de Belges*.
1891–1893	First mate on *Torrens*. English passenger (Jacques) reads the first nine chapters of *Almayer's Folly*, offers encouragement; meets John Galsworthy aboard the ship. Visits uncle Bobrowski in Poland.
1893–1894	Second mate on *Adowa* (London–Rouen–London). Ends his career as seaman on January 14, 1894. Uncle Bobrowski dies on January 29, 1894. In April Conrad sends *Almayer's Folly* to T. Fisher Unwin.
1894–1895	Writes *An Outcast of the Islands*.
1896	March 24, marries Jessie George.
1897	Completes *The Nigger of the "Narcissus"*; friendship with R. B. Cunninghame Graham.
1898	Son Alfred Borys born January 14. In October moves to Pent Farm, Kent.
1899	In February completes *Heart of Darkness*.

1900	Finishes *Lord Jim*.
1904	*Nostromo*. Writes *The Mirror of the Sea*. Wife ill, practically an invalid.
1905	Spends four months in Europe.
1906	Spends two months in France. Second son John Alexander born August 2.
1907	Children ill in France. Returns to Pent Farm in August. *The Secret Agent*.
1908	*A Set of Six*.
1910	In June moves to Capel House, Kent. Seriously ill.
1911	*Under Western Eyes*.
1912	*'Twixt Land and Sea, Tales*.
1913–1914	*Chance*. Writes *Victory*. Leaves for Poland in July 1914; meets Stefan Żeromski in Zakopane; caught by the war in August; escapes and returns to Capel House November 3.
1915	*Victory. Within the Tides*.
1916	Borys fights on the French front.
1917	*The Shadow-Line*. Writes prefaces for a new collected edition of his works.
1918	Borys, gassed and wounded, is hospitalized in Le Havre.
1919	*The Arrow of Gold*. Moves to Oswalds, Bishopbourne, near Canterbury, where he spends the last years of his life.
1920	*The Rescue*.
1921	Visits Corsica. *Notes on Life and Letters*.
1923	Visits New York (April–June). Reading from his *Victory* at home of Mrs. Arthur Curtiss James, May 10. *The Secret Agent, Drama in Four Acts* (adaptation of the novel). *The Rover. Laughing Anne,* a play (adaptation of "Because of the Dollars").

1924   Jacob Epstein does Conrad's bust. In May Conrad declines knighthood. Health deteriorates and he is bedridden. His wife is also ill. Both sons and Richard Curle are with them. Dies of heart attack August 3. Buried in Canterbury.

1925   *Suspense* (incomplete). *Tales of Hearsay.*

1926   *Last Essays.*

1928   *The Sisters* (written in 1896; incomplete.)

1936   Jessie Conrad dies December 6. Buried near her husband at Canterbury.

1978   Alfred Borys Conrad, the elder son of Conrad, dies on November 13.

Chapter One

Beyond the Life of Ships[1]

The Polish Heritage

Most portraits and photographs of Joseph Conrad, which the average reader finds in editions of his books or anthologies, present him as a grizzled old man, his eyelids drooping, his gaze ponderous, and his noble face encased in a brown beard. His massive figure is immaculately draped in a suit of Victorian style.

It is the familiar image of Conrad the great novelist, Conrad the thinker and artist, and also Conrad the aged seaman, whose face seems deeply lined with memories of his adventurous past, a suffering older man. It is a sad and wise face, and many of his readers must have wondered what he looked like as a boy. How did he develop into that paradoxical figure of a Pole, turned seaman, turned master of English prose? What were the real causes of his expatriation from Poland? Why did he become a sailor? And, finally, what made him give up his professional connection with the sea and embark on a far more hazardous and painful voyage—into the realm of English literature? How can one explain his pessimism, his indifference to Christianity, although he was brought up as a Roman Catholic? How to account for his prejudices, his dislike of Dostoevsky, his political conservatism, and the fact that he had such a profound compassion for the common man?

Conrad's is a most personal art, woven out of his intimate memories and transmuted by his artistic conscience and labor into the final product. Yet the extraordinary care Conrad took to stand aside from his fictional material, to place the "objective" narrator between himself as a novelist and the core of the story to be told, indicated his ardent desire to escape from his true self, or perhaps to disguise it beyond recognition in the folds of his fictional mantle. In this respect, his reserve was, proverbially, more British than any Englishman's could have been. "It

1

may be my sea training acting upon a natural disposition," Conrad wrote, "but the fact is that I have a positive horror of losing even for one moving moment that full possession of myself which is the first condition of good service."[2]

That full possession of himself is obviously something Conrad learned in his years of service with the merchant marine, and he had carried his notion of good service from his earlier into his later life. But this was not the way he was as a child, or as an adolescent, or even as a young man who landed in Marseilles in 1874. And Conrad himself does not give us too many clues about the early phase of his life, although he does offer a few significant ones. His reticence to speak and write of his childhood and youth, both of which had been marked by a sense of loss and anguish, later took the form of an unconcealed reluctance (if not downright refusal) to write about his early life in Poland in a straightforward manner.

Conrad's Polish heritage looms large in most of his important works, but his specific experiences as a child or adolescent do not appear directly in his fiction. Only two of his works clearly reveal the Polish theme: the largely autobiographical *A Personal Record,* and the short story "Prince Roman." Another short story, "Amy Foster," is set on the shores of the Eastbay in England, and its hero, the Carpathian peasant Yanko Goorall, owes his existence to Conrad's encounter with an anonymous Polish sailor in "The Sailor's Home" in Saigon. Finally, the protagonist of "Il Conde" is based on Conrad's acquaintance with Count Joseph Szembek, whom the Conrads met in Italy, but this is not really a *Polish* story.

This is not to say that Conrad denied his national origin; on the contrary, he retained a good knowledge of the Polish language, and raised his voice in the defense of Poland in such essays as "Note on the Polish Problem" (1916) and "The Crime of Partition" (1919), to mention but two. He went to Poland in 1890 and again with his family in 1914, when he was caught in Cracow by the outbreak of World War I. He wrote a long account of his last visit, "Poland Revisited," and from that time on maintained closer ties with the country. Before his death he even contemplated moving to Poland. Still, he failed to produce a single novel devoted to his native land. Unlike other Polish writers living abroad, such as the great Romantics Adam Mickiewicz and Juliusz Słowacki (both favorites of Conrad), he never took Poland as the central theme of his work; in fact, he shunned it.

Perhaps a partial explanation of his phenomenon can be found in Conrad's early years, which were marked by sadness and loneliness. His life in Poland had given his character a distinct cast which he could never shake, and the tragedy of that country had become his personal tragedy as well. He grew up in the atmosphere of national defeat and frustration that followed the ill-omened Polish insurrection of 1863. Tsarist Russia ruled Poland with an iron hand, suppressing any manifestation of nationalism; even the teaching of the Polish language was illegal. The aristocracy was small but haughty and ever-ready to fight the three powers which had partitioned the land: Russia, Austria, and Prussia; the bulk of the population were the peasants, for the most part illiterate and in the eastern provinces largely Ukrainian stock. There was no middle class in the present sense of the word, although there were small merchants and a few industrial enterprises. The nobles were wrapped up in their own political squabbles, their elaborate etiquette, and largely out of touch with the sociological or political realities of their country or the world. Their chivalry and romantic notions of grandeur were of no avail against the savage retributions of the occupying powers.

Conrad's parents came from families that sacrificed property, liberty, and life in the futile struggle for independence. And the failure of Conrad's father as a rebel, the sorry fate that befell his mother, were symbolic of Poland's lot. Conrad himself recalled the situation of the Polish nation in a letter to Joseph Spirydion Kliszczewski, a fellow Pole who settled in England: "We have passed through the gates where *lasciate ogni speranza* is written in letters of blood and fire, and nothing remains for us but the darkness of oblivion. . . ."[3] This letter, dated October 13, 1885, is an illustration of the profound effect his Polish heritage had upon him. Indeed, no childhood such as his could ever be forgotten, but one can understand his reluctance to dwell upon it.

He was born on December 3, 1857, in Berdichev (or its vicinity), in the Polish Ukraine. and his full name was Józef Teodor Konrad Nałęcz Korzeniowski. His father, Apollo Korzeniowski, was a romantic dreamer of an unsteady disposition and an amateur poet and dramatist. Having lost his own inheritance through lack of business acumen, he became a manager of other people's estates—and failed in this venture as well. His marriage to Evelina (Ewa) Bobrowska came only after eight years of waiting, since the bride's father opposed the union, and only after his death did the mother give in to her daughter's pleas.

From his father Conrad received his literary talent and his artistic imagination; and from his mother, a certain spiritual uneasiness and a tendency to constant worry, and from both an exalted view of fidelity to a cause. Apollo Korzeniowski's poetry was not particularly distinguished; its main appeal lay in a sincere lyricism and a noble concept of love for fatherland. It was poetry full of pessimism, disappointment, and melancholy. Its themes were mainly patriotic, social, and religious, and the recurrent idea (borrowed from the great poet Zygmunt Krasiński) was that Poland's martyrdom constituted a sacrifice on behalf of all enslaved peoples; numerous compositions were devoted to social problems, especially to the vices of the nobility.

Apollo's own martyrdom made an indelible impression on young Conrad; he was to remember it all his life, often imparting the mood of resignation and despair to his fictional heroes. When Conrad was three his father went to Warsaw to pursue a literary career. There he joined a radical patriotic group which was working for another uprising. Ironically, he was arrested and sent to exile on October 9, 1861, some two years before the uprising finally did break out in 1863, and before he had a chance of doing anything. The investigation failed to break his spirit and Apollo maintained his silence. He continued writing poetry in his prison cell. Then he was sentenced to exile in distant provinces; in his case it proved to be the Vologda region in northern Russia.

His wife and son went with him, too. The journey and the hardships of exile broke the frail health of Evelina, who died in 1865. Thus, at the age of seven Conrad was left with a gloomy and tubercular father. After his wife's death Apollo was permitted to go to southern Russia. There young Conrad saw the Black Sea—his first acquaintance with the element that was to be his home for nearly two decades. When Korzeniowski was at length allowed to go home, he was a dying man. His public funeral in 1869 in Cracow was followed by the granting of the freedom of the city to his son three years later.

The years spent at the side of his dying father, without friends of his own age, deprived of normal children's pursuits, deeply affected young Conrad. He could not help noticing, and indeed absorbing, " . . . that appalling feeling of inexorable fate, tangible, palpable, a figure of dread, murmuring with iron lips the final words: Ruin—and Extinction."[4] It was a mature artist who wrote these words in 1915. Twenty years earlier, he said the same thing in his first Author's Note to *Almayer's Folly*. The mood of hopelessness and resignation became a pervasive quality of his work.

Apollo Korzeniowski feared that the harsh realities of the exile might impair his son's emotional life and freeze his young heart. But Conrad's heart was not withered. Endowed with a rich imagination young Conrad reacted to the oppressive atmosphere of his household and later to the conditions of exile by a silent withdrawal into himself and into the imaginary world of fictional heroes. He was a solitary, nostalgic child, and in his moods of total immersion in his own imaginative life he resembled Apollo Korzeniowski.

It was a fortunate thing that he was a reading boy, and a creative reader at that: "I don't know what would have become of me if I had not been a reading boy. . . . I suppose that in a futile, childish way I would have gone crazy. But I was a reading boy . . . I read! What did I not read!"[5]

There is no doubt that both Conrad's early reading fare and his father's literary work were responsible for his dream of the sea. He read the sea stories of Marryat and James Fenimore Cooper, Sir Leopold McClintock's *The Voyage of the "Fox" in the Arctic Seas* (A Narrative of the Discovery of the Fate of Sir John Franklin and His Companions), and, while his father lay desperately ill, he read about three Scottish explorers in Africa, James Bruce, Mungo Park, and David Livingstone. Of the French authors, Louis Ambroise Garneray, artist and sailor, was his favorite; Conrad read his *Récits, Aventures et Combats*. When he was only eight he read to his father the proofs of his translation of Victor Hugo's *Travailleurs de la Mer* [Toilers of the Sea] and Alfred de Vigny's *Chatterton*. He also perused his father's translations of Shakespeare's *The Two Gentlemen of Verona, Much Ado About Nothing, As You Like It, A Comedy of Errors,* and *Othello*.

Shakespeare must have exercised an abiding influence upon Conrad, for many of his stories and novels have Shakespearean figures: men like Hamlet, destroyed by their sensibility and inability to act, or like

Macbeth, driven to evil and corruption by ambition, to cite but two examples. The vehemence of the Renaissance era, the sheer vitality of Shakespearean tragedy, and the pessimism of his great tragedies along with their quality of compassion must have fascinated young Conrad. One recalls that Lord Jim carried a tattered edition of Shakespeare on his journeys; and one ought to remember that when Conrad himself set out on his adventurous course he took, along with family photographs and a number of Polish books, a well-thumbed copy of Adam Mickiewicz's *Pan Tadeusz*.[6]

Conrad also read Walter Scott, Byron, Thackeray, and Trollope. He singled out Dickens's *Bleak House* as

. . . a work of the master for which I have such an admiration, or rather such an intense and unreasoning affection, dating from the days of my childhood, that its very weaknesses are more precious to me than the strength of other men's work. I have read it innumerable times, *both in Polish and in English*; I have read it only the other day. . . .[7]

Apollo Korzeniowski translated Dickens's *Hard Times,* whose antiutilitarian ideas must have appealed to the romantic exile.

Conrad devoured history, voyages, and novels of adventure in Polish and French. He knew *Gil Blas* and was particularly fond of *Don Quixote,* a fact noted by his collaborator Ford Madox Ford (Hueffer), who also adds that Conrad was very partial to his own sea Don Quixote, Lingard.

At the age of eleven Conrad entered St. Anne High School in Cracow, which he attended rather sporadically. The education he received placed great emphasis on the classics and German, and he had acquired a fair knowledge of French from a governess at home, which he further improved during his stay in France.

"My main purpose," wrote his father, Apollo, before his death, "is to bring up little Konrad not as a democrat, aristocrat, demagogue, republican, monarchist or some servant or lackey of any one of these parties—but only as a Pole."[8]

Young Conrad had a tutor from 1870 to 1874, a medical student at the University of Cracow, Jan Marek Pulman. After his father's death Conrad was brought up by his maternal uncle, Tadeusz (Thaddeus) Bobrowski, who acted as his legal guardian and also served as his mentor until his death. Uncle Tadeusz was a most practical man, a great critic of the Korzeniowski family, a firm believer in a nonviolent adjustment under the Russian rule without sacrificing his Polish identity.

Even as a boy of eleven Conrad betrayed his incipient literary talent. Quite frail in health, he was not an athletic child, but was capable of great merriment. During his holidays with friends and family in Lwów little Conrad composed comedies and produced amateur plays. He displayed an excellent literary background by his ability to quote from the works of Adam Mickiewicz. Thus it is quite obvious that Conrad's childhood and youth had provided him with some sort of initiation into the realm of literature.

It is small wonder that he found his high-school studies dull except for geography, and even this discipline was not taught properly: "And their geography was very much like themselves, a bloodless thing with a dry skin covering a repulsive armature of uninteresting bones."[9]

It is hard to say what exactly triggered Conrad's determination to go to sea. It was, undoubtedly, a desire, not unusual for a boy of his age, to travel and have adventures; but for him it was more than that. In a sense, it was an escape from his bleak past, from a hopeless future as a son of a political exile.

The pangs of unrequited teen-age love in September 1873 could have been another contributing factor to Conrad's wish "to get away from it all." Conrad biographer Jocelyn Baines asserts that the writer's allusions to his childhood love life are contradictory. Actually there appear to have been two girls for whom he had formed a romantic attachment: the biographers are divided as to the identity of the girls. Janina (or Kamila) Taube and Tekla Syroczyńska are Baines's choice, and he also claims that Janina Taube served as a model for Antonia of *Nostromo*. But the Polish writer Róża Jabłkowska suggests another person: Ophelia Buszczyńska, whom she also believes to be the original Antonia. Frederick R. Karl, the most recent of Conrad's biographers, does not shed any new light on the matter by suggesting that the novelist's romantic memories could apply to either Janina or Tekla and that in any case there was no proof of Conrad's early Byronic romances.

Whoever the girls were, one of them must have humiliated Conrad severely. In a passage deleted from *The Arrow of Gold* Conrad recalls the incident, whose echoes can be heard in many an anguished cry of his unfortunate lovers.[10]

Conrad's tutor Pulman tried to do his best to dissuade the boy from his decision to go to sea, and, failing to do so, called him "an incorrigible, hopeless Don Quixote." This happened when Conrad was fifteen, and he confessed to having felt flattered "at the name of the immortal knight turning up in connection with [my] own folly, as some people would call it to [my] face."[11]

Actually, aside from the romantic aspects of Conrad's wish to leave the country, there was a very important albeit prosaic problem of his choice of citizenship. The family decided that the boy should become an Austrian citizen. Uncle Tadeusz paid 20 rubles to a lawyer to get the proper papers for the boy, but the Austrian authorities refused to grant citizenship to a young man "with a political past," hence Uncle Bobrowski paid a further amount of 80 guldens to the lawyer "who successfully labored on [your] naturalization in Austria."[12] This was one more reason that made Conrad's earnest guardian relent in his two-year-long resistance to his nephew's demands that he be allowed to join the merchant marine. When one thinks of the succession of "homes" Conrad had by the time he was fifteen, one should not be surprised at his desire to go to sea. His residences were in Debreczynka, Żytomierz, Warsaw, Vologda, Czernichów, Kazimierówka, Lwów, and finally Cracow.

Yet his immediate family and friends were shocked at his "quixotic" dreams, and this precipitated a conflict with his community and, what proved even more momentous for the shaping of his character, a conflict within himself. Grandmother Bobrowska, called "a woman of iron," whose opinion was highly respected in family councils, and his father's friends and his uncle's friends—all contended that young Conrad was too young and inexperienced, that his health was delicate, that he lacked initiative, and could not be permitted to embark on a life among strangers. Besides, there was no Poland and no Polish sea; nor could he serve in the Austrian or Russian navy. And, finally, Conrad's relatives voiced their indignation that his seafaring plans could not be reconciled with his birth and the tradition of Polish landowner class into which he was born. Nor could it be reconciled with the ideals of Polish patriotism. After all, wasn't it his father's chief ambition to make of him a good Pole?

Young Conrad, however, defied everybody, for he could not follow his dreams in the city of Cracow. Like the knight of La Mancha, he could not be a good citizen of his country. The charges of treason and desertion leveled against him hurt Conrad so deeply that he was to remember them thirty-five years later.[13]

The magnitude of this commotion over Conrad's desire to leave the country may be partly responsible for his attitude toward seamanship. His uncle was against his going to sea, but when he submitted to Conrad's wish, he urged him to attain proficiency and excellence in his chosen field. Thus, when Conrad left Poland he had to prove to himself as well as to Uncle Tadeusz that he could indeed master his profession. Similarly, after he abandoned his career as a sailor he once more had to justify himself by proving successful in his second adventure—again in response to a mysterious impulse—to become an English writer, and again taking "a jump out of his racial surroundings and associations."[14]

What he did not know at that time was that "a sailor is not an adventurer" (as he later observed in *Chance*). But the intimation of this truth was long in coming. Meanwhile, Uncle Tadeusz financed the venture, the trip to Marseilles, and undertook to send the young man the sum of 600 rubles (or 1,200 francs) annually. He also gave him several letters of introduction to his French friends. Following the old Polish emigrant route to France, through Vienna, Geneva, and Lyon, Conrad left Cracow for Marseilles on October 26, 1874. He would be seventeen only six weeks later, but he was not merely a thoughtless youth in search of adventure. The heritage of an unhappy land, the personal loss and tragedy weighed heavily upon his spirit. He had by now acquired a somewhat melancholy disposition which would deepen with years. His elaborate manners and the air of aloofness protected him from strangers and enhanced his essential state of loneliness. Still, there was enough in him of the naive and romantic to yearn for the pure spirit of adventure, so beautifully expressed in his story "Youth." The romantic feeling of reality, as he put it, was in him an inborn faculty, but it was largely the romance of youth.

His years of maritime service turned the exaltation and enthusiasm of young Conrad into a somber vision of the sea and of man's lot upon this earth. It was a long, arduous, often perilous voyage that eventually transformed the young exile from Poland into a writer, and its first stage was set in Marseilles.

Worthy of the Service

Conrad arrived in Marseilles with letters from Uncle Tadeusz to the wealthy Delestang family of shipowners, and to Babtysta Solary and Victor Chodźko. The former introduced the young man to a group of royalist sympathizers; Solary had been a sailor in his youth and now lived in Marseilles; he knew many families connected with the sea, and young Conrad entered into the world of salons as well as that of the waterfront. He rubbed shoulders with harbor pilots and later began to ship out of Marseilles to the West Indies and to Central and South America. While the initial period of his stay in the French port was full of excitement for young Conrad, it also led to his involvement (without any earnest political interest) in the hopeless cause of Carlism and an unfortunate love affair with a girl who was described by the novelist as the Doña Rita of *The Arrow of Gold.*

Some years before his death, Conrad himself commented on the nature of the Carlist enterprise in a letter to a critic, and labeled it "a very straightforward adventure conducted with inconceivable stupidity and *a foredoomed failure* from the first."[15] When Conrad joined the band of gunrunners, however, he gave no thought whatever to the ridiculous aspects of the cause of Don Carlos, the mediocre pretender to the Spanish throne whom the Delestangs supported. Superficially, it might appear as though Conrad was following the age-old Polish tradition of fighting for lost causes—a tradition richly reflected in Polish literature, which abounds in heroes sacrificing their lives chivalrously for a cause doomed to failure. Yet the truth of the matter is that young Conrad was totally indifferent to the squabbles for the throne of Spain although he was ready to risk his life and spend his money (to be accurate, also Uncle Tadeusz's funds) in what appealed to him as a dangerous and romantic enterprise. The chief virtue, if not the only one, lay in the deliberate risk the gunrunners were taking; otherwise, the whole affair was rather dull, and it ended in disaster and a profound shock to the young man.

Conrad captured the mood of those days in *The Arrow of Gold* and also in *The Mirror of the Sea.* He described the relationship with Dominic Cervoni, the skipper of the tartan *Tremolino,* bought by Conrad and three of his friends. Braving high seas and the danger of detection by

Spanish coastguard cutters, the four men brought supplies and guns to the remaining supporters of Don Carlos in northern Spain. On their third trip they were driven ashore. Conrad's description of this episode in *The Arrow of Gold* is a good illustration of the sad experience he was to undergo many a time—the discovery of the great chasm between dream and reality.

The little vessel, broken and gone like the only toy of a lonely child, the sea itself, which had swallowed it, throwing me on shore after a shipwreck that *instead of a fair fight left in me the memory of a suicide.* It took away all there was in me of independent life. . . . Even Dominic failed me, *his moral entity destroyed*. . . . I found myself weary, heartsore, my brain still dazed and with awe in my heart entering Marseilles by way of the railway station, *after many adventures, one more disagreeable than another,* involving *privations, great exertions, a lot of difficulties* with all sorts of people who looked upon me evidently more as *a discreditable vagabond* deserving the attention of gendarmes that a respectable (*if crazy*) young gentleman. . . . I must confess that I slunk out of the railway station shunning its many lights as if, invariably, *failure made an outcast of a man.* [16]

These experiences were hardly the attributes of a great romantic adventure such as young Conrad had in mind when he had set out for Marseilles.

And this wasn't all. The second momentous adventure of this phase in his life was the affair with the mysterious Doña Rita, which came on the heels of the gun-running exploit. This affair Conrad recalled vividly at the age of sixty and in semifictional form, without clearly revealing the identity of the girl, and bequeathing a knotty issue upon his future biographers. Jean-Aubry made no attempt to find out who Doña Rita was, simply assuming the whole story was fully autobiographical, and, apparently, Conrad never bothered to tell Aubry this wasn't so.

The story is fairly simple. Monsieur George is the young Conrad who comes back to Marseilles after the loss of the *Tremolino.* He has been unsuccessfully courting Rita but now is finally accepted and the two go off to a secluded village in the Maritime Alps for an idyllic and totally isolated spell of happiness. This idyll lasts briefly, probably during the last two weeks of 1877 and the beginning months of 1878. Conrad (or

Monsieur George) goes to Marseilles to get some money. There a royalist friend reports to him that a Captain J. M. K. Blunt has been spreading rumors about Rita's having fallen "into the hands of an unscrupulous young adventurer whom she was keeping,"[17] whereupon Monsieur George challenges Blunt, and the two men meet in a duel late in February 1878. The former wounds Blunt in the right hand. Blunt fires with his left, wounding his adversary in the left side of his breast bone.

The real story is a bit more prosaic. Uncle Tadeusz is informed of his nephew's gunshot wound and comes all the way from the Ukraine to his bedside, only to find the wound almost healed; he pays the young man's debts, scolds him for his folly, and goes back to the Ukraine with a stern warning to Conrad to stay within his income of 2,400 francs a year. What makes this account so interesting is the fact that, as Jocelyn Baines contends, Conrad's duel never took place, but that Conrad attempted suicide, shooting himself after having gambled away the rest of his money in Monte Carlo. Baines bases his thesis on a long-lost letter from Tadeusz Bobrowski to a friend of Conrad's father, Stefan Buszczyński. The letter relates how Conrad tried to kill himself with a revolver, and how Bobrowski has told everyone that his nephew was wounded in a duel.

Indeed, there are several reasons that could have prompted young Conrad to attempt suicide (and later to become preoccupied with the theme of suicide or self-destruction in his novels and stories): the loss of the money lent to Conrad by his German friend, Richard Fecht, and the *Tremolino* investment; despondence after the *Tremolino* disaster; the unhappy ending of the love with "Rita"; possibly, also, the fact that when he reached the age of twenty-one he would no longer be allowed to serve in the French merchant marine (since the French law forbade the enlistment of foreigners who might be called to military service by their native governments).

When one studies Conrad's heroes who take their own lives, one is struck by the psychological similarity between their motivations and those that impelled Conrad to kill himself, the most interesting being loss of social position or honor, failure in a romantic exploit, a pessimistic view of life in general, the feeling of being an outcast, social or spiritual, and, finally, disappointment in love. Little wonder, then, that in recalling the *Tremolino* affair Conrad was left with "the memory of suicide."[18]

Whatever the cause of the wound Conrad sustained in Marseilles, this was an important episode in his life. In her book *The Thunder and the Sunshine* (1958) Jerry Allen identified "Rita" as Paula de Somoggy (or Somogyi), who, according to her, was not a Basque, as Conrad described her in *The Mirror of the Sea,* but a Hungarian peasant girl who was raised in her native hills by her uncle, a parish priest. When she was eighteen she was "discovered" by Don Carlos, who fell in love with her and took her to Paris. There she was presented as a favorite of "the King" under the assumed name of Baroness Paula de Somoggy. From Miss Allen's portrait of this strikingly beautiful, blond woman it appears that she was also endowed with an extraordinary intelligence. She learned to speak five European languages and carried herself with royal grace. This identification is discarded by Mr. Baines, who contends that it rests on very flimsy evidence, for, on the basis of chronology alone Paula could not have been the "Rita" of Conrad's real experience. The two views of Paula clash, and while some of Mr. Baines's objections are justified, he has not disproved Miss Allen's claim that Paula was educated; nor has he come up with the time identity of "Rita." As it is, even Mr. Baines reluctantly admits certain similarities between the life of Paula and that of "Rita."[19]

Whoever the girl was, he could never forget her. And, perhaps like the young George of *The Arrow of Gold,* he looked at all women "and each reminded him of Doña Rita, either by some profound resemblance or by the startling force of contrast."[20] And as failure in adolescent loves could have been partly responsible for Conrad's desire to leave Poland, so the end of the affair with "Rita" certainly made him wish to escape the city of Marseilles. The man who boarded the Scottish ship *Mavis* in 1878 on a voyage to Constantinople and Lowestoft was no longer the starry-eyed youth seeking romantic adventure. His four years in France were over, and although he had gone through exciting adventures, three voyages to the West Indies, a hapless love affair and a suicide attempt; although upon arrival in London "no explorer could have been more lonely," he was still young and romantic enough to say:

I was elated. I was pursuing a clear aim, I was carrying out a deliberate plan of making out of myself, in the first place, *a seaman worthy of the service,* good enough to work by the side of the men with whom I was to live; and in the second place, *I had to justify myself, to redeem a tacit moral pledge.* . . . How simple seemed the problem of life then, on that hazy day of early September in the year 1878, when I entered London for the first time.[21]

Conrad was a perfect stranger in England; he had neither friends nor acquaintances; he carried no letters of introduction, as on his arrival in Marseilles. Above all, he did not know English. In a moving story, "Amy Foster," Conrad was to recall the terrifying experience of an exile lost among total strangers. Indeed, the first years in England and on British ships were years of loneliness, boredom, and hardship. The weeks and months spent ashore brought no relief. During the years 1878–1894 he knew closely only two people, a businessman, Adolf Krieger, and a retired sailor, G. F. W. Hope. However, he maintained contact with his uncle Bobrowski (whose letters, though frequently full of reproaches and admonition, reflected the older man's love of his nephew) and set about the goal of becoming an officer of the merchant marine. He had wasted a great deal of money and had gotten nowhere. He was still totally dependent on Uncle Tadeusz's financial support and his own modest income from the Ukraine. But now the Marseilles period was over. After a short and bleak stay in London he went on a voyage to Australia, then to the Far East, making steady progress in English and his profession and eventually passing all the examinations until he became captain.

This was no mean achievement for a man of his temperament, and it required the singular tenacity of will and purpose which he maintained throughout his life. Still in the grip of his adolescent passion for the sea, he was fascinated by the struggle of the crew against the treachery of the elements. Yet the prosaic severity of the work aboard ship wore him down, and the tedium of the daily routine was a far cry from the adventures he had expected in each voyage. He spent long months in the company of men with whom he had nothing in common, as isolated aboard the ship as the ship itself was in the ocean. Though he had risen from ordinary seaman to captainship, he gained no security. There were frequent periods of unemployment. Even when he received his British citizenship (in 1886), he was still regarded as an alien, and he had trouble competing with other men for jobs. His letters from those years bear ample evidence of plans that failed, and his exasperation at being often without a berth. His sundry financial ventures collapsed; the voyages brought him but modest remuneration and no prospect of security.

In 1866, the year in which Conrad received his master's certificate, he also wrote his first story, "The Black Mate," which he submitted unsuccessfully to a prize contest in *Tit-Bits*. Conrad did not receive the prize, and the story is interesting not merely because it is Conrad's first piece of fiction, but because of its theme of the handicapped man. But it lacks true literary merit and is an imitation of Maupassant.

The hero of this slight piece is a mate whose premature grayness prevents him from obtaining a job. He solves his problem by dyeing his hair black and then finds a berth. His bottles of dye are broken during a stormy passage, and he tries to mask his predicament by an ingenious tale that smacks of the supernatural. In his mature work Conrad would never rely on a purely superficial plot scheme, practically devoid of psychological delineation of character. But the very fact that at this early stage Conrad attempted fiction, is significant. It shows that the transition from sailor to writer was not sudden but, rather, a slow process that had begun already in his adolescent literary games in Poland. Yet the year 1866 was a turning-point, for Conrad could now feel secure in the knowledge that he had attained his objective of becoming a sea captain, while at the same time he began to realize the essential triviality of the profession for a man like himself. It is not surprising, therefore, that in the two years that followed Conrad must have kept a diary, which he was to continue later in the Congo, and in 1889 he began work on his first novel, *Almayer's Folly.* I rather doubt that we can take seriously Conrad's contention in his *A Personal Record* that the conception of a planned book was quite outside his mental range when he began to write. Literature was in his blood, and it only had to be liberated by a favorable set of circumstances. On the other hand, Conrad declares: "All I can claim after all those years of devoted practice . . . is the right to be believed when I say that if I had not written in English I would not have written at all."[22]

He was right. There were several reasons why Conrad steadfastly refused to write in his native language or in French (which he knew well), the most important being the fact that he matured intellectually and artistically at a time when English became his daily tongue. He had declined his uncle's suggestion to write for Polish magazines; he found French too "crystallized." But perhaps the best answer is that his choice of English as his medium of artistic expression was mostly unconscious, and that it was closely bound up with his alleged "desertion" of Poland. In a sense, Conrad could become a great artist only if he remained a solitary. He had to succeed as a novelist despite the financial hardship, poor health *and* the problem of writing in English. The latter problem was not only that of mastering a foreign language; it also became a moral issue for his compatriots and, eventually, for Conrad himself.

There was nothing unusual about a Pole living abroad, and had Conrad remained a sailor or had he succeeded in his business enterprises, his fellow Poles would have hardly taken the trouble to notice him. Thus it was not Conrad's emigration that enraged some of the Polish intellectuals, but the emigration of a man of genius, who, they felt, ought to have dedicated his talents to Poland. One Polish novelist, Mme Eliza Orzeszkowa (1842–1899), violently assailed Conrad, accusing him of being a mere careerist who wrote popular and lucrative novels in English. Ironically enough, when this indictment was made,[23] Conrad was still struggling against poverty. A personal letter from her so hurt Conrad that fifteen years later (in the autumn of 1914) he was still furious with Eliza Orzeszkowa. Yet Conrad must have found more than a grain of truth in the accusations of Polish critics, for he protested vehemently (in excellent Polish) that he simply didn't know the language well enough. He also assured his critics that his own literary work was unworthy of Polish literature and he wrote only to earn a living.[24] "To write in Polish," Conrad was quoted as having said, "that's a great thing, for that one must be a writer like Mickiewicz or Krasiński. I am a common man, I write to earn my living and to support my wife, in the language of the country where I found refuge."[25] Indeed, it would be perfectly natural for a man who became a British citizen and was a captain in the British merchant marine to use the language of his adopted country.

Thus, when in 1889 Conrad faced another period of unemployment he sat down to write his first book, *Almayer's Folly.* Boredom played an important part in this endeavor and perhaps Conrad did not think of a writing career at this time. Surely, however, we cannot suppose that the notion of writing for a living did not occur to him as he began to spin out the tale of the hapless Almayer, still clinging to his maritime career. But he was looking for new avenues; he considered an old plan of whaling in arctic waters, giving up the idea when he accepted the job of first mate on a Congo steamer on April 29, 1890.

Jean-Aubry thought that the adventure in the Congo made Conrad turn from the sea to a vocation of writing, and he had a good point.

Instead of romance, Conrad found the horror of the jungle and its savage laws, the utter degradation of man isolated in the wilderness. The rapacious immorality of the Belgian explorers and traders filled him with disgust. He began to question the existence of any purpose in life, which he found full of unextinguishable regrets. The journey into the heart of the Congo, which had once inflamed his childish imagination, turned out to be a gray, somber struggle for survival—a most unexciting contest which offered neither glory nor victory. Moreover, the Congo voyage seriously impaired Conrad's health. Frequent spells of illness enhanced his habit of reverie and often made him feel demoralized. It is small wonder that with perfect sincerity he sometimes wished himself dead. He yielded to haunting memories and vague regrets. He reflected on his disappointed hopes and the somewhat poor consolation that one must live when one has had the misfortune to be born. He began to be aware of a certain duality in himself. The romantic sailor had turned into a lonely thinker with a passion for introspection. His concern was now with his own fate and that of humanity, with the meaning of failure and success, fidelity and faithlessness. Conrad the sailor was dead, despite his return to sea on the *Torrens* until July 26, 1893, and on the *Adowa* for a mere crossing of the Channel to Rouen and return trip to London on January 18, 1894. He never sailed again; out of his misery and disenchantment Conrad the writer was born.

Chapter Two
The First Outcasts

While Conrad served abroad the *Torrens* on a passage to Australia (as first mate) he became acquainted with a young former Cambridge student, W. H. Jacques, to whom he showed the manuscript containing the first nine chapters of *Almayer's Folly*. In response to Conrad's anxious queries, Jacques replied that the novel was worth finishing, and that it was interesting and perfectly clear. The laconic encouragement given to Conrad at that time must have meant a great deal to the strange first mate of the sailing ship. The manuscript was completed and sent to T. Fisher Unwin on July 4, 1894. Impressed by the exotic richness of the novel and the originality of its style, a young reader at Unwin's, Edward Garnett, not only recommended that it be published but expressed the desire to meet the author, and then warmly urged him to write another book, not knowing that Conrad had, in fact, begun working on his next novel. Yet he had not given up entirely his desire to continue his seafaring life, for as late as September 1898 he was still looking for a command. But the die was cast. From the life at sea, Conrad descended within himself towards "that lonely region of stress and strife" in which the artist "finds the terms of his appeal"[1]

It was not an easy descent, and Conrad's life as a writer was not easier than his life as a seaman. However, his background was not without its advantages. He had stored a rich fund of impressions and recollections, which he would later use in his fiction. Both his travels and his Polish heritage gave the novelist an element of exoticism that appealed to the English and American readers.

Yet, from the beginning Conrad did not regard himself as a spinner of sea yarns or a mere entertainer. He took his writing as seriously as he had regarded his former profession. With a rare dedication Conrad "wrestled with the Lord" (as he had said of his work on *Nostromo*) for the right word, the right atmosphere, the right fictional technique.

Almayer's Folly, Conrad's first book, appeared in 1895. It is not one of his great novels, but its appearance had a certain impact on the English novel, even though it took the author another two decades to reach world recognition. Conrad was so unsure of himself as a writer that before he received the first galley proofs of the novel from T. Fisher Unwin he had made plans to issue the novel in a partnership with his "Aunt" Marguerite Poradowska in the *Revue de Deux Mondes,* Mme Poradowska was to translate the book into French and be featured as the author, while Conrad would be briefly mentioned in a note as a collaborator under the pseudonym "Kamudi," the name he used when he sent the manuscript to his publisher. Despite this grotesque scheme and his feeling of inadequacy, however, he had already conceived the idea for his next story, "The Two Vagabonds," which was to develop into his second novel, *An Outcast of the Islands.*

From the beginning, Conrad's preoccupation was with men handicapped by a destructive passion or idea, ridden with guilt or doubt, isolated from society by nature, their fellow men or their own transgression. His first novels and stories were usually set in the Malayan islands, against the backdrop of an immense jungle; his first heroes were white men placed in alien surroundings and generally defeated by them. Conrad viewed the native society and nature as two destructive powers that undermined the white man's integrity and sapped his vitality.

Like so many of Conrad's heroes, Kaspar Almayer is a loner and a man possessed by a dominant dream that both enhances his isolation and proves destructive in the end. Almayer's folly is not only the unfinished, sumptuous house in the wilderness of Borneo; it is, more accurately, his dream of wealth and power or, as it will be for many other Conradian heroes, his "illusion." This dream makes communication with others virtually impossible and, in Almayer's case, it is used to rationalize his breach of the white man's code.

Almayer and Willems (the hero of Conrad's second novel) have broken this code. Each takes a woman of a different race, Almayer in pursuit of his dream of wealth and Willems to gratify his passion. Both women remain total strangers and come to hate their white men. Almayer's wife abandons his civilized existence for a native hut; Aïssa turns Willems into a traitor to his own group, and finally kills him.

Almayer's case is complicated by the fact that he is rejected by two women, his wife and his beautiful half-breed daughter, Nina, whom he loves dearly and through whom he hopes to redeem himself in Holland, after finding Lingard's gold mine. His dream proves his undoing, for it clouds his common sense, and makes him blind to the reality of his surroundings. His end is piteous, as he remains alone, betrayed by Nina, who prefers the native Dain to her father. Almayer has wrestled with many problems but this final act of his daughter is beyond his comprehension: he is too wrapped up in his own personality.

How important the theme of betrayal is to Conrad can be seen from the fact that the two works which had given him the most trouble, *The Rescue* (begun in 1896 and completed in 1920) and *The Sisters* (given up in 1896), contain this motif. Actually, the first two novels and *The Rescue* are, in a sense, a trilogy with one central character who appears in all three books—the mysterious and romantic Captain Tom Lingard. The chronology of *The Rescue* (first called *The Rescuer*) is not so strange when one remembers that it was laid aside many times. The story was so crucial to Conrad that some notes for it can be found on the manuscript of an early draft for his novel *Lord Jim.*

In *The Rescue* Lingard turns traitor to the natives who have trusted him. The hero of *The Sisters*, Stephen, betrays his home and parents. Almayer has betrayed his Dutch heritage, and Willems both his patron, Lingard, and his racial code. In each case there has been a breach of solidarity of a group, and the transgressor is punished severely.

Almayer cannot live like a native, nor can he lead a civilized existence in Borneo; his attempt to erect a pretentious mansion in the wilderness is as futile as his dream of a triumphant return to the Old World, for the Old World will not accept his daughter. But even if it did, Nina would not go, for she has learned to hate the white race, and she loves Dain. Of this Almayer is totally unaware, since he scarcely regards her as a young woman. She is merely the idealized projection of his own personality.

Thus, Almayer is left alone, betrayed by his Malay wife, his daughter, his patron, and his ally. With two symbolic gestures he tries to blot Nina and his dream out of his memory: her erases her footprints in the sand and erects little tombs over them; then he burns his house—deluding himself with the idea that Nina is merely a burden he must shake off. The burden takes his life.

The thematic similarities between the first two novels are numerous. *An Outcast of the Islands* introduces the main characters of *Almayer's Folly* from an earlier period. The downfall of Almayer is paralleled by the disintegration and death of Willems. In both novels the jungle provides the dark, sinister setting, and the two protagonists are destroyed by their passions.

A fugitive from a Dutch ship in a port in Dutch Indies, Willems is helped by Lingard, who takes him aboard his own ship. But Willems does not last long in this job, so Captain Lingard installs him as a clerk in a shipping business in Macassar. There Willems makes progress, marries the natural daughter of the boss, but when he is harrassed by the wife's relatives he begins to steal money from his firm. As he is about to complete his restitutions to the firm's till, his embezzlement is discovered, and Willems is disgraced. Thus, for the second time in his life, he becomes an outcast—rejected by his wife (who does not want to leave her home) and by the local society.

Another chance comes, again through the generosity of his former patron, Lingard. Left at a trading post up a rocky river in Borneo, Willems stays with Almayer, waiting for Lingard to procure for him another position. It is then that Conrad's jungle drama is enacted. Time in this drama is of essence, for, along with nature, it is corrosive in character. Had Lingard returned in six weeks, as he had promised, Willems would have come to no harm. But the boredom and isolation of the wilderness get hold of him and he succumbs to the fascination of Aïssa, whose "somber gaze" fits well into a picture of the great solid and somber trees of the jungle.

His sexual infatuation means loss of freedom for Willems, for he now becomes a pawn in the struggle between Malay chieftains and the white traders. Primitive though she is, Aïssa has no difficulty to ensnare Willems and make him a tool in the plot against Almayer and Lingard. That she also has conceived a passion for him and wants him to become a leader of her own people, is another ironic twist Conrad adds to the story.

Completely overcome by his passion, Willems agrees to betray Captain Lingard's secret—the unknown channel leading from the river to the sea—for which he is to become a partner of Abdulla (Almayer's Arab rival) and Aïssa's husband. He has tried to persuade Aïssa to go away with him, but her tribal loyalty is stronger than his, and so Willems takes Abdulla up the river, and is set up as a trader in partnership with him. Only now does he begin to see that he can never become a member of Aïssa's social group. Moreover, he seems to have awakened from his love spell and what enchanted him before now repels him. Aïssa is a constant reminder of his own cowardice, treachery, and sinfulness. His dreams of rescue are mingled with attacks of hysterical fear. No longer can he rely on his previous conviction that he would muddle through—somehow. His dream of greatness, like Almayer's dream of wealth, is elusive; his love of Aïssa has turned to hatred.

Aïssa cannot understand it any more than she could comprehend his love for her. He baffles her completely, too, and evokes in turn bewilderment, apathy, and despair. He had come to her as the great white man, the future chief of her people, and she was to rule by his side. Suddenly he is transformed into a pitiful weakling. Vaguely she hopes for a change, but Willem's momentary lapse into his previous sexual passion (ironically to seek forgetfulness in that which he has come to hate and despise) does not satisfy her. Neither does it satisfy Willems, for, the brief ecstasy of lovemaking over, he is again in the throes of despair. The picture of these two lovers, clasped in each other's arms, yet so utterly torn apart, is indeed a pathetic sight. Their isolation has reached the limit.

Those two, surrounded each by the *impenetrable wall* of their aspirations, were *hopelessly alone,* out of sight, out of earshot of each other; each the centre of dissimilar and distant horizons; standing *each on a different earth, under a different sky.* [2]

To break out of this intolerable state of isolation Willems must commit his final betrayal, now of Aïssa and her Malay world. But this last desertion proves fatal. The dark, tumescent forest has claimed another victim.

Lingard (who himself turns a traitor in *The Rescue*) brutally condemns Willem's act of treachery. "You are alone . . . ," he says to him. "Nothing can help you. Nobody will. You are neither white nor brown. You have no color as you have no heart."[3] Indeed, there is no doubt that Willems is a multiple traitor; he betrays his company, Lingard, his wife, his class, and finally even the woman who was to be his refuge from the world—the savage Aïssa.

Willem's lust for her denotes his utter degradation and his loss of civilized status. She is part of the primeval forest which will become for Conrad the symbol of the implacable destiny that closes in upon the white man and destroys him.

The jungle with its destructive forces is the setting of early Conrad works and, interestingly enough, it precedes the purely maritime background of the raging or quiet sea and man's struggle against it. Conrad's treatment of nature suggests that he views it as a symbolic framework or a power. Both the impenetrable, somber forests and the vast solitude of waters, to use his familiar epithets, become factors that affect or shape the destiny of his heroes. From his seafaring experience Conrad developed the notion of man's contest with the elements, either as an individual or in a group such as a ship's crew. Many of his works deal with this contest. The measure of man is shown in his struggle against the elements. It is a test which often brings self-knowledge but which can also prove to be the undoing of the person thus tested.

The special character of Conrad's early fiction derives from his desire to bring to his reader an essentially authentic recollection, usually taken from one or several autobiographical sources but transformed into a sophisticated fictional fabric. Like Marcel Proust, Conrad must practically withdraw from the world in order to render artistically the elusive recollection of his own past. Yet he knew that mere recollection of things past was not sufficient:

My task which I am trying to achieve is, by the power of the written word, to make you hear, to make you feel—it is, before all, to make you *see*. That—and no more, and it is everything.[4]

The first books and stories are indeed powerful in their evocation of the physical scene, of sound and color, no less than in their themes of violent emotions and moral predicament. The greatest skill of Conrad the artist is manifested in those works where he combines magnificent descriptions of nature with a convincing portrayal of men and women in their strengths and weaknesses. In Conrad's fiction there is an essential difference between the sea and the jungle. The sea, for all its immensity or indifference to man's fate, for all the hard knocks it deals the sailor, can still be a place of romance. The terror, perfidy, and violence of the sea are a test of man's solidarity, as are the conditions of isolation in the jungle. Yet the sea has some aspects which cannot be found in the darkness of the primeval forest. It has a charm and "a sort of unholy fascination;[5] it is "the moral symbol of our life."[6]

The jungle cannot serve such a symbolic purpose in Conrad's stories and novels dealing with its disintegrating influence on the white man. The hidden terrors of the primeval forest do not prod men to band together in solidarity, inspire no ideals of service, and not only do not "keep men morally in order"[7] but, on the contrary, corrupt them. The jungle is thus the opposite of a moral symbol—it stands for the savage in man, for his utter isolation and his moral collapse. This symbolic view of the jungle is fully developed in *Heart of Darkness*.

In *Almayer's Folly* Conrad weaves the descriptions of the jungle and its moods into the narrative in order to enhance the desolation of his heroes. Nature itself does not bring about the downfall of the central character. It is, rather, a contributing cause: it makes Almayer want to escape; it not only suggests but seems to hasten his moral deterioration. The two lovers (Nina and Dain), however, are not affected by the wilderness although they are surrounded by the fecund and fetid growth of the tropical forest.

The first kiss Nina gives to her lover is against the background of an immense and dark jungle, not exactly a romantic place. The highly adjectival description of the tropical forest is used merely as an ornamental piece of tapestry; it serves no dramatic purpose and is rather rhetorical and florid.

In his next novel, however, Conrad's use of scene-painting indicates greater maturity as a storyteller. Nature in *An Outcast of the Islands* reflects and enhances the mental and moral character of the heroes and is, moreover, a direct *deteriorating* agent. It is symbolic of decay and sloth, the moral and intellectual inertia into which so many of Conrad's characters fall.

Both novels are concerned with symbolic darkness, and although *An Outcast of the Islands* shows greater technical mastery in the handling of imagery and characters and greater detachment of the author from his characters, it too suffers from the initial practice of romantic scene painting, in which the mountains, the rivers, the sea, the moon and the sun become infused with human traits. And both Almayer and Willems are at times suicidal and, in a sense, responsible for their own destruction, without, however, exhibiting anything remotely resembling the "tragic flaw" of the later characters like Jim or Nostromo.

Neither Almayer nor Willems has the courage to perform the actual act of self-destruction but death is symbolic for both. Conrad often regards death as the absolute sacrifice and the supreme moment of a man's life. To Almayer it spells freedom from his torment—final oblivion. There is a difference between this early treatment of death and the later, as in *Lord Jim*. Almayer seeks only escape and relief from anguish, while Jim craves punishment, self-knowledge and self-fulfillment, and he meets death almost ecstatically. To Willems death reveals for the first time the joy and the beauty of sunshine. Upon dying he melts into the natural scenery.

In the later, more complex novels, death and the images of light and darkness assume more profound aspects, as, for example, in the ironic victory by death of Lena (in *Victory*). Never a dogmatist, Conrad does not use these images consistently. Thus, in the first three novels, *The Nigger of the "Narcissus"* (1897) being the third, the images of light indicate the simple, good life of the seaman, while those of darkness are associated with the evil and mystery of the jungle, the corruption of the life on the land. Yet in *Heart of Darkness* (1899) it is whiteness that is truly sinister and evil, for it symbolizes the immoral scramble for loot by the unscrupulous and unfeeling Belgian traders in ivory and human flesh; the whiteness of ivory is also contrasted with the blackness of the natives whose lives must be destroyed for its sake. The darkness of the jungle, on the other hand, can serve a twofold function; it can spell an imminent lapse into savagery to Marlow and Kurtz, but it is at times presented as a symbol of an upright existence, full of vigor and promise. The ambiguity of this usage may suggest the moral ambiguity of human life.

The themes of early Conrad are simple enough, although the style and method of narration show the promise of the future master. His early heroes are morally weak men whose predicament of lost honor or lost social position is heightened by their isolation in unfamiliar surroundings of the East.

Artistic progress was not smooth for Conrad, for the very process of writing was difficult for him, often a tortuous struggle. When he wrote *Almayer's Folly* he was still a sailor, and the writing apparently came easily to him. The second novel, begun enthusiastically, soon became a desperate task, punctuated by days of total mental blankness. The next two projects were the *Sisters,* which he never completed, and *The Rescuer,* which proved a lost cause, only to be picked up again many years later. The young author was beset by doubts and plagued by financial uncertainty; he had sustained a substantial single loss of investment in a South African gold mine. Now a married man, he felt he had to write in order to make both ends meet, and this strain greatly affected (at this time, at any rate) the quality of his writing. Hence both *The Sisters*[8] and *The Rescuer* abound in very weak, inflated, and often turgid prose passages.

As Conrad was wrestling with *The Rescuer* during his honeymoon with Jessie in Brittany, they met a couple with idiot children. The experience resulted in a short story, "The Idiots," which was first rejected by the magazine *Cosmopolis* but then printed by the *Savoy.* Although it reads well, it is a very slight piece of work, done (as Conrad himself admitted) under the direct influence of Maupassant. The only significant thing about it is perhaps Conrad's choice of such a theme while being on a honeymoon. It is a story of two unhappy parents, Jean-Pierre and Susan Bacadou, who have four idiot children and feel guilty about it. Jean's attempts to appease his fate by turning a devout Catholic are of no avail; he then tries sexual abstinence, but when he attempts to make love to Susan, she is revolted, and kills her husband. Running away from the house, the hysterical Susan is frightened by a strange weed-gatherer, leaps into the sea from a cliff, and drowns.

There may be no apparent connection between the first two novels and this story, yet once again Conrad is exploring the problem of guilt. The white man's code is broken by Almayer and Willems, and the latter also commits several acts of treachery. What is the transgression of the unfortunate Bacadous? Not any untoward action but merely their inability to produce normal children, or, in other words, a natural handicap they cannot overcome. Bunter in "The Black Mate" finds an ingenious—if morally superficial—way out of his problem; for the Bacadous there is no way out except by death, as for Almayer and Willems.

The "psychoanalytic" critic will be tempted to derive a special meaning from the fact that Susan kills her husband by stabbing him in the throat with a pair of scissors (obviously a phallic symbol); he will suggest that Jean-Pierre's failure as a father is an indication of Conrad's own fears of sexual impotence during the early period of his marriage; he might also consider his treatment of sex in the first two novels and this story as a confirmation of Thomas Moser's view that love was an uncongenial subject to Conrad.[9]

According to Mr. Moser, the shift in Conrad's themes from explorations into moral failure in the masculine world to those of love and sex is responsible for Conrad's artistic shortcomings. The former enabled him to attain artistic success; the latter proved frustrating and resulted in failure and decline. Mr. Moser's thesis is, briefly, that Conrad's negative attitude toward love should not be shocking, for Conrad views man as being lonely and morally isolated, and that his gloomy view could not be reconciled with a belief in the stability of family existence or the panacea of love. Hence, he claims, the effect of sexual subjects on Conrad's creative processes was both inhibiting and crippling.

The psychiatrist, according to Dr. Bernard Meyer, detects two attitudes in Conrad's writing: ". . . a masochistic wish that is responsible both for the fear of and the fascination with women."[10] The analyst explains that this implies a reversal of sexual roles; the man is emasculated and debases himself before the image of the monolithic woman; the man wishes to deny a latent sadistic element in his sexual makeup. On a deeper psychological level, the origin of this attitude to sex comes from the craving for the protecting embrace of an all-powerful mother.

Dr. Meyer's investigations offer many original insights into the workings of Conrad's mind, notably that Conrad "turned to fiction as a means of effecting a corrective vision of a painful reality"[11]—a position recently developed by Jeffrey Berman in his *Joseph Conrad: Writing as Rescue.*[12] Many readers, no doubt, will be more than ready to adopt the psychoanalytical interpretation of rescue fantasies which, according to Dr. Meyer, contain "consistent allusions to the Oedipus Complex, namely, derivatives or the daydreams of a small boy of gaining undisputed possession of his mother."[13]

Viewed from this perspective, *An Outcast* "epitomizes Conrad's reiterated insistence upon the destructive and devouring nature of a woman's love. In short, Aïssa's love is likened to being eaten alive."[14]

Dr. Meyer further suggests that there is a link between the treatment of love in *An Outcast* and his own neurotic suffering during the early months of his marriage; yet he also observes that, neurotic suffering notwithstanding, Conrad managed to create a true masterpiece, *The Nigger of the "Narcissus."*

It is largely a question of emphasis. Conrad's jungle imagery of trees, creepers, and flowers may be interpreted as symbolic of his subterranean emotions concerning love; but it may be regarded also as symbolic of man's inescapable loneliness and his moral dilemma. Mr. Moser sees the description of the forests, fertility, and death in *Almayer's Folly* as Conrad's subconscious desire to underline the femininity of the destructive jungle life, and the consummation of love between Dain and Nina as associated with death. Yet in "Youth," where there is no woman character and no love or sexual theme, Mr. Moser himself observes the symbolic use of similar imagery: the mysterious East appears to Marlow: "silent like death, dark like a grave," but no significant sexual symbolism can be traced here.

I suppose it is possible to dissect Conrad's fiction in a thoroughly "clinical" fashion and to show that some of "immobilized" loves are either impotent or voyeuristic—and this Mr. Moser does quite well. It is debatable, however, whether this kind of analysis will shed more light on the more subtle meaning of Conrad and the universal significance of his insights into man's moral nature, his mastery of style or novelistic structure. Mr. Moser's implication, albeit made with due reservations concerning Conrad's own sexual impotence, will surely be questioned by many critics no less than readers who have come to regard Conrad as a "masculine" writer.

My own feeling is that love itself was not necessarily an uncongenial subject with Conrad, but that his treatment of love and sex simply falls into his general vision of mankind. Conrad's heroes dream of honor, passion, and glory but when they discover the disparity between their dreams and reality they become aware of their essential loneliness. Sexual love promises the closest union between man and woman, but, in Conrad's fiction, it usually brings pain, solitude, or destruction. This may be Conrad's way of dramatizing man's isolation, the great distances between man and woman (or, for that matter, between man and man) that cannot be bridged by sexual contact. For, essentially, Conrad's luckless and frustrated lovers are not different from his luckless and frustrated seekers of romantic adventure and honor. Their inability to love is not necessarily sexual impotence; it is their inability to approach others closely; it is their expression of irremediable individualism. This is consistent with Conrad's professed view of life:

Everybody must walk in the light of his own gospel. . . . No man's light is good to any of his fellows. That's my view of life—a view that rejects all formulas, dogmas and principles of other people's making. These are a web of illusions. We are too varied. Another's truth is only a dismal lie to me.[15]

This extreme belief in individualism is hard to reconcile with the idea of a romantic merging of two bodies and souls. Perhaps this is one reason why Conrad strikes the contemporary critic as a modern is his treatment of love, Victorian in his avoidance of revealing details and in his air of reservation and respectability, and at the same time psychologically complex in that it shows that man does not shed his basic isolation.

But sex alone does not account for the passivity of his women or for the diffidence of his men. Other important keys can easily be found to unlock the secrets of their behavior, such as Conrad's reading of Polish and European romantic writers, his experience as a sailor (conveniently ignored by some psychoanalysts), and last, but certainly not least, the tradition of patriarchal Polish landed gentry from which Conrad originated. These are only some of the *other-than-sex* factors that undoubtedly influenced Conrad's treatment of love. It seems, therefore, that Conrad's attitude toward women and love comes *partly* from what he himself accepted as the romantic, chivalrous tradition of the Polish landed gentry in the Ukraine, and from the tradition of Polish Romantic poetry.

Some of the significant leitmotivs in the work of the "big three" of Polish Romantic poetry (Adam Mickiewicz, 1798–1855; Juliusz Słowacki, 1809–1849; and Zygmunt Krasiński, 1812–1859) are easily traced in Conrad's work. The Polish Romantic heroes are consumed by an inner conflict, but they are usually defeated by the forces of destiny more than by their own imperfections. Conrad's ironic, often detached vision of man robs some of the ostensibly heroic characters of the heroism they appear to possess. This is especially true of the later, more complex protagonists like Jim, Nostromo, and Marlow.

It is also possible to relate the peculiarities of Conrad's style in his first two novels to the *fin-de-siècle* literature, more specifically to the poetic mannerisms of Arthur Symons (whom Conrad admired), to W. B. Yeats and Ernest Dowson (in their early phases), to D. G. Rossetti and William Morris. Thus Frederick Karl finds an affinity between "Conrad's early work and the language of decadence; itself a carryover from the French *symbolistes*," and he recognizes "how significantly he was part of the 1890s milieu."[16]

Eschewing any romantic involvements, Conrad continued to explore the theme of "the white man's burden" in the story "An Outpost of Progress" (1897), which he himself called "the lightest part of the loot I carried off from Central Africa, the main portion being of course *The Heart of Darkness*."[17] Conrad was quite right in his judgment, for "An Outpost" is a much lesser story, although both are set in the Congo. Yet it is an interesting seminal tale, anticipating *Heart of Darkness* and marked by a rather macabre quality. Conrad claimed that he wrote it "with pleasure if with difficulty."[18] Its two Belgian antiheroes, Kayerts and Carlier, are ushered in with poignant brevity as grotesque figures. Kayerts is "short and fat"; Carlier, "tall, with a large head and a very broad trunk perched upon a long pair of thin legs" (86). Their director, a "ruthless and efficient" man, indulges at times in "grim humor" (87). In a speech to the two men, he offers them an "exceptional opportunity . . . to distinguish themselves . . . as a favor done to the beginners. Kayerts was moved almost to tears by his director's kindness" (87–88). The director, however, regards them as two imbeciles, two ridiculous human specimens.

With fine irony, Conrad shows the two Belgians engaging in interminable and silly discussions about the plots of novels left at the station by their predecessor. "In the centre of Africa they made acquaintance of Richelieu and of D'Artagnan, of Hawk's Eye and of Father Goriot . . ." (94)—the very people, incidentally, young Conrad encountered in his youth in Poland. But this unusual reading fare did not inflame the imagination of these two dull men; unlike Jim, they remain untouched by ideas or by the destructive element of the romantic dream. They share, however, Jim's terrifying loneliness, albeit without his moral predicament. Kayerts and Carlier peruse old copies of a home paper and discuss a piece called "Our Colonial Expansion," praising "those who went about bringing light, and faith and commerce to the dark places of the earth" (94). Though they feel somewhat elevated by these words, the pathetic pair are incapable of doing anything. The contact with "pure unmitigated savagery" has turned them into frightened children. They "lived like blind men in a large room . . . unable to see the general aspect of things" (92). After being cut off from supplies for eight months, demoralized and debilitated, they fight over some lumps of sugar which Kayerts has locked away. In a confused collision, Kayert's gun goes off and Carlier is killed. As the steamer carrying the Managing Director of the Great Civilizing Company sounds its whistle, Kayerts gropes his way through the fog, looking upwards, looking round "like a man who has lost his way" (116). He is, indeed, a lost man, utterly crushed by his deed yet unable to feel any remorse. Symbolically, he hangs himself on the cross standing over the grave of the former chief of the outpost. "And, irreverently, he was putting out a swollen tongue at his Managing Director" (117). The outpost is not of progress but an outpost of regression: from the platitudes of civilized conduct into a moral wilderness, and thence to mindless murder and suicide.

When Conrad mentioned his writing of "An Outpost" to Garnett on August 5, 1897, he also added: "The one I am writing now I hammer out of myself with difficulty but without pleasure. It is called 'The Lagoon,' and is very much Malay indeed." Conrad changed his mind after the piece was praised by his friends and said (in a letter to Miss Watson, the fiancée of his friend Edward Sanderson):

I am right glad to know you like "The Lagoon." To be quite confidential I must tell you it is, of my short stories, the one I like the best myself. I did write it to please myself. . . .[19]

Perhaps one of the reasons why Conrad favored this piece is the conscious or unconscious association of its principal themes with two literary sources that were to form the most pervasive of literary influences: Shakespeare and Polish Romanticism. The tonalities of the story clearly show such association. Conrad's choice of a Shakespearean epigraph for the collection in which the story appeared, *The Tales of Unrest*, further strengthens this aspect. It is from *II, Henry IV*: "Be it they course to busy [not *being*, as originally printed in the book] giddy minds/With foreign quarrels." The tales in the collection reiterate the main preoccupations of the play with divided loyalty, betrayal and guilt; moreover, "The Lagoon" uses *theatrum mundi*, the world viewed as if it were a theater, as its chief metaphor. The theatricality of the story, its dialogue and imagery, bespeak Shakespearean cadences and images.

But they also reveal remarkable affinities with the rhetorical devices of some Polish Romantics, especially those of Adam Mickiewicz. And the theme of star-crossed lovers can be traced to Mickiewicz's ballad "Romanticism" (1821) as well as to *Romeo and Juliet*. The symbolic use of light and darkness and the linking of love with death are but two of the many correspondences between Conrad's story and these two literary sources.[20] In a sense, Shakespeare's influence worked upon Conrad twice; from his direct acquaintance with the Bard's works, and from his discovery of the abundant presence of Shakespeare in Mickiewicz.

The story might have pleased Conrad; on the whole, however, it is, like all the stories in the collection *Tales of Unrest* (in which it is the last tale), quite mediocre and, in fact, quite below the first one in the book, "Karain: A Memory." Its language is verbose, adjectival, and the postpositioning of adjectives in his descriptive sentences suggests French or Polish usage, e.g., "The forests, somber and dull. . . . immobility perfect and final. . . . darkness, mysterious and invincible; the darkness scented and poisonous of impenetrable forests" (187–89). Conrad was still awkwardly groping for his distinctive style. In one sentence (in the second paragraph) he repeats the word *every* five times without any artistic effect. In "Youth" there will be many such repetitions but they will be artistically controlled—and they will form an essential ingredient of his poetic prose. The symbolism of the story is not much of an improvement, if any, on that of the first two novels. The night journey invites a Freudian or a Jungian reading, but the menacing images of nature, the opposition of light and darkness, lose their symbolic value simply because they are too frequent and too obvious. The final words of the story, another description of poor Arsat, will illustrate my point: "He stood lonely in the *searching sunshine*; and he looked beyond the *great light* of a *cloudless day* into *the darkness* of a world of *illusions* (204).

Conrad had not yet embarked on a new theme, but was continuing that of his first two novels. Thus Arsat, the protagonist of "The Lagoon," resembles Willems in his total immersion in a romantic passion, the price of which is betrayal of his brother. Arsat and Diamelen are two lovers who serve in the court of a Malayan Rajah; upon the latter's refusal to let them leave the palace in order to marry, they leave the state, incurring the Rajah's wrath. Arsat's brother assists them in their escape, but when they are overtaken by the Ruler's men Arsat saves himself and Diamelen, abandoning his brother. After Diamelen's death Arsat remains in a state of anguished loneliness. His sole relief lies in the telling of his story to the white man.

He is thus very similar to Willems, who cannot be loyal to Aïssa and to Lingard at the same time; his passion for the girl has further corroded his sense of duty and turned him into an outcast. Arsat prefers the status of outcast to that of loyal courtier. Love and duty cannot be reconciled. Since Conrad was wrestling with *The Rescuer* at the time he wrote his Malay stories, his treatment of this theme is quite significant in the final product *The Rescue,* in which Part V is entitled "The Point of Honor and the Point of Passion." *The Rescue* is not so much a story of adventure as an account of what happens to a man who is suddenly possessed by an uncontrolled passion for a woman. Lingard's loyalty to Hassim (an exiled Malayan prince who had saved his life, and whose kingdom he now attempts to restore) cannot be reconciled with his love for Edith Travers and his concern for the party of the whites. His romantic passion for Mrs. Travers makes him lose his customary powers of thought and action. And the irony of the story lies in the fact that his love is actually an illusion—or so Conrad would like the reader to believe, and a most paralyzing illusion at that. Thus the famed adventurer turns into

. . . a stranger to all men, and abandoned by the All-knowing God. . . . The fierce power of his personality seemed to have turned into a dream.[21]

"Karain: A Memory" is significant in several ways. It repeats the motif of betrayal which obviously preoccupied Conrad during the first years of his work as an English writer and continued to haunt him throughout his writing career. The theme is important, for Conrad's own emigration and his writing in a foreign language can be compared to the betrayal of his race by a protagonist (Almayer, Willems, Arsat, Matara's sister, Karain) or failure to be loyal to one's social group. Conrad's hypersensitivity on this point can be illustrated by his own words, addressed to his namesake, Józef Korzeniowski, a Polish historian:

. . . I have in no way disavowed either my nationality or the name we share for the sake of success. It is widely known that I am a Pole and that Józef Konrad are my two Christian names, the latter being used by me as a surname so that foreign mouths should not distort my real surname—a distortion which I cannot stand. It does not seem to me that I have been unfaithful to my country by having proved to the English that a gentleman from the Ukraine can be as good a sailor as they, and has something to tell them in their own language.[22]

"Karain" anticipates *Lord Jim* in its treatment of the problem of guilt and remorse, and also in the introduction of a patient listener and a narrator who tells the story of Karain as well as his own. It also deals with the theme of life being a dream (taken from Calderón) which Conrad will introduce into many of his later works. It establishes Conrad as a writer who uses a Malayan setting but whose real interest is man's moral complexity.

The introduction of the first-person narrator is an improvement on the "I" of *The Nigger of the "Narcissus"* (where it is actually the novelist's voice), for it spells the appearance of Conrad's ubiquitous Marlow, the *engaged* narrator of "Youth," *Heart of Darkness, Lord Jim,* and *Chance.*

Moreover, the style shows a growing mastery over the language and the manipulation of plot: the attainment of a plausible speaking voice, the building up of suspense, and a greater subtlety in the use of irony and natural imagery. Altogether, then, "Karain" is Conrad's first "complex" story. It is actually divided into sections in the story-within-a-story method, the unity lying in the limitations of the subject matter; the plot deals with *one* major episode of Karain's life: his crime and its consequences.

Once again definite affinities with Mickiewicz manifest themselves: the confession of Karain recalls the account of his crime by Robak, one of the main characters in *Pan Tadeusz*; the plot itself resembles another work of Mickiewicz, his ballad "*Czaty* [The Watch], a Ukrainian Ballad." It is a story of an elderly *wojewoda* ("governor of a province") whose young wife is having a nocturnal tryst with her lover. The governor summons his cossack Nahum, and the two take up a watch behind a bush, loading their rifles. When the cossack tearfully confesses he cannot kill the girl, the governor orders him to shoot; without hesitation the cossack pulls the trigger, killing—his master.

Although not told in a simple manner, the plot of the "Karain" is simple enough. Karain, a ruler of a small Malayan state, has a good friend called Pata Matara. The latter's sister has eloped with a red-haired Dutchman, breaking her marriage contract to marry a Malay. Karain agrees to assist Matara in his task of finding his sister and killing her. They look for the couple for years, but Karain dreams of the girl himself, for he is in love with her. When they finally come upon the Dutchman and Matara's sister, Karain shoots not the red-handed culprit but his own friend Matara. This "involuntary" action saves the girl's life but it brings a ghost into his own—the specter of Matara which now begins to haunt him. For a while he is relieved when an old sorcerer exorcizes the ghost, but when he dies Pata Matara again begins to haunt the guilt-ridden Karain.

His problem is solved when he arrives at the English ship and tells them his story, asking for their help. One of the white officers presents Karain with a "magic" talisman: a necklace with a Jubilee sixpence bearing the image of Queen Victoria. Assured by the white men of the talisman's potence, Karain returns to his land, freed from his specter at last. His deliverance from his anguish is thus made ironic, for it is effected by dint of a white man's compassionate lie. The white man's talisman reinforces Conrad's theme of the power of illusion in man's life. Karain has lost his peace of mind because of an illusion and again has regained his peace of mind by trusting an illusion. Other heroes, like Lingard or Willems, also *lose* their peace of mind by yielding to illusions.

In "The Return," the other non-Malayan story in *Tales of Unrest* (along with "The Idiots"), written after "Karain," Conrad tried to

explore the psychological darkness of a married couple, and this time he
failed badly. The story gave him trouble from the first, and upon
concluding it he expressed his own doubts in a letter to Edward
Garnett: "The work is vile—or else good. I don't know. I can't
know. . . . I have a physical horror of that story. I simply won't look at
it any more. It has embittered five months of my life. I hate it."[23] And
in the Author's Note to *Tales of Unrest* he condemns the piece frankly as
"a left-handed production." There seems to be, therefore, ample justifi-
cation for the critic to ignore or dismiss "The Return" as serious
writing; but if the story fails artistically, it affords the reader an added
insight into Conrad's development by showing his difficulties and
frustrations with his fictional material, and his continued obsession
with isolation.

During the years 1894 (the year he completed *Almayer's Folly*) to
1897 Conrad produced works which are often called his "Malayan"
phase. Except for the advance shown in "Karain" Conrad had managed
to write only one book which foreshadows his great, mature novels: *The
Nigger of the "Narcissus,"* completed in February 1897 and published the
same year. The two novels and *Tales of Unrest* established him as a
promising English novelist, assailed for his rhetorical verbiage but
praised for the freshness of his vision, the power of his imagination and
the poetic quality of his prose.

None of his characters, thus far, even approached the dimensions of a
tragic hero; Almayer and Willems are, at best, pitiful men and their
lives are lived out against the backdrop of the dark jungle, which
thwarts the white man, reducing him to torpor and nothingness.
Conrad's symbolic images of the jungle, the river, and the sea were not
significant literary innovations, but his portrait of the tropical world
and the outcasts in it, his emphasis on the moral dilemma of man,
however simple his nature—these were clear indications of the directions his work would take. But it was *The Nigger of the "Narcissus"* that
brought Conrad's first artistic manifesto and it was also his first major
novel.

Chapter Three

The Great Light and the Profound Darkness: *The Nigger of the "Narcissus"*

Ostensibly, *The Nigger of the "Narcissus"* is a sea yarn in which there are a violent storm, a ship in danger, the crew's struggle for survival, and, finally, the docking of the ship in a port. But, fortunately, there is much more in the book. It is a tale of a ship called *Narcissus* but also of a man called James Wait, and of the strange relationship between him and the crew; it is a story about the ship as a microcosm, in which man's destiny, his goodness and evil, are symbolically revealed; about Conrad's love and hate of the sea; above all, it is about the problem of an outcast's conflict with a social group.

The social group in question is the crew of a ship, cut off from the land and exposed to entirely different dangers and living conditions; therefore governed by different concepts of morals and justice. This social group lives in isolation, and its leader, the captain, while sharing his men's lot, must at the same time bear the responsibility of command—a powerfully "separating" agent. He is thus doubly isolated.

The task of a ship's crew is to keep the vessel afloat and to reach a given destination. It can be performed only if the work is executed by a compact body of sailors obeying the commands of their officers. The fury of the elements may destroy this valuable solidarity. In fact, any conflict aboard the ship may undermine it.

The Negro sailor of the *Narcissus* is, in Conrad's own words, "the center of the ship's collective psychology," and the pivot of the novel's conflict and its action. "A Negro in the British forecastle," Conrad observes, "is a lonely being" (ix), for he has no friends. But *The Nigger* is not at all a story of racial discrimination. James Wait is different not only because he is black. He is set apart in many other ways. His very appearance and name are fraught with symbolic meanings. From the moment the crew sets their eyes upon him, he holds their attention until his death and even after it.

Wait has missed muster and when he utters his name, it is taken for the command "Wait!" and for a moment it upsets the routine aboard. "Wait" thus appears to be a symbolic cry to stop the work; Wait proves a malingerer and later the crew *waits* on him while *waiting* for him to die. The sound of his name also means "weight," which is exactly what he becomes to the twenty-five men aboard, and even to the ship, which, after his burial at sea, "rolled as if relieved of an unfair burden" (160).

From the first, the novel is full of symbolic or ironic ambiguities. Social outcast though he is, James Wait stands far above the rest of the crew by dint of his powerful physique, his voice, manner of speech, and superb bearing. "I belong to the ship," he declares, unaware of the irony in his statement. Although he is stronger than the others, Wait stirs up a conflict by refusing to do his share of work on the pretext that he is ill. Conrad leaves the reader no doubt as to the Negro's unscrupulous nature, but Wait does not know that the part of the dying man, which he assumed as a confidence man, will bring about his own undoing. Thus, both Wait himself and the crew are fooled by his deceit. He belongs to the ship indeed, as he has stated at the outset, but in a profoundly ironic and symbolic manner, not as a true member of the crew, who undertakes his share of the group solidarity, but as a "disintegrating power" that is elemental in nature and in humanity, a symbol of Fate itself.

But Wait is not the sole arrival from the outer dark to disrupt the ship's collective solidarity. Actually, another "startling visitor from the world of nightmares" comes aboard the *Narcissus* before James Wait, and becomes a hypocritical champion of the Negro's rights. He is Donkin, the Cockney malingerer, whose parasitical deceit is, in a sense, parallel to that of Wait, and he too is identified with darkness. What unites Donkin and Wait is that neither wishes to work and, moreover, each disrupts the ship's normal life.

Wait's convincing fits of coughing earn him the status of a sick man, and begin a raging controversy aboard the ship. Confined to his quarters by the chief mate Baker, James Wait elicits the sailors' sympathy, then chides them for laughing too loud or leaving the deck wet. He succeeds in creating a state of perpetual turmoil and discontent among the crew and the officers.

Therein the paradox of the situation. The crew members hate him, argue about his case and fight for him. James Wait is in a shelter, specially constructed for him on the deck when a storm hits the *Narcissus.* The ship keels and for about sixty hours the crew hangs on the perilously sloping deck. The solidarity of the crew has been restored temporarily by the exigencies of the storm and Captain Allistoun's unfailing calm and resolution. Wait has been forgotten during the first few hours of the storm, then his submerged shelter is noticed and the most symbolic scene of the book is enacted: the rescue of the trapped Negro. The paradox of the relationship between Wait and the crew has reached its height. Although he is now truly a victim, close to death and not merely a faker, he still exercises a spell over those who would save him at the risk of their own lives; in fact, he still terrorizes them, and they are baffled by their love-hate emotions for him.

The bearded old carpenter, Singleton, calls Wait a "jinx," attributing magical powers to him, and claiming that he has brought the storm to the *Narcissus*; the ship will not reach land safely until Jim dies.

The ship and Wait have been saved but now another ironic situation arises. The captain's firmness has restored the identity and the unity of the crew at a moment when fear has turned them into unthinking animals. Now that Wait is found alive he resumes his reign of terror, repaying the crew's solicitude with insults.

He was demoralizing. Through him we were becoming highly humanized, tender, complex, excessively decadent: we understood the subtlety of his fear, sympathized with all his repulsions, shrinkings, evasions, delusions— as though we had been overcivilized, and rotten and without any knowledge of the meaning of life. (139)

Perhaps James Wait had really been sick all the time? Nobody knows it with certainty. But after the storm there is no doubt that he is really gravely ill, possibly because he had spent hours in his flooded deckhouse. Moreover, now he is truly afraid to die and, ironically again, feigns good health, asking Captain Allistoun to allow him to go back to work. When the captain refuses the crew comes close to mutiny.

Once more, however, Captain Allistoun prevails over the crew and restores the discipline, but not Wait's spell over his men. The ship and the men must be rid of their burden before the voyage of the *Narcissus* is ended. Wait thus becomes a composite symbol of death, darkness and the subconscious.

Conrad's use of James Wait as a symbol of black Africa may be a clear anticipation of *Heart of Darkness,* where a similar figure (the female temptress) and the dark jungle are the disintegrating forces that bring Kurtz to ruin. Is Conrad a racist in his treatment of Wait? Eugene B. Redmond has no doubts about it. In his essay "Racism, or Realism? Literary Apartheid, or Poetic License? Conrad's Burden in *The Nigger of the 'Narcissus'* " he expounds on the subject of the etiology of racism in Anglo-Europe, suggesting that Conrad was a "willing victim of latent racist thoughts and attitudes," who developed, in James Wait, "a straw-man, a scapegoat on whose back he can take a symbolic journey through the world of the White Man's Burden. . . . Conrad reveals both his own and the white world's love-hate attitude towards Blacks."[1]

While one cannot deny that Conrad regarded the Negro, especially the natives of Africa, as being inferior to the white man, we ought to be wary, I think, of applying to him the social and political criteria of the 1960s or 1970s; rather, we ought to view his anti-Negro, anti-Russian, anti-German, and anti-Semitic strains from a proper historical perspective. Thus, Conrad was one of the first writers of the century to exhibit a savage indignation at the white man's atrocities committed against the natives of the Congo. His portrayal of James Wait is, essentially, no more negative than that of the cockney Donkin. To regard *The Nigger* as a racist piece of invective is no more justified than to consider *The Merchant of Venice* as an anti-Semitic treatise.

Though Conrad drew on his personal experiences and the acquaintances with sailors and ships for his fictional material in this novel, his selection of characters and the conflicts which beset them are carefully orchestrated to bring out Conrad's own interpretation of human solidarity. Thus, James Wait is singled out, as is Donkin or Singleton or Captain Allistoun, not to subscribe to the racist theory of the White

Man's Burden, but to illumine the problem of survival at sea, to expose the danger of fragmentation among the crew. The characters are grouped into symbolic units so as to dramatize the ship's ordeal.

And color is an essential element in this symbolic scheme which Conrad employs not only in the *Nigger* but throughout his work. In this novel, however, the opposition of white against black, light against dark, may invite social or political implications clearly not intended by the author. The very first paragraph of the novel shows this *visual* symbolic intent: the contrast between light and darkness:

Mr. Baker, chief mate of the ship *Narcissus,* stepped in one stride out *of his lighted cabin into the darkness* of the quarter-deck.

The second paragraph continues the theme:

The main deck was *dark aft,* but the halfway from forward, through the open doors of the forecastle, two streaks of *brilliant light* cut *the shadow of the quiet night* that lay upon the ship . . . in the *illuminated doorways,* silhouettes of moving men appeared for a moment, *very black,* without relief, like figures cut out of sheet tin. (3)

The appearance of the tall, statuesque Negro aboard the *Narcissus* is, in itself, a similar contrast of light and dark.

The lamplight lit up the man's body. He was tall. His head way away up in the *shadows* of the lifeboats that stood on skids above the deck. *The whites* of his eyes and his teeth *gleamed distinctly,* but the face was *indistinguishable.* (17)

After filling the deck with his deep and sonorous voice and his disdainful manner, he is set off from the rest of the crew. Separated by his color and nature from all the other white men, Wait is further isolated from them as he dwells in the shelter away from the men's quarters. Significantly, however, he does not make any attempt to come close to them. On the contrary, it is the men who keep coming to him, and his deckhouse turns into a symbolic abode of evil, which Conrad draws with his usual emphasis on color: Wait is now presented as a black idol who receives a homage of the other sailors, while the ship is seen as an image of light, far less real than the darkness of James Wait.

From this emphasis on the image as it is *seen* Conrad developed his art of producing a series of impressions of things and people in terms of color, motion, or immobility. The preoccupation with the image as well as Conrad's Polish background may be responsible for his preference for long sentence cadences, alliterations, and his frequent use of words beginning with im-, in-, il-, and ir-. Conradian pages are strewn with adjectives like impenetrable, irremediable, inscrutable, imperturbable, immense, immobile, and their derivatives. It may be that Conrad loves these words because of their sonority, but their negative meanings fit well into the melancholy portrait of the universe he was painting.

The Nigger of the "Narcissus" contains many felicities in style but some critics find in it passages they consider overwritten and somewhat repetitious or too much like a dictionary of epithets. Yet the book is the first fully controlled narrative and, unmistakably, it contains some splendid examples of his prose, especially in passages describing and indeed imitating the motions of a ship:

The hard gust of wind came brutal like the blow of a fist. The ship relieved of her canvas in time received it pluckily: she yielded reluctantly to the violent onset; then, coming up with a stately and irresistible motion, brought her spars to windward in the teeth of a screeching squall. Out of *the abysmal darkness of the black cloud* overhead *white hail* streamed on her, rattled on the rigging, leaped in handfuls off the yards, rebounded on the deck—round and *gleaming* in the *murky* turmoil like a shower of pearls. It passed away. (53)

The Nigger is a symbolic story of a disintegrating force on the deck of a ship, in the minds of men, and the equally disintegrating power of the sea; it is a dramatic account of men locked in a complex psychological conflict; also a tale of the contrast between sea and land. The *Narcissus* docks, meeting the world of land which Conrad describes as symbolically as he painted the sea and the ship. The docking of the ship, partly told in the passage above, creates the impression of "abysmal darkness" and of "murkey turmoil." Conrad adds several other images that give away his feelings about land (at that time, at any rate): "the steaming brows of millions of men," "begrimed walls," "a vision of disaster," "a mysterious and unholy spell" (164).

The Nigger is a tale of the sea, as the title of the American edition indicates: *The Children of The Sea: A Tale of the Forecastle.* The landfall of the *Narcissus* is as symbolic as the story's unfortunate hero, James Wait, whose centrality, however, this title distorts by the omission of "The Nigger."

The *Narcissus* came gently into her berth; the *shadows of soulless walls* fell upon her, the dust of all the continents leaped upon her deck, and a swarm of *strange men,* clambering up her sides, took possession of her in the name of *the sordid earth.* She had *ceased to live.* (165)

The *Narcissus* has ceased to live as a ship, and her crew are no longer the same men. Now they come in contact with the land "to get the wages of their glorious and obscure toil." The clerk paying them thinks them to be quite stupid for they hardly bother to count the money, and the venerable, white-bearded Singleton comes in for special abuse because he cannot write and is clumsy:

. . . his hands, that never hesitated in the great light of the open sea, could hardly find the small pile of gold in the profound darkness of the shore. (168)

The patriarchal sailor is only a "disgusting old brute" to the nameless clerk, but to Conrad he symbolizes the grand old man of the sea, with "a long record of his faithful work" (168–69). His name connotes his single-minded devotion to duty, as Donkin's suggests the unattractiveness of a donkey. Singleton and his fellow shipmates joined in a tie of loyalty to the ship "upon the immortal sea," indeed "wrung out a meaning" from their sinful lives. They were "a good crowd." Thus Conrad concludes his tale of the sea with a nostalgic remembrance of his days as a seaman. The *Narcissus* voyage was over; Jimmy Wait laid to rest in the dark depths of the sea, and Donkin gone elsewhere to earn his bread "by discoursing with filthy eloquence upon the right of labor to live" (173). The contact with the earth is not very pleasant to Conrad. The paid-off crew of the *Narcissus* will be met by men "with brutal faces and in shirtsleeves" who "dispense out of varnished barrels the illusions of strength, mirth, happiness; the illusion of splendor and poetry of life . . ." (171). Conrad begins and ends the story on a note of irony. The crew is totally unaware of the splendor and poetry of their labors upon the sea, for only Conrad the Romantic could see the seaman's task in this alluring light. Although they are no longer isolated on the endless waters of the sea or locked in the psychological strife with Wait and their own consciences, Conrad still observes them through the prism of their own solitude. Once again he sees the men of the *Narcissus* in terms of the visual contrast between the white and the black. His sailors step on "the white stones," but they seem to be "creatures of another kind—lost, alone, forgetful and doomed." Clouds break overhead. Sunshine streams down "the walls of grimy houses." And, finally, "the *dark* knot of seamen drifted in the *sunshine*" (172).

The Nigger of the "Narcissus" is an important book in Conrad's career as a novelist. It was accompanied by a "Preface" which defined the author's beliefs concerning art. Moreover, it clearly marked his break with his seafaring past. In a note "To My Readers in America" written after the first appearance of *The Nigger,* Conrad said:

After writing the last words of that book, in the revulsion of feeling before the accomplished task, I understood that I had done with the sea, and that henceforth I had to be a writer. (ix)

If the progress of the heroes of *The Nigger* was from light to darkness, the movement in Conrad's artistic growth had certainly been in the opposite direction. For, with this third novel (not counting the stories), he has formulated his credo as a novelist. Conrad defined art as

. . . a single-minded attempt to render the highest kind of justice to the visible universe, by bringing to light the truth, manifold and one, underlying its every aspect. It is an attempt to find in its forms, in its *colors,* in its *light,* in its *shadows,* in the aspects of matter and in the facts of life what of each is fundamental, what is enduring and essential—their one illuminating and convincingy quality—the very truth of their existence. (xi)

This Conrad has accomplished in *The Nigger* and, indeed in all his mature work. What is enduring and essential about this tale is not the adventurous passage of the *Narcissus* from Bombay to Dunkirk, but the manner in which Conrad made the ship *live,* the moral and psychological complexity with which he endowed his simple-minded protagonists, and, for all the apparent pessimism of his utterances on the treacherous qualities of the sea, his noble vision of the ship's crew as a compact social unit bound by an unwritten law of fidelity to their task, and by the solidarity of their calling.

In almost all of his works Conrad transformed his own experiences and bits of information available to him through hearing or from hearsay, into the terms of his fictional art. The men who served with him on the real *Narcissus* and the ship itself became the models for the future characters of *The Nigger*. The latter is not a mere record of a sea voyage but an intricately conceived novel, yet superb in the simplicity of its design; it is, quite often, a poem in prose, and it makes Conrad a poet in fiction.

Conrad must have understood this first artistic achievement, for he wrote:

It is the book by which, not as a novelist perhaps, but as an artist striving for the utmost sincerity of expression, I am willing to stand or fall. Its pages are the tribute of my unalterable and profound affection for the ships, the seamen, the winds and the great sea—the molders of my youth, the companions of the best years of my life. (ix)

The Nigger is certainly not Conrad's most outstanding novel, but it is his *first* symbolic masterpiece. Little wonder, therefore, that it is a rich source material for critics who find in the ambiguous symbols of the book a fertile ground for their interpretations. The more assiduous reader will have to decide which of these to embrace: the view of the rescue scene as a symbolic childbirth (Albert Guerard) or the apocalyptic nature of the novel's outline (Vernon Young),[2] to take but two recent examples. But if the multifariousness of critical interpretations of Conrad's symbols in *The Nigger* may baffle the uninitiated student or the average reader of Conrad, neither of them can fail to notice the central symbol of death and, more specifically, the symbol of a death journey. The ship is in danger of being lost on her voyage; and the twin messengers of death are Wait and Donkin, both of whom are the debilitating agents, sowing unrest and dissention in the crew. Wait dies; Donkin is dismissed in contempt; the remaining members of the crew straggle away as the ship's voyage, and therefore (in Conrad's view) her life, has come to an end.

Yet both the crew and the ship *are* alive, the reader will protest with justice; alive in our imagination, by dint of the novelist's art, whose task Conrad thus describes in the concluding paragraph of the "Preface":

To arrest, for the space of a breath, the hands busy about the work of the earth, and compel men entranced by the sight of distant goals to glance for a moment at the surrounding vision of form and color, of sunshine and shadows; to make them pause for a look, a sigh, for a smile—such is the aim, difficult and evanescent, and reserved for only a very few to achieve. But sometimes, by the deserving and the fortunate, even that task is accomplished. And when it is accomplished—behold!—all the truth of life is there: a moment of vision, a sigh, a smile—and the return to an eternal rest. (xvi)

The oft-anthologized "Preface" has stirred considerable critical turmoil among those who questioned the ambiguity or obscurity of its pronouncements; its grammatical and logical structure; and the validity of Conrad's general artistic credo. Ian Watt gives an excellent summary of the heated controversy offering his own interpretation of the "Preface" and the novel.[3] He points out that Conrad himself had reservations about the "Preface." Watt agrees with some objections of David Goldknopf, to whom he refers as a "contumelious infidel" who dared question the sacred cow, though apologetically, in his essay "What's Wrong with Conrad: Conrad on Conrad."[4]

Goldknopf objects to "the volley of rhetorical words and phrases"; to the raising of "the most profound metaphysical and esthetic issues" which are then "passed in a series of flourishes"; and finally considers the concluding statements of the preface "as simplistic as the rest." He then comments on the last words: "Form, color, sunshine, and shadows—a moment of vision, a sigh, and a smile. And what returns to eternal rest I must leave to an abler intuition than my own."[5] Watt attempts to answer this charge while accepting the fact that "Conrad's referent has been slipping; in the first sentence of the paragraph the person spoken of is the reader, who is made to pause; the referent of 'it is accomplished' can only be the successful work . . . however, we are back to the reader again, since he must be the recipient of the 'moment of vision.' This, however, won't do either; after all, we are naturally led to expect that, after finishing the book, the reader will get back on the job, and certainly not, as the text seems to say, find that its contact is lethal."[6]

In Watt's opinion, Conrad used the word "eternal" to remind the reader of an earlier reference to "Art is long and life is short," but "unfortunately the implication of 'eternal rest' conflicted with what had been said about the reader and the work of art, and this confusing conflation of grammatical subjects made the essay end in a logical blind alley."[7] In his argument concerning the meaning of the "Preface," Ian Watt shows that though there may have been some influence of Walter Pater, Maupassant, and Schopenhauer, he was not a hedonist like Pater, and his "formulation and combination of similar ideas is personal and undoctrinal."[8] The "Preface," he concludes, has attained a deserved fame not because Conrad has disclosed his narrative method but because he has conveyed his intimate feelings "about writing within the general context of other human activities in the ordinary world."[9]

In fact, Conrad's "credo" does not necessarily correspond to his fictional practice. Conrad's central idea, his statements on existential meaninglessness notwithstanding, is the affirmation of mankind's solidarity; this, however, stands in opposition to man's illusory view of human life and of the world itself. One of the frequent paradoxes of Conrad's fiction is the notion of truth being founded on an illusion which negates meaninglessness. The "Preface" thus cannot represent Conrad's own consistent creation of protagonists, who are marginal and deracinated men whose conduct usually signifies a breach of solidarity.

Moreover, solidarity itself in *The Nigger* must be distinguished from sympathy which is clearly presented as posing a danger to the safety of the *Narcissus*. Sympathy implies an imaginative identification with suffering humanity, whereas solidarity can be exemplified by men who totally lack imagination, men like Singleton, who looks "upon the immortal sea with the awakened and groping perception of its heartless might"; who "saw it unchanged, *black* and foaming under the eternal scrutiny of the stars . . . an immensity tormented and *blind*. . . ." Singleton will not allow the blind and meaningless fury of the elements to interfere with *his* commitment to solidarity. "He stood, still strong, as ever *unthinking*" (24). As the storm lashes the *Narcissus,* his erect figure is alone by the helm. "He steered with care" (89).

The story of *The Nigger* is told by an omniscient narrator whose voice at times becomes that of the author as in the final passage. In the beginning, the narrator's stance is quite objective and detached, punctuated by observations that would normally be the author's; then, as his membership in the crew is disclosed, the narrative voice acquires the intimate authenticity of a subjective point of view, that of a close observer and participant in the action. There are some inconsistencies in this method for if the story is told by one of the seamen aboard the *Narcissus,* he could not possibly report a verbatim account of conversations or incidents which he has not witnessed directly; nor can he be in possession of the inner thought processes of Wait and other characters.

The changes in the point of view may irritate some readers, but it is doubtful whether a Marlovian narrator would enhance either the drama of the tale or the poetic qualities of its style, despite Conrad's lapses into grandiloquence and near-sentimentality. Nor would a thoroughly objective third-person omniscience serve Conrad better. Perhaps the very vacillation between "he-they" and "I-we" captures the ambiguities of the crew's moral and emotional responses to the tests put before them.

The titles and the subtitles of the English and the American editions; the epigraph from the diary of Samuel Pepys ("My Lord in his discourse discovered a great deal of love to this ship."); and the dedication ("To Edward Garnett This Tale About My Friends Of The Sea") all point to Conrad's emphasis that this work is a sea-yarn *and* a *tale* rather than a novel: therefore it is endowed with the element of the fabulous, and it suggests oral narration.

The Nigger's being a *tale* may explain if not explain away the story's shifting perspective. But it is, Gerald Morgan argues in "Narcissus Afloat," a great deal more than merely a tale of a ship and its crew. Conrad represents the sea as a mirror both physically and metaphysically. He conceives of Narcissus as a vessel, implying "that if, like the chastened crew of the *Narcissus,* one enters unselfconsciously into one's voyage upon 'the immortal sea,' the 'mirror of the infinite,' one may possess at least the universe."[10] Narcissus, Morgan continues, is the proper mythical emblem for our time. He observes that there are no women in the ship the *Narcissus.* "Conrad's women, as a rule, don't take seriously the complicated masculine game of self-deception."[11] Echoing Moser's view that Conrad's heroes are not good at loving, Morgan terms his thesis that Conrad fails in treating sexual themes as an erotic fallacy. The Conradian hero is too preoccupied with his ideal conception of himself "to inspire anything but despairing self-sacrifice in women. . . . The failure seems to be less in Conrad than in his characters, since Conrad portrays faithfully the vagaries of Narcissus, in plots which are adequate comments on the failure of communication, which is today the agonizing concern of authors and dramatists."[12]

Chapter Four

The Disintegrating Power

Isolation from All Land Entanglements: "Typhoon"

The crew of the *Narcissus* bore the impact of the sea as well as the evil influence of Wait and Donkin. In another account of a sea voyage, "Typhoon,"[1] Conrad again subjects the seamen to a series of trials, testing their individual courage and their solidarity as a social group. Like the crew of the *Narcissus*, the men aboard the *Nan-Shan* voyage into death; their main trial, as the title of the story indicates, is the ship's struggle against the storm which attacks with singular fury, threatens the cohesion of the crew and thereby their survival.

This is *the disintegrating power* of a great wind: it *isolates one from one's kind.* An earthquake, a landslip, an avalanche, overtake a man incidentally, as it were—without a passion. A furious gale attacks like a personal enemy, tries to grasp his limbs, fastens upon his mind, seeks to rout his very spirit out of him. (40)

A man endowed with a lively or an unusual imagination will easily falter under the onslaught of "a great wind." Captain MacWhirr, however, lacks this quality, and although his officers and crew ridicule him for it, it is precisely this shortcoming that is responsible for the safety of the *Nan-Shan*. For Captain MacWhirr cannot be distracted from his task by an obscure or insistent dream, by an illusion of his exaggerated worth, nor by a romantic attachment. His own wife's only secret "was her abject terror of the time when her husband would come home to stay for good." His two children "were but slightly acquainted with their father." Captain MacWhirr is a man of very few words and an indifferent, almost ridiculous appearance. This silent man is presented by Conrad, obviously for the sake of a future dramatic suspense, as a man who has so far not experienced "the wrath and fury of the passionate sea," but merely "dirty weather (14, 18–19).

The point of the story, of course, is that this seemingly unprepared man must face a most violent typhoon and an explosive situation aboard his ship. He succeeds in his task far beyond the expectations of his crew. Jukes, the first mate, has a low opinion of his captain and is more intelligent than MacWhirr. But at the very first moment of the crisis his superiority disappears. The very presence of Captain Mac-Whirr cheers the seamen on deck, but he himself "could expect no relief of that sort from anyone on earth. Such is the *loneliness of command*" (40). The burden as well as the magic of command separates the captain from his crew. Despite his taciturnity and his unimaginative nature, Captain MacWhirr is also capable of introspection and moments of doubt. In the solitude and the darkness of his cabin, he speaks to himself, as if addressing another being stirred within his breast. Even to *his* feeble imagination of the burden of command becomes intolerable. The senselessly destructive wrath of the gale causes not only overwhelming bodily fatigue, but also severe mental stress. It is a kind of an insidious fatigue that penetrates into man's soul and makes him crave for peace.[2] It may cause a man's mind to turn upon himself in aimless concentration. But Captain MacWhirr resists the temptation to allow the brute force of nature to destroy him. More sensitive men, like Jukes, are apt to engage in do-nothing heroics in times of acute stress. The fury of the hurricane renders them indifferent and irresponsible. Had Jukes not had Captain MacWhirr on board, he would have faced the predicament of Lord Jim, who was also a victim of this sudden paralysis in a moment of danger. But Captain MacWhirr was there, silent as ever, facing the problem resolutely, the unheroic hero whose courage and sense of justice prevail over the chaos brought about by nature's wrath and men's passions.

Like all Conrad's sea tales, "Typhoon" is not really about the sea but about men locked in one or more conflicts. The calm manner of MacWhirr aids the crew in battling the storm. They are quite helpless, however, in dealing with the storm that Conrad creates *below* the deck. There, two hundred Chinese coolies are sitting out the gale, each man holding on to his possessions, especially to his box, in which he has locked "a small hoard of silver dollars."

As the crew fights the typhoon on deck, the tossing of the ship scatters the passengers and breaks up their baggage. Now the coolies are fighting, too—against one another and for what represents survival to *them:* the possession of the silver dollars. This truly macabre situation could prove disastrous to the *Nan-Shan,* had not Captain MacWhirr ordered his men to string up ropes across the hold so as to immobilize the passengers. The silver dollars are then collected and locked in an empty coalbin. The Chinese coolies remain imprisoned until the *Nan-Shan* arrives in Foochow.

Once more Captain MacWhirr displays his fortitude and good sense by his handling of this predicament. The crew is afraid that the coolies might overpower them and start their scrabble for the dollars, and is frightened even more when MacWhirr orders the release of the human cargo. The captain then solves the problem by proposing to the Chinese an equal division of the silver dollars among the passengers, since it is impossible to refund each man's precise amount. Should they not accept his proposal, the money would be turned over to a Chinese court, and thereby the bulk of the sum will be lost. To the amazement of the crew the Chinese accept the captain's decree. MacWhirr has won his second battle—not by doing anything imaginative or exceptional but simply by exercising his sense of fairness. "I think that he got out of it very well for such a stupid man" are the concluding words of the story—the reluctant appreciation of the first mate.

Thus Conrad portrays the adventurous tale of the *Nan-Shan* not in a straightforward way but in his usual ironic, double vision. The hero of the story, Captain MacWhirr, is deflated while at the same time revealed as the only man who could save the ship and her men, and whose very stolidity is a guarantee of order. The ironic vision is also enhanced by Conrad's narrative technique. The story is told in several, parallel methods: the "ordinary" third-person narrative is immediately spiced by bits of dialogue and excerpts from letters from MacWhirr to his parents and his wife, from Jukes, from Solomon Rout, the engineer, to their respective wives. Conrad attains yet another narrative voice by the wives' reading of the letters to the family members. For instance, Rout's wife selects what she considers important passages from her husband's reports and yells them to his elderly, deaf mother. This produces a humorous effect of contrast. On the one hand, we have the men and the captain of the *Nan-Shan* waging a truly heroic battle against the fury of the seas; on the other, the folks "back home," totally indifferent to the real nature of the seaman's toil.

There is a fascinating sociological as well as psychological aspect in these ironically presented relationships. For one thing, they emphasize the essential loneliness and isolation of each man aboard the ship; the crew members really have no point of contact with their families. The typhoon stresses this condition further by isolating each man from his fellow sailor, for the gale appears to each as a personal enemy; and finally, the crew is cut off from their captain and their human cargo of Chinese coolies.

A careful reading of this and other "sea" stories by Conrad shows that he was not concerned with the seaman's experience as such, but rather with individual or group psychology, and with nature's impact upon mass. He was annoyed by the critics who called him a "sea" novelist— and he had a good reason to be. For in *The Nigger* and in "Typhoon," indeed in all stories and novels with a setting of the sea, Conrad deals not with the problem of the sea but "merely a problem that has arisen on board a ship where *the conditions of complete isolation* from all land entanglements make it stand out with a particular force and coloring."[3]

The complexity of "Typhoon" is evident not only in the narrative technique but also in the treatment of the subject matter. For the story is really not about the storm but about the seamen of the *Nan-Shan*, and the diversion below the deck is not accidental. It is a basic element of the narrative, as the Donkin-Wait disturbance is central to *The Nigger of the "Narcissus,"* by showing that the real struggle aboard the *Nan-Shan* (and aboard the *Narcissus*) was among the men themselves. The secret self of the sailor is not revealed to fellow-seamen or to the members of his family. It is shown only to the reader who alone can put the pieces of the "jigsaw puzzle" together. Even the simplest of Conrad's men are often people of dual personality; their true identities are hidden or ambiguous and sometimes cannot be fathomed at all, therein summarizing (on Conrad's own terms) the human condition.

The Supreme Disaster:
"Amy Foster," "To-Morrow," "Falk"

The identity of Conrad's characters has always intrigued his readers and critics, especially since so many of his stories and novels are based on his own experiences. Yet although there are many Polish motifs in Conrad's fiction, there are only two Poles in the entire fictional output of Conrad, and of these one is a Carpathian peasant, Yanko Goorall (the Polish *góral* means mountaineer or Highlander), who could be called a Slav as well as a Pole. The other Pole is quite clearly identified as the protagonist of the story "Prince Roman" (discussed in Chapter 5).

Yanko, the hero of the story "Amy Foster," is an important minor character, for his fate is the keynote of so many works of Conrad: he is rejected by the people of the village of Brenzett, on the shores of Eastbay in England, and subsequently betrayed by his wife. Yanko is a humble mountaineer in the Carpathians who leaves his native shores in search of a better future in the New World. Shipwrecked off the English coast, this innocent "adventurer" has committed no crime save being different from the people in a village of Kent or Sussex, whose deep-seated hostility toward the outlandish looks and the ways of strangers makes Yanko a despised pariah.

Ah! he was different; innocent of heart, and full of good will, which nobody wanted, this castaway, that, like a man transplanted into another planet, was separated by an immense space from his past and by an immense ignorance from his future.[4]

To the stolid citizens of Brenzett and vicinity the stranger is simply unacceptable. The schoolmistress sees him as a "horrible-looking" man although he is actually handsome. Boys throw stones at this "funny tramp." The people have heard of a shipwreck but at first fail to connect the appearance of Yanko with the event. Nobody will stop to help the poor man, who is looking for food and shelter. The driver of a milk cart lashes him with a whip right over the face. A Mrs. Finn hits him "courageously" with her umbrella over the head; dogs bark themselves into a fit. Finally Mr. Smith does "his duty to the community by shutting up a wandering and probably dangerous maniac" (119–21).

His neighbor, Mr. Swaffer, takes Yanko to his farm and offers him food, lodging, and work, but the stranger lives there alone, shunned by everyone.

These were the people to whom he owed allegiance, and *an overwhelming loneliness* seemed to fall from the leaden sky of that winter without sunshine. All the faces were sad. He could talk to no one, and had no hope of ever understanding anybody. (128–29)

His tragedy is, from the beginning, one of incommunicability and estrangement.

He is tolerated by his employer and the only friendly soul in a menacing world is Amy Foster, the farmer's hand who had brought him a loaf of bread. Yanko's wish to marry her is opposed by everybody until he saves the granddaughter of Swaffer. The old farmer then allows Yanko to eat in the kitchen, and gives him title to a cottage and about an acre of land. But Yanko remains an unaccepted stranger to the community and, as he soon discovers, to his own wife as well.

She is infatuated with him at first and appears to be happy, despite their mutual isolation from the rest of the village. But the birth of a son to them shatters the brief period of their contentment. Cut off from everybody (his wife included), Yanko begins to teach his boy his own language, "so that he could have a man to talk with in that language that to [our] ears sounded so disturbing, so passionate, and so bizarre" (137). Amy resents this and snatches her son out of Yanko's arms when he sings to him. The passion he has evoked in her, perhaps by being so different and strange, has now turned to repulsion.

He falls ill, and when he is lying feverish, Amy refuses to allow the patient upstairs, as the doctor has directed, but keeps him in the drafty hall below, afraid to be alone with him, and especially to hear him speak his native tongue. On a stormy night his frantic supplications for water, uttered in that tongue, frightens her out of the house. Thereupon Yanko is found in a puddle, outside the wicker gate, face down. Although he is conscious, the realization of the terrible betrayal of his wife crushes his resistance. " 'Gone!' he said distinctly. 'I had only asked for water—only for a little water.' " He utters a poignant "Why" and is answered only by wind and rain. He then dies with the word "Merciful!" on his lips. The immediate cause of his death is found to be heart failure, and the narrator observes: "His heart must have indeed failed him, or else he might have stood this night of storm and exposure, too." Amy Foster has turned from a savior into a hunter whose spear "had entered his very soul" (141). Instead of finding a new land of future, this pathetic young foreigner is "cast out mysteriously by the sea to perish in *the supreme disaster of loneliness and despair*" (142). No human being understands this "lost stranger, helpless, incomprehensible . . ." (113), not even his wife, who forsakes him at the moment he needs her most. He has evoked no pity in the dwellers of the Eastbay shores, nor has he left any marks on Amy's mind. His memory disappears from her dull brain as a shadow traverses a white screen. His solitary singing in the fields, his dancing in the tavern, and his Slavic mannerisms are misunderstood by the people of Brenzett. It is indeed poor consolation to Yanko Goorall that his son was called Johnny by Amy Foster.

The autobiographical or, more specifically, the Polish character of the story is of further interest although Yanko is presented to the reader not as a Pole but as a Carpathian peasant from Central Europe. The description of Yanko and his early experiences takes us back to Conrad's childhood and the summer vacation he spent with his grandmother in the mountainous area of Krynica. The subject itself was also familiar to Conrad from his reading of Polish literature. The large and often unhappy emigration of Polish peasants to America and Europe was dealt with in many stories. Henryk Sienkiewicz's (great Polish novelist and Nobel Prize winner, best known abroad for his historical novel *Quo Vadis?*) well-known stories "The Lighthouse Keeper" and "After Bread"[5] described the fate of Polish wanderers in search of a more prosperous life. Perhaps Conrad's choice of the name for his hapless hero can be related to another story by Sienkiewicz, "Yanko the Musician" (1878). Like Conrad's Yanko, the gifted peasant boy in Sienkiewicz's story is guiltless but is treated by society as if he were a criminal. Both stories end on a note of bitter irony. Both Yankos die because they are total aliens in their communities.

Even if Conrad had not thought consciously or unconsciously of Sienkiewicz's and other similar Polish stories, there was plenty in Conrad's own experience to suggest the tragedy of this "supreme disaster." Consider, for example, Conrad's arrival in England, which he himself defined as a very lonely exploration. Or his solitary years at sea and the lack of true contact between him and other sailors; or the hardship and the unreality of being an English writer; the self-consciousness at his inability to speak English without a heavy foreign accent; or his ambiguous if not downright misogynous feelings toward his young English wife, who could not understand him and to whom he remained a stranger to the end of his days; or the inability of the English critics, friends and admirers included, to understand what he was trying to say in his fiction; or finally, his financial troubles.

Any of these experiences would have made Conrad think of his own fate when he wrote of Yanko: "He must have been a real adventurer at heart, for how many of the greatest enterprises in the conquest of the earth had for their beginning just such *a bargaining away of paternal cow for the mirage of true gold far away*" (117).

Conrad's "desertion" of his fatherland for the quixotic dream of adventure as a seaman was not much different in terms of the psychological analogy. The story is undoubtedly based on Conrad's profound feeling of loneliness and even on his personal experience not unlike that of Yanko himself. According to Jean-Aubry and Jessie Conrad, when Conrad fell ill in France in 1896, he found himself in a situation that parallels that of Yanko. The former bases his account on what is obviously Jesse Conrad's own recollection of an attack of gout suffered by her husband while they were staying on Île Grande:

For a whole long week the fever ran high, and for most of the time Conrad was delirious. To see him lying in the white canopied bed, dark-faced, with gleaming teeth and shining eyes, was sufficiently alarming, but to hear him muttering to himself in strange tongue (he must have been speaking Polish), to be unable to penetrate the clouded mind or catch one intelligible word, was for a young, inexperienced girl truly awful.[6]

But Conrad tried to make the story universal in its message: the rejection of an innocent, amiable foreigner by an unimaginative and dull native social group, and the inevitable punishment by death meted out to that foreigner. He was most careful to avoid any direct identification between himself and the protagonist; hence the story is told through the device of a conversation between an impersonal (because undescribed) "I" who introduces the real narrator, Dr. Kennedy, a country doctor made intimate by the epithet "my friend." The "I" provides the listening audience, Dr. Kennedy the speaking voice. The former also gives all necessary explanations, summaries and reported dialogue. It is through him, a humane and sympathetic Englishman who never loses his temper but is capable of bitter indignation, that we hear the passionate voice of Yanko Goorall, and learn of the inert passion of his Amy. To render Yanko's emotions more accurately, Kennedy attempts to capture the childlike, terrifying vision of the world as it appeared to the young, Polish emigrant. The patient listener, the "I" provides the continuity of the narrative, and gives it the dimension of time, e.g., "Kennedy discoursed. . . . He remained silent. Then he went on. . . ." Kennedy does not overtly condemn the cruelty of his insular fellow citizens, yet his narrative leaves the reader with a terrifying vision of a stranger's rejection by a hostile community, of a woman's unthinking betrayal of her husband.

H. G. Wells considered "Amy Foster" to be a caricature of an autobiography, and Conrad's own self-torment caused by the experience of his own foreignness. Guerard called it "the best expression of Conrad's sense of isolation," and "the most personal of his works, since it dramatizes an obscurely unsuccessful marriage and the rejection of the Carpathian peasant Yanko Goorall by the British."[7] Apparently, Conrad himself had a high opinion of "Amy Foster," for in his letter to A. Knopf of August 24, 1913, he wrote that the story and "Falk" were "the most highly finished of [my] stories."[8]

He did not think that highly of the second story in the collection *Typhoon and Other Stories,* "To-Morrow." When Conrad sent it to his agent, J. B. Pinker, he referred to it as " 'Conrad' adapted down to the needs of a magazine, but 'by no means a potboiler.' " Conrad relied on the suggestion of his collaborator, Ford Madox Hueffer (later Ford), in creating the main character, Harry Hagberd. According to his wife, Jessie, he did not like the piece, but he considered it good enough to be used as a basis of a one-act play (with which Hueffer was also helpful), *One Day More* (begun in 1904, performed on June 25, 1905).[9]

The situation in "To-Morrow" is, to some extent, a reversal of Yanko's plight in "Amy Foster," but here too we have an innocent soul, overtaken by loneliness and despair. This time it is the woman who is utterly crushed in her pursuit of happiness. Like most women of Conrad, Bessie Carvil is a silent and passive sufferer. A daughter of a blind, retired boat builder she lives alone with her tyrannical father in a cottage rented from her neighbor. The latter is an old, retired coasting-skipper, Hagberd, whose son Harry has run away from home. The Hagberds begin advertising for their son in the London papers, but after the wife dies the old captain grows miserly and abandons his efforts. He seems to recover "from the disease of hope" (248), but is now possessed by a new "formula of hope," a fixed idea that his son will return "tomorrow." The old man keeps digging up the front plot of his land without planting anything, "not till our Harry comes home to-morrow" (250). He assures Bessie that Harry will marry her upon his return. When the long-lost son does come back, after an absence of fifteen years, his father does not recognize him and throws a spade at the young man. Harry meets Bessie, who wants to know why he has returned. He tells her he has come to collect five pounds, which he needs after a drinking spree. He has become a wanderer and has no intention of staying in "this dead-alive place" (263). All he gets, however, is a half-sovereign from the girl. He showers "kisses on her face with a silent and overmastering ardor" (275) and leaves her ". . . overcome by fate," tottering "silently towards her stuffy little *inferno* of a cottage" (276).

This sad story is not very effective or moving; at best it offers yet another example of Conrad's preoccupation with the theme of frustrated love, his awkwardness in describing sexual intimacy, and, last but not least, his treatment of the dreamer. For Bessie is not without blame, though she has done nothing to deserve her lonely life. However, her acceptance of the demented Hagberd's notion that Harry was her future husband and her submission to his "hopeful craze" are a challenge to, perhaps a betrayal of, reality. The futile dream has come true, wreaking havoc in her heart, leaving her more isolated than she was before.

"Falk" also begins on this note of rebuttal. Like Yanko, Falk is not accepted by the community. However, the reason for his status as an outcast is not his foreign origin but the dark deed committed in his past. This silent tugboat captain in the Dutch East Indies is different from everybody else; he does not eat meat; moreover, he does not explain his peculiarity. The mystery about him is augmented by his

unexplained, sudden termination of his courtship of a lady in the city. If
Yanko Goorall reminded the narrator of "Amy Foster" of a child of
nature, and "a wild creature under the net . . . of a bird caught in a
snare," Falk strikes the narrator of the story as a mythological beast—a
centaur whose image he had once seen in a book.

The two men are separated from their respective social groups, but
the stigmas that brand them lead to different—in fact, opposite—
endings, which is perhaps why Conrad thought of these two stories as
"highly finished," for he had a clear design of the purpose each man
would serve. Yanko's separateness cannot be overcome and it proves
deadly. Falk's is merely an indication of his superior will to live; Falk is
the epitome of human self-preservation, the preservation of the body
and of its senses. The dark secret of the man is a memory of a desperate
struggle aboard an isolated and lost ship. Falk survives by killing the
ship's carpenter and eating him with the rest of the crew members; then
the stronger men kill and eat the weaker ones until only one man
remains alive and is rescued—Falk.

His plight must be distinguished from the predicament of so many
Conradian heroes who torture themselves with a feeling of guilt, who
cannot live except by expiating that guilt, and rarely do. He simply has
a most profound horror of death and "will guard his own life with the
inflexibility of a pitiless and immovable fate" (236). In a sense, Falk is a
symbol of this fate, of blind natural forces, and therefore he must
prevail. He has deserted the human race by his act of killing and
cannibalism, and he enters it again through the experience of confession
and love. He attains the same kind of determination that enabled him
to survive aboard the stricken ship.

"Falk" could have been as interesting a story as "Amy Foster" because
it too is autobiographical (Conrad based it on his long and frustrating
period of waiting for a voyage from Bangkok), but, the author's view
notwithstanding, it simply lacks cohesion as a narrative, although the
plot has many possibilities. Falk, the only man with a tugboat, refuses
to escort the narrator's ship down the river, suspecting him (mistakenly)
to be a rival for the affections of the nameless niece of Captain Hermann. After some complications, the narrator promises to intervene on
Falk's behalf since Uncle Hermann is against the marriage but finally
leaves it all to the girl's decision. Falk makes a full confession of his

crime and promptly moves the girl, who then agrees to marry him, uncle or no uncle.

The theme of love between Falk and the girl is not handled well. For one thing, the girl never materializes as a full-fledged person, and she utters not a single word in the whole story. The silent girl is supposed to resemble Falk's mythical appearance: she is "built on a magnificent scale," and she "could have stood for an allegoric statue of the Earth." A fitting companion for a "man strong and elemental." It is hard to say whether Conrad failed in "Falk" because he may have tried to introduce a comic treatment into a story about a case of cannibalism and love. Altogether, the elements of the story are not well mixed and Conrad's verdict is, unfortunately, quite untrue. "Falk" is *not* one of his finished stories. In fact, it isn't even interesting. Perhaps Falk's transgression and his separateness never became the "supreme disaster" of Conrad's tragic heroes.

What may be interesting, however, are Conrad's references to *grotesque* images (223), the *profound conviction* of Falk's cry (236), and the introduction of the comic German, in fact, *two* comic Germans, Schomberg and Hermann. The interest in the grotesque will be fully developed in *The Secret Agent,* and Falk's conviction foreshadows Jim's triumphant conviction, Kurtz's desperate cry, the Intended's illusory conviction, and, of course, Prince Roman's and Lord Jim's triumphant convictions. Schomberg will appear both in *Lord Jim* and in *Victory*.

Though intended to be an archetypal story of man's survival under conditions of extreme stress, rivaling the theme of *Heart of Darkness,* "Falk" is more like a melodramatic romance, its string of symbolic clues notwithstanding. The latter, however, have aroused the voracious appetites of symbol-hunting critics who are floored by Conrad's preoccupation with eating and sex. And since eating and speaking both require the use of the mouth, it and language itself or the absence thereof are made into central metaphors. The reader is urged to note the verbosity of Hermann, the almost nonlingual speech of Falk, and the silence of the corpulent niece, whose body obviously speaks volumes.[10] The story has invited sweeping comparisons with other writers as the critics ranged from Wagnerian and Zolaesque motifs to the philosophical themes of Schopenhauer, Darwin, and Jack London.[11] Recently a reassessment of "Falk" has been attempted by critics like Joel R. Kehler who plead for it a higher place in the "hierarchy of excellence," suggesting that the nameless narrator is the focal figure and not Falk; that the story is actually another Initiation tale and its narrator has more affinity with Kafka's Joseph K. than with the Marlow of *Heart of Darkness.*[12]

Chapter Five

The Triumphant Conviction

The Triumphant Conviction of Strength: "Youth"

"Youth" (1898) is a typical product of early Conrad, with a dose of atypical cheerfulness. Although Conrad calls the story simply a "Narrative," he feels compelled to distinguish it from *Heart of Darkness*. Thus he considers "Youth" a feat of memory . . . a record of experience . . . [which] in its inwardness and in its outward coloring, begins and ends in [myself]" (xi). Conrad clearly implies in his subsequent comments that *Heart of Darkness* goes far beyond the autobiographical elements. Yet although "Youth" is simple, it does introduce a new technical device—Conrad's celebrated narrator, Marlow. Except for the opening three paragraphs, a few descriptive interjections toward the end of the story (e.g., "He drank"), and the concluding paragraph, the entire story is related by Marlow to his silent four companions: a company director, an accountant, a lawyer, and the author. The five men are united by "the strong bond of the sea, and also the fellowship of the craft" (3) and the reflection of their faces bent over the polished table is the image with which Conrad begins and ends the tale.

Marlow's is a nostalgic story of his youth, its glamour and intoxication. He was twenty at the time of the adventure, which was his first voyage to the East as a second mate. This was also the first command for the captain of the *Judea*. Marlow's account captures Conrad's "romantic feeling of reality" when Conrad himself was young and full of illusions about life and the sea, and when he voyaged from London to Bangkok, and his ship, laden with coal, went through severe trials.

The delays in getting the ship loaded, the vicissitudes during the voyage: leaks, culminated by a fire and finally escape by lifeboats—these provide the material of the narrative. Marlow, whose indomitable spirit of youth triumphs over all difficulties, gets his crack at first command—of a lifeboat rather than a ship, but first command nevertheless—and it proves to be a totally exhilarating experience for him. Marlow's first glimpse of the Far East is somewhat sentimental but the imagery and cadence of that description are rich and sufficiently ambiguous to invite many exercises at unearthing symbolic meanings. It is as if Conrad tried to freeze his memories into a motionless piece of sculpture:

And then I saw the men of the East—they were looking at me. The whole length of the jetty was full of people. I saw brown, bronze, yellow faces, the black eyes, the glitter, the color of an Eastern crowd. And all these beings stared without a murmur, without a sigh, without a movement. They stared down at the boats, at the sleeping men who at night had come to them from the sea. Nothing moved. The fronds of palms stood still against the sky. Not a branch stirred along the shore, and the brown roofs of hidden houses peeped through the green foliage, through the big leaves that hung shining and still like leaves forged of heavy metal. This was the East of the ancient navigators, so old, so mysterious, resplendent and somber, living and unchanged, full of danger and promise. And these were the men. (40)

The structure of the story is not merely a literary convention to enable the author to unfold the story, although it must be noted that it came naturally to Conrad; it serves the special purpose of creating the illusion of Marlow's youth, nostalgically remembered after twenty-two years. The frame for this recollection is provided in the four men surrounding Marlow, who nod in approval, their faces marked by the experience of age. The contrast between these weary faces and the intensity of Marlow's account enhance the dramatic quality of his vision. Conrad needs these aging men about Marlow to emphasize the true feelings of youth.

Young Marlow's romantic attitude to the world implies a belief that man is infinite, an attitude that produces the disparity between what is the romantic's expectation of his achievement and his actual performance. Or, in other words, the disparity between illusion and reality. Thus the experience of life, in retrospect, has the qualities of absurdity. The view of the East affords young Marlow mysterious delight, but the older Marlow knows it as an illusory experience, often a depressing one. His memory of youth is deeply touched with sadness.

The story, however, is much more than the aging Marlow's recollection of his youth, though it is not as profound or as artistic as *Heart of Darkness*. In both stories Conrad subjects his protagonists to a crucial test. In "Youth" Captain Beard and his crew are tried by a series of misfortunes that beset the *Judea*. The sundry mishaps of the doomed ship culminate in its destruction. Up to this point Captain Beard and his crew (which includes Marlow) have had to face the unpredictable disasters and the fury of the elements as one social unit, welded together by the force of solidarity. After the ship goes down Marlow exultantly sets out on his first command, purposely drifting away from his companions so that he can fully taste the meaning of adventure—alone.

It is here, in this naive, romantic pursuit of excitement, that Conrad emphasizes the difference between the youthful Marlow and the aged Captain Beard. The latter is old and experienced; although hopeful that his ship will pull through he knows the true meaning of mortality. Marlow, on the other hand, is totally intoxicated by the glamour of youth. Like a child, he cannot conceive the notion of death. Wrapped up in the boundless egoism of his quest for adventure, young Marlow regards himself as an indestructible being. Nothing can touch him— neither the wrath of the ocean nor the inadequacy of men. In a sense, he foreshadows Lord Jim before the *Patna* incident by being so romantically absorbed in his dream.

Were the story told from young Marlow's point of view, it would have little or no affinity with *Heart of Darkness* or *Lord Jim*. The story is narrated by the *aged* Marlow, whose recollection of his younger self and the *Judea* adventure is nostalgic, but the narrative strikes a note of profound pessimism. There is a glimpse of glamorous youth, but also the death of a ship. In fact, death is intimately linked with Conrad's portrayal of "indestructible" youth; hence the implied irony of the story. Thus, at the very highest moment of Marlow's success, the arrival of his lifeboat in a Far Eastern port, he alone watches the men of the East. His crew "slept . . . in the careless attitudes of death" (41). Later, we learn of Captain Beard's death. Marlow's final conclusion is that youth is but a few moments, that youthful strength and the glamour of adventure are but illusions, that life must inevitably end in disenchantment, in weariness, in death.

The name *Judea* may be nothing more than a simple transcription of the actual experience by Conrad himself. The barque *Palestine* on which

Conrad sailed suffered the same disaster. In his desire to capture the feeling of reality Conrad frequently retained the actual names of people with whom he came into contact, or changed the names slightly, as if fearing to lose the tie that bound him to their identities. Yet "Youth" (like many other stories based on Conrad's own experiences (transcends the confines of a personal remembrance.

The characters are carefully arranged so as to bring out the contrasts in ironic terms: the elderly gentlemen bent over the polished surface of a table, drinking silently as Marlow recounts his adventures, are the first visual tableau which Conrad draws before the reader. The same group will appear at the very end of the story, serving as a kind of refrain, a formal closing of the story. That Marlow the narrator is one of them and is speaking of himself as another man is one contrast. But there are others, such as the contrast between Marlow and Captain Beard, and the humorous aspect of their relationship is further enhanced by the fact that despite his advanced age Captain Beard's command of the *Judea* is the first one—and, ironically, also his last one.

Youth and old age intermingle from the first. "You'll admit it was time," Marlow remarks of his skipper's first command, since he was "sixty if a day" (4). But the captain has a youthful aspect: "And he had blue eyes in that old face of his, which were amazingly like a boy's . . ." (4). The second mate had "a snow-white, long beard," and "between those two old chaps [I] felt like a small boy between two grandfathers" (5). The *Judea* is also old, "all rust, dust, grime . . .," but the motto below her name belies her age—"Do or Die." Marlow recalls: ". . . it took my fancy immensely. There was a touch of romance in it, something that made me love the old thing—something that appealed to my youth!" (5).

Like her husband, Mrs. Beard combines old age and youth. She was "an old woman, with a face all wrinkled and ruddy like a winter apple, and the figure of a young girl" (7). She treats Marlow as if he were her own child and insists on repairing his shirt. As she overhauls Marlow's clothes he reads, significantly enough, *Sartor Resartus* by Thomas Carlyle (also Burnaby's *Ride to Khiva*). Marlow observes that he "preferred the soldier to the philosopher at the time; a preference which life has only confirmed" (7). And, once again, he cannot resist repeating the main idea of the story: "However, they are both dead and Mrs. Beard is dead, and youth, strength, genius, thoughts, achievements, simple hearts—all die. . . . No matter" (7).

Irony is piled upon irony. As Mrs. Beard is mending Marlow's torn outfit, Captain Beard is vainly trying to overhaul the ancient ship. The obvious corollary suggested here is that life, perhaps like old clothes and the ship, must be worn out *irreparably.* But men are not always aware of this process. The rats desert the old ship, while men remain behind, as if to affirm the youthful motto of the ship. The Captain and Marlow are on trial, but so is the *Judea,* for Marlow, at any rate:

O youth! The strength of it, *the faith of it,* the imagination of it! To me she was not an old rattletrap carting about the world a lot of coal for a freight—to me she was *the endeavor, the test, the trial of life.* (12)

The ship is on fire; its black cargo burns, and fire is both life and death. The whole experience becomes "like an absurd dream" (24). Yet when the ship burns, after all futile efforts to save her, Marlow "thought it fine and the *fidelity to the old ship* was fine" (30). Therein Marlow's (and Conrad's) simple thesis: Life is an absurd thing, and it can be understood only in terms of its opposite—death. What matters in life is not mere survival, but the individual or collective code.

Even the ship is capable of this sense of fidelity, and the death of old *Judea* is in the nature of a reward and a triumph:

A magnificent death had come like a grace, like a gift, like a reward to that old ship at the end of her laborious days. The surrender of her weary ghost to the keeper of stars and sea was stirring like the sight of a glorious triumph. (35)

This "glorious triumph" is the same kind of victory that Marlow attains by the exercise of his "triumphant conviction of strength" (37)—a delusive, romantic notion that belies the facts. For the ship's motto "Do or Die" does not help the ship or the crew. As the ship goes down to her final "triumph" so goes Marlow's youthful and romantic idealism after he has ignored the lesson of the *Judea.* At the moment of the ship's death Marlow is in the throes of his romantic infatuation; totally immersed in his own interpretation of the event (tragic for Captain Beard and certainly not glorious for any other crew members), he can regard it only through the prism of his own egoism, as Jim views the sinking of the *Patna* solely in terms of his own romantic commitment to honor. It is the older Marlow, the narrator of the story, who provides the more objective perspective by his constant references to the brevity of the human endeavor and human life. His vision is a memory of the past, and Marlow himself is a simple man, slightly touched with the sadness of an advancing age.

The Appalling Face of a Glimpsed Truth: *Heart of Darkness*

The transformation of this narrator into the Marlow of *Heart of Darkness* represents a great artistic stride forward. Once again there is the familiar group of listeners whose common bond is the sea, seated on the deck of the *Nellie,* a cruising yawl: the Director of Companies, the Lawyer, the Accountant, Marlow, and the initial storyteller who provides the description of the Thames, the four men, and sets the mood for the journey that will lead into the "heart of darkness," starting Marlow on his long discourse. But this time it is not a straightforward tale of adventure. From the first Conrad gives warning of his serious purpose, and later in the story Marlow takes great pains to assure himself that his audience is following him:

Do you see him? Do you see the story? Do you see anything? It seems to me I am trying to tell you a dream—making a vain attempt, because no relation of a dream can convey the dream-sensation, that commingling of absurdity, surprise, and bewilderment in a tremor of struggling revolt, that notion of being captured by the incredible which is of the very essence of dreams. (82)

Perhaps Conrad is straining a bit this device of creating an air of verisimilitude, but he succeeds splendidly with the story as a whole. For *Heart of Darkness* is not really a tale about a man called Kurtz, told by Marlow to a group of his friends. It is about Marlow and, no doubt, about Conrad himself. The story, as one of Conrad's letters to William Blackwood indicates, is about "the criminality of inefficiency and pure selfishness when tackling the civilizing work in Africa. . . ."[1] It turned out to be much more—an illuminating personal confession, a profound discussion of man's moral complexity, and, last but not least, a remarkable short novel whose literary merit is not lessened by its being at once an adventure story and a psychological thriller.

Once more Conrad examines the plight of the white man in the wilderness of the jungle. As in "Karain" and the first two novels, the images of light and darkness, of sound and stillness, abound, but their function is more effective here; they are not only more numerous and varied, but they are used on three different levels: literary, intellectual, and psychological. The jungle becomes the symbol of the savage in man and a symbol of man's isolation. The white man in the darkness of the primeval forest wages a double battle against the destructive powers that prey on his body, and also against the forces that undermine his moral integrity. People who live in an organized, civilized community, protected by law and police, cannot understand the powers of darkness.

Neither did Marlow—*before* he went to the Congo, and his search for Kurtz began in the depths of the primeval forest symbolically representing man's quest for self-knowledge. This quest, which appears in almost all of Conrad's works, is the core of his literary method, and especially so in the two stories and two novels featuring Marlow, the spinner of yarns engaging the attention of his audiences. In each case the reader is drawn not merely into Marlow's narrative about other people but also into an exploration of Marlow's own personality. Of course, this happens also in other tales, e.g., in "The Secret Sharer," where the Captain reaches a measure of self-knowledge only after he has totally identified himself with the problem of the confessed murderer, Leggatt, whom he shelters from punishment. In *Lord Jim* Marlow is joined by Brierly and Stein in his painstaking and painful efforts to understand Jim's motives, and each of them ends up with self-examination. Similarly, Marlow's unflagging pursuit of Kurtz is an attempt to fathom his own soul, conducted with accents of self-mockery.

The tone of Marlow's narrative is easy to understand when one recalls Conrad's own experiences in the Congo and his comments on his interest in geography and the strange fascination exercised upon his boyish mind by Sir Leopold McClintock's *The Voyage of the "Fox" in the Arctic Seas*:

The great spirit of the realities of the story sent me off on the romantic explorations of my inner self; to the discovery of the taste of poring over maps. . . . Only once did that enthusiasm [geographical] expose me to the derision of my schoolboy chums. One day, putting my finger on a spot in the very middle of the then white heart of Africa, I declared that some day I would go there.[2]

What Conrad discovered when he did go to Africa some eighteen years later was no romantic dream or exalted adventure but "the distasteful *knowledge* of the vilest scramble for loot that ever disfigured the history of human conscience and geographical exploration."[3] Little wonder Conrad was melancholy and lonely there in the heart of the African continent, and was prompted to observe with considerable bitterness: "What an end to the idealized realities of a boy's daydreams!"[4]

Yet the Congo journey was valuable to Conrad beyond supplying him with material for his fiction. Before it, he said, he was a mere animal.[5] After it, he lost his illusions, perhaps, but not love of humanity in general. Thus, in discovering the horrors of exploitation, the brutality and hypocrisy of the Belgian colonists, Conrad also discovered (as Marlow did) a terrifying feeling of affinity with the savagery of the jungle.

Marlow alone, among the members of the expedition, can understand the nature of Kurtz's fall *because* he has experienced the same temptation. But though the wilderness, to use his own phrase, has patted him on the head, he does not succumb to its momentary spell (144). He may feel alienated from his fellow men, both in the jungle and upon his return to the civilized world, but he has not cut himself off from the whole world, as Kurtz did.

The potent suggestiveness and the dreamlike quality of Kurtz's words shake Marlow profoundly, but he keeps his head, though not his soberness. The fate of Kurtz is a symbolic warning to Marlow to beware of the danger of extreme isolation. Kurtz ". . . had kicked himself loose of the earth . . . he had kicked the very earth to pieces. . . . He was alone . . ." (144). This is the penalty he must pay for having yielded to the dark powers of the forest *and* to the darkness of his own soul.

Kurtz had arrived in the Congo with a notion of being considerably more than a mere producer of ivory. He believed that the whites were regarded by the savage natives as superior beings, and he meant to reform them. Instead of overcoming the savages' ignorance, however, Kurtz became one of them—as their demigod, to be true. He submitted to adulation and rites in his own honor (probably involving cannibalism and therefore not described but merely suggested); he resorted to violence in extorting ivory for his company. Yet he came to hate the natives. The paper for the International Society for the Suppression of Savage Customs, which the idealistic Kurtz had once written, bore a scrawled note, "Exterminate all the brutes!" obviously jotted down much later.

For all his degradation, Kurtz stands, morally speaking, one notch above the manager of the company, who never wanted anything but financial gain for himself. In comparison with the manager Kurtz's corruption is rather attractive, for it lacks the manager's hollowness; and because of Kurtz's eloquence it is dramatic, so much so, in fact, that it casts a spell on the young bepatched Russian trader and on Marlow, for whom Kurtz's lot becomes "the nightmare of [my] choice." Marlow is fascinated but not overcome by the power emanating from the face of the dying Kurtz. It seems to him that a veil had been lifted from Kurtz's ivory face. Having glanced over the edge of the precipice, Marlow knows the meaning of Kurtz's stare on his deathbed.

"Droll thing life is," Marlow declares, "that mysterious arrangement of merciless logic for a futile purpose. The most you can hope from it is some knowledge of yourself—that comes too late—a crop of *unextinguishable regrets*" (150).[6] Yet Marlow considers Kurtz a remarkable man because his cry "The horror!" was ". . . the expression of some sort of *belief*; it had candor, it had *conviction* . . . it had the appalling face of a *glimpsed truth* . . ." (p. 151). That is why Marlow remains loyal to Kurtz; the latter "had stepped over the edge" while he, Marlow, was "permitted to draw back [my] hesitating foot" (151). Therein, he observes, lies the whole difference. Kurtz's cry represents a revulsion against his darker self, a sign that he has not been lost completely. In fact, Marlow believes, "It was an affirmation, a moral victory . . ." (151).

After he recovers from his illness Marlow comes to Brussels, full of disgust for its people, who are intruders because they cannot possibly understand his state of mind. He walks about the city, bitterly grinning at people, haunted by the vision of Kurtz on the stretcher. The gloom of the jungle and the beating of the drums are still vivid in his imagination. When he brings this vision with him to Kurtz's "Intended," he realizes that he can never stop seeing that eloquent phantom as long as he lives. The memory of Kurtz is like a dream (or rather like a nightmare) he can share with nobody else. Kurtz's "Intended" is isolated by her grief and her illusion of Kurtz's integrity and greatness, as the Russian youth was cut off from the rest of the white colonizers by his fervent belief in Kurtz's eminence. This woman is endowed with a ". . . mature capacity for *fidelity,* for *belief,* for *suffering*" (157).

Marlow's efforts to find Kurtz and to understand him represent, essentially, his search for truth. It is natural, therefore, that he cannot abide falsehood. Seeking the truth about himself, too, and a true way to tell his story, he concludes that it is impossible

to convey the life-sensation of any given epoch of one's existence—that which makes its truth, its meaning—its subtle and penetrating essence. (82)

It is one of the major ironies of the story that Marlow, for all his dedication to truth, must stoop to a lie. Kurtz's fiancée asks what the dying man's last words were, and Marlow cannot tell her the truth, that Kurtz's last cryptic message to the world was an agonizing cry, "The horror! The horror!" He cannot because "It would have been too dark—too dark altogether . . ." (162). Marlow caustically observes that the heavens didn't fall upon his head when he uttered the lie. Truth has become a rather ambiguous thing, and so has the notion of darkness. For, while Kurtz's voice reaches Marlow ". . . from the threshold of an eternal darkness" (159), he bows his head before the faith that was in Kurtz's Intended, ". . . before that *great and saving illusion* that shone with an unearthly glow in the darkness, in the *triumphant darkness* from which I could not have defended her—from which [I] could not even defend [myself] . . ." (159). Marlow gives the young woman what she wants, something to treasure for the rest of her life; he tells her that the last word Kurtz pronounced was her name. Conrad belabors the irony of the situation. The woman's ". . . cry of inconceivable triumph and of unspeakable pain" indicates that "She knew. She was sure . . ." (162).

Marlow was not; having proven his loyalty to the darkness of Kurtz does he thereby prove that her illusion is true light? After all (to continue the symbolism of dark and light), she remains in the dark about her beloved Kurtz. Conrad does not give a clear answer. Despite the light of her belief, the "ashy halo" about her head, the room of the Intended has grown darker, and she is "all in black . . . floating . . . in the dusk" (156–57).

Marlow has emerged from the depths of the jungle a wiser and a sadder man. The contact with Kurtz has given him something valuable, a heightened perception of life's complexity. He no longer takes things for granted; nothing is either black or white, for the two merge into each other. The supreme lesson he has learned is to respect man's faith, any faith or sincere conviction. He harbors a secret he cannot divulge to other people. Man must forever remain shut within the shell of his own personality. Like the captain in "The Secret Sharer," whose special knowledge sets him apart from his crew, Marlow is unable to communicate with others. He doubts whether his experience can ever be conveyed to his listeners. He has come to believe that ". . . we live as we dream—alone" (82).

Marlow is right in expressing this doubt, for many a reader of Conrad occasionally fails to distinguish between the literal and the symbolic aspects of his fiction. Yet the symbolic level is a most essential feature of the writer's method. As Conrad's use of the central narrator enables the author to remove himself from his subject matter, so his symbolism and his images convey and enhance the doubts, ambiguities, and moral predicaments of his heroes.[7]

Ivory is *white* and it is craved by the white man but it also represents moral darkness; the two white women in the Company's offices knit *black* wool; ". . . It seems to me," Marlow says, "I had stepped into the gloomy circle of some Inferno" (66). As he proceeds to fathom Kurtz's mystery, he perceives that its essentials ". . . lay deep under the surface, beyond [my] reach . . ." (100). Because Marlow's story goes beyond the obvious it carries an abundance of suggestive words or images, e.g., silence, stillness, blazing heat, immobility, somber trees, decay, somber and brooding ferocity, skulls on posts, blind whiteness of a fog, overcast sky, impenetrable darkness. Thus, the memory of an actual experience is transformed into a symbolic and deeply ironic account of a modern descent into Hell.

We see, therefore, that *Heart of Darkness* is not a simple story. The symbolic journeys of Kurtz and Marlow are one theme. Another, perhaps no less important, is the political issue of Belgian colonialism. Conrad, his own conservatism notwithstanding, indignantly condemns Belgian imperialism in the Congo.

The first narrator connects the story that is to come from Marlow with some comments on the history of the Thames and the conquerors who had gone out on that river. He paves the way to Marlow's opening

words, spoken against the setting of a falling dusk and the lights of
moving ships, "And this also . . . has been one of the dark places of the
earth" (48). Marlow takes up the theme of man's conquest, briefly
mentions the Romans, the fascination of the mystery in the wilderness,
and then, before he makes the most significant observation, he assumes
"the pose of a Buddha preaching in European clothes and without a
lotus flower" (50). Marlow speaks of the ancient conquerors:

They grabbed what they could get for the sake of what was to be got. It was
just robbery with violence, aggravated murder on a great scale, and men
going at it blind—as is very proper for *those who tackle a darkness*. The
conquest of the earth, which mostly means the taking it away from those who
have a different complexion or slightly flatter noses than ourselves, is not a
pretty thing when you look into it too much. What *redeems* it is *the idea* only.
An *idea* at the back of it; not sentimental pretence but an *idea*; and an *unselfish
belief in the idea*—something you can set up, and bow down before, and offer *a
sacrifice to*. . . . (50–51)

This is a fitting prelude to the picture of the Belgian exploitation of the
Congo Marlow paints later on, as he plunges into his narrative. With
biting irony he describes the activities of a French man-of-war, an-
chored off the coast, and shelling the bush although there was not a shed
in sight. This was indeed a passage into places which had a deadly but
also a farcical aspect. During this nightmarish pilgrimage Marlow
comes upon a chain-gang of native slaves and then a group of black
shapes crouching among the trees and dying. This is one of the most
powerful and shocking evocations of man's brutality, an indignant
indictment of the white man's inhumanity to the black man in the
Congo.

They were dying slowly—it was very clear. They were nothing earthly now,
nothing but black shadows of disease and starvation, lying confusedly in the
greenish gloom. Brought from all the recesses of the coast in all the legality of
time contracts, lost in uncongenial surroundings, fed on unfamiliar food,
they sickened, became inefficient, and were then allowed to crawl away and
rest. These moribund shapes were as free as air—and nearly as thin. (66).

Little wonder Marlow has some strong words for the so-called Eldorado
Exploring Expedition. These explorers were merely buccaneers who

lacked the idea, the only redeeming quality of the necessary brutality. They only wanted to wrest the treasure from the land with ". . . no more moral purpose at the back of it than there is in burglars breaking into a safe"(87).

Heart of Darkness can thus be regarded as a study of Belgian colonialism, and not a very complimentary one at that. Like *The Nigger of the "Narcissus,"* however, it has provoked ire among some more extreme black writers of our age. For example, Chinua Achebe, the African novelist (*A Man of the People* and *Things Fall Apart*), in a paper entitled "An Image of Africa," presents a central and strident thesis "that Conrad was a bloody racist."[8] He fails to see anything else in *Heart of Darkness* and does not mention any other works of Joseph Conrad. Achebe's parochial and rather simplistic view of Conrad's achievement in this short novel is underscored by the recent avalanche of references to *Heart of Darkness* in the media, following the disastrous war in Vietnam and the macabre events in the jungle of Guyana which ended with the mass murder-suicide of the followers of Rev. Jim Jones. The popular appeal of the story is further shown in Francis Ford Coppola's film *Apocalypse Now,* which uses Kurtz's name and the metaphor of the boat going up the river and draws on several other motifs of the novella, whose title has entered the language as a term for the drama of fanaticism, the dark mystery of the bush, and the darkness of the human soul.[9]

Yet it is a great deal more. Its many-leveled ambiguities and apparently inexhaustible literary allusiveness (conscious or unconscious) have inspired or baffled numerous critics questing for an explanation of its symbolic design and significance. Some, like E. M. Forster (in *Abinger Harvest*), assailed Conrad for his mistiness. The secret task of Conrad's genius, Forster asseted, contained a vapor rather than a jewel. There was no point discussing the philosophy of Conrad in this work or in other works of Conrad, for they had no creed worth discussion. Others, like F. R. Leavis (in *The Great Tradition*), while agreeing with some tenets of Forster, considered *Heart of Darkness* one of Conrad's best performances. T. S. Eliot found in it a fitting epigraph for his "The Hollow Men"—"Mistah Kurtz, he dead." One could argue its appropriateness, for Kurtz is anything but hollow. It is people like the Manager, or Kayerts and Carlier (in "An Outpost of Progress") who qualify for the epithet.

Like any good work of art, this novel affords many interpretations, so many, in fact, that they would fill several thick volumes. I shall mention a few only, to illustrate some critical possibilities. Lilian Feder suggests an analogy of Marlow's journey with Vergil's visit to Hades in the sixth book of the *Aeneid*.[10] Robert O. Evans calls it a "descent into the underworld."[11] Paul Wiley compares Kurtz's lot with the Christian myth of man's fall from innocence, Kurtz being the man expelled from the Garden of Eden.[12] Zdzisław Najder detects allusions to the legends about Alexander the Great.[13] Feder's view may offend some as being too forced a literary exercise, and Wiley's as not quite in keeping with Conrad's own attitude to Christianity or the conventional understanding of the Christian dogma. Marlow is no Christ-like figure, nor is Kurtz the Christian Satan. Najder's parallel with the death of a great military leader is fascinating, but it is treated almost parenthetically in a note and thus never fully developed. Cedric Watts (in *Conrad's "Heart of Darkness": A Critical and Contextual Discussion*)[14] attempts a definitive answers to all other critics of the novel, as he weaves into his argument "references to Dr. Johnson, T. S. Eliot, Vergil, Darwin, T. H. Huxley, Shakespeare, Beckett, Berkeley, Ionesco, Pound *et al.* (for this is only a partial list). . . . He rejects 'allegorizing a non-allegoric work' as Robert O. Evans's treatment of Dantean illusion. He rejects Hillis Miller's whole approach as being 'so vehement a tribute to Conrad's nihilism that his ingenuity was strenuously exercised by the fact that Conrad had put pen to paper at all;' this has led to Miller's neglect of 'the nobility of Marlow's humanity and of Conrad's moral and political indignation.' He rejects Guerard's 'night-journey' theory, 'the prime weakness' of which is that we lose more by it than we gain." Watts's credo is simple enough but, like all other theories that preceded it, it hardly offers an end to the continued exegesis of this work: "The better the interpretation of a text, the larger the number of salient narrative facts that interpretation will (in principle or in demonstration) accommodate, and the fewer it will contravene."[15]

Perhaps the familiarity with Conrad's biographical background of this novel and the existence of his *Congo Diary* are partly responsible for the elaborate aesthetic and psychological interpretations which may obscure the author's basic preoccupation with man's guilt (as in "Karain" and "The Lagoon"), and thereby man's moral stance tested in the darkness of a jungle. Conrad did not *choose* vagueness or mistiness in order to confuse or mystify his readers or critics. Such mistiness, if one agrees with Forster, as there is results from Conrad's narrative method (which makes the narrator a major protagonist of the story, thus placing a distance between him and the author) and his symbolic language. In a sense, it is precisely this sense of mistiness, which I prefer to call mystery, that is one of Conrad's stylistic traits. The author cannot reveal the mystery without the reader's participation. Conrad's heroes (in this and in other novels) include both the Marlows who tortuously seek self-knowledge and the Kurtzes who leap into moral darkness and are swallowed by it. The contact between the two, sometimes the conflict, must be shared by the reader who is asked to experience a kind of moral and aesthetic ephiphany: the revelation of his own affinity with the nether regions of the human soul or an indentification with the tragic triumphs of heroes who assert their elusive glory by exalted idealism or misguided conviction.

A Sinister Clearness in a Darkening Universe: "The End of the Tether"

Captain Whalley in "The End of the Tether" has both idealism and conviction, which earn him this elusive glory. The story was originally conceived as "End of the Song," suggested by Ford Madox Ford. On June 23, 1902, a lamp exploded on Conrad's desk, and the second part of the story went up in flames. Conrad had to race against time to complete the story for the next installment of the magazine *Maga*. This haste may explain, in some measure, Conrad's own doubts about the artistic merits of the piece. In his Author's Note of 1917 he says this of the facts of the story: "More skill would have made them [the facts] more real and the whole composition more interesting" (xii). And he adds: "It is not very likely that I shall ever read 'The End of the Tether' again. No more need be said. It accords best with my feelings to part from Captain Whalley in affectionate silence" (xii). This emotional commitment of the author makes the story more interesting than it would be otherwise, although it is not without intrinsic literary worth.

Despite his sixty-seven years, Captain Whalley has retained great vigor. The failure of his bank forces him to sell his barque, the *Fair*

Maid, so that he can assist his daughter. He then becomes a partner of Massy, an engineer who owns an old steamboat, the *Sofala*. Since Whalley is aware of Massy's dubious reputation, his act is not in keeping with professional integrity. To make things worse, he is losing his sight, but he fails to reveal his condition for fear of losing his investment of £500, and he decides to finish the term of his command. Thus, again he betrays the ethics of his profession. He feels humiliated by the falsehood into which he has drifted ". . . from paternal love, from incredulity, from boundless trust in divine justice meted out to men's feelings on this earth" (324). He does not want much from life, only to be close to his daughter, to see her once again, and to provide for her. So, he holds on to his deception. But his idealized love for Ivy, his symbolically named daughter ("She had twined herself tightly round his heart . . ." [174] and his misguided conviction that he could compromise with his conscience do not evoke divine justice. Like all traitors of Conrad, Whalley must pay the supreme penalty.

Although the story drags a little, Conrad manages to impart a sense of danger and suspense aboard the *Sofala*. The captain's predicament is portrayed against the background of another strife—Massy's persistent efforts to get more money from his captain, whom he regards as a rich man, and the attempts of the mate, Sterne, to betray Whalley's secret to Massy. As in "To-Morrow," "Youth," and *Heart of Darkness,* Conrad depicts the image of an inferno, into which his protagonists descend, or from which they escape: the cottage of Bessie Carvil, the burning *Judea,* the smoldering Heart of Darkness of the African Congo, and now the hell aboard the *Sofala*. It is not, however, hell in the physical sense, as in the other three stories, but rather in terms of the human spirit. The relations among Whalley, Sterne, Massy, and Jack (the second engineer) are a twisted maze of emotions and conflicts; each of these people cannot help torturing at least one of the four white men aboard.

There are echoes of Conrad's first novel in this story. Massy resembles Almayer in his dream of success, the power he will attain by accumulating wealth; like Almayer, he is irritable and morose, and his life is ". . . a sort of *inferno*—a place where his *lost soul* had been given up to the torment of savage brooding" (ibid.). As Sterne is being ejected from the cabin by Massy, who refuses to listen to the mate's revelation about Whalley, the ship comes close to the bank covered by a "gigantic wall of leaves . . . the *darkness of the primeval forest* seemed to flow into that bare cabin with the odour of *rotting leaves,* of *sodden soil* . . ." (ibid.). The darkness of the human soul is emphasized by the surrounding muddiness of nature. Sterne is drowning in the morass of his moral turpitude; he will do anything, betray anybody for the sake of a permanent position. Massy nourishes the erroneous "conviction that, in the course of years, every number was bound to have its winning turn" (267). Jack is periodically drunk and in one of his spells he gives Massy the idea of sinking the *Sofala.* And Captain Whalley, always still and alone winds up having ". . . nothing of his own—even his own past of honor, of truth, of just pride, was gone. All his spotless life had fallen into *the abyss*" (319). As Almayer's dreams collapse, so does Whalley's hope for divine providence. Like the blind Oedipus or the crazed Lear, old Captain Whalley begins to see clearly now that he cannot see.

In vain. In the steadily darkening universe a sinister clearness fell upon his ideas. In the illuminating moments of suffering he *saw* life, men, all things, the whole earth with all her burden of created nature, as he had never *seen* before. (324)

The clearness of Whalley's vision is of a moral kind; it is sinister because it implies self-destruction.

Almayer burns his "folly"—the expensive house he erected; Massy ". . . wondered at his *folly.* He had thrown away the substance for the shadow" (268). He realizes that what he really wants is the "notion of absolute idleness" and not merely the power of being a shipowner. Both Massy and Whalley are guilty of an act of destruction: Massy causes the shipwreck; Whalley is responsible for it to some extent, and he in turn takes his own life. In fact, even the father-daughter relationship reminds one of *Almayer's Folly* if only in the intensity of Whalley's love for Ivy. Another strain of resemblance is the figure of Van Wyk, the wealthy Dutch plantation owner who lives like a hermit but whose function in the story is that of Marlow in *Heart of Darkness,* although he is not the narrator. Van Wyk is a foil to the other characters, standing outside, as it were, trying to help Whalley by neutralizing Sterne, then keeping silent about the captain's dark secret, and, finally, by suddenly going back to Europe in the wake of Whalley's death. It is as if he, like

the Marlow of *Heart of Darkness,* suddenly discovered the true nature of
man, and he no longer cares to pursue his dream in the wilderness. His
point of view is presented along with those of Massy, Sterne, and
Whalley in a truly Flaubertian manner of indirection and objective
realism, and in the sustained tone of irony. Only once (on p. 321) does
Conrad refer to "our conduct" lapsing momentarily into the part of the
narrator. Each of these characters presents his own visual impressions to
the reader; those of Whalley are amazingly accurate, undoubtedly
reflecting Conrad's own recollections of the "Eastern port" which was
Singapore.[16] In its metaphorical sense, thus, it is a story about the
ability to *see.* It opens with a description of sunlight streaming upon the
sea, "a dazzling vapor of light that *blinded the eye* and wearied the brain
with its unsteady brightness" (165). Whalley loses his sight *before*
blindness sets in, for he does not see the world as it really is, in his blind
trust of God's divine mercy and justice. Above all, he no longer sees
himself as he is, falling into self-deception.

After Massy contrives to deflect the boat's compass needle, and it
runs into a reef, Whalley at last realizes that he has destroyed his moral
reason for living. As in the other stories, the self-cognition is rendered
in terms of color symbolism.

. . . for Ivy he had carried his point, walking in his *darkness* to the very verge
of a crime. God had not listened to his prayers. The *light* had finished ebbing
out of his world; not a *glimmer.* It was a *dark* waste. . . . He must pay the
price. (333)

Unlike Lord Jim, Captain Whalley does not heed the cries "Leap!" He
makes sure that he goes down with his boat by putting iron into his
pockets. The ending is bitter irony, not unlike that of *Heart of Darkness.*
No blame is attached to Whalley's memory when the daughter (like
Kurtz's Intended) receives the final message from her father. But
although Ivy learns of his anguish she does not learn the whole truth.
And it is doubly ironic that it is only now that Whalley is dead that she
can afford the time to stand still and think about him, ". . . the letter
folded between the two buttons of her plain *black* bodice." Appropriately she remains there ". . . till *dusk,* perfectly motionless, giving
him all the time she could spare." Her final question; "My God, is it

possible?" strikes another ironic note since the reader knows by now that it is indeed possible; there is no divine mercy for the man who has lost his honor and little if any redemption in his final act of self-sacrifice and the daughter's protestation that she "had loved him after all" (399).

The Religion of Undying Hope: "Prince Roman"

The self-sacrifice in "Prince Roman" is of a different nature. The story was published in 1911 (it appeared in the United States under the title of "The Aristocrat") but, as Ludwik Krzyżanowski suggests, the first sentence indicates that it was written in 1901: "Events which happened seventy years ago. . . . Of course the year 1831 is for us an historical date . . ." (91).[17] Prince Roman, the only clearly identified Pole of Conrad's fiction, is little more than a shadowy figure. The story is, in form and in its origins, a personal recollection. Indeed, according to Jessie Conrad, it was to have formed part of a collection of reminiscences; it closely resembles the passages in *A Personal Record* (see Chapter 9 for further discussion) describing Conrad's childhood, especially the meeting with Prince Roman Sanguszko, a participant of the 1831 uprising against the Russians, on whose life the story is based. "Prince Roman" is a fairly compelling narrative. But the Polish critics have tended to exaggerate the importance of this tale of Polish patriotism, and others have often dismissed it with a casual comment. The story deserves neither treatment. Admittedly, it is not one of Conrad's greatest achievements; it can hardly compare with "Youth" or *Heart of Darkness*. Perhaps Conrad's profound emotional involvement with the subject matter made it more difficult for him to present a full-blooded Pole than, ironically, a fully developed Russian, in whose case he could muster artistic objectivity.

"Prince Roman" has a typical Polish Romantic hero whose most distinctive characteristic is his capacity for boundless self-sacrifice. When Conrad revealed that he modeled the beautiful Antonia of *Nostromo* on his first love he wrote that she was ". . . the standard-bearer of faith to which [we]were all born, but which she alone knew how to hold aloft with an unflinching hope! . . . she was an uncompromising Puritan of patriotism . . ." (*Nostromo,* Author's Note, xiv). What moved Conrad so deeply was Antonia's power of conviction and her

Puritan self-denial. It is this quality in Prince Roman that appeals to the author. The prince's devotion, with something of the national ideal is like Nostromo's "faithful devotion, with something despairing as well as desperate in its impulses" (xii). Prince Roman loses a young wife and falls into despondency from which he recovers only when he dedicates himself to the cause of his nation. He is thus one of the few protagonists of Conrad to recover from adversity and isolation. At first the prince languishes in indifference to the fate of his fellow beings. Then the sight of his countryside and the example of his countrymen in arms stir him from his moral torpor. He throws himself into the struggle with great abandon, and when he is caught and appears before the Military Commission he has a chance to escape punishment owing to his family's influence. The judges hopefully wait for words of penitence from the young man. But the prince defies the offer of clemency and writes on a sheet of paper (maintaining a symbolic silence): "I joined the national rising *from conviction*" (147).

This moral transformation is a familiar theme in Polish literature, particularly of the Romantic period. Prince Roman's change of heart, to give a few examples, is quite similar to that of Father Robak (the former adventurer Jacek Soplica turned priest under the assumed name which in Polish means "a worm") in Adam Mickiewicz's epic poem, *Pan Tadeusz*. To expiate a sin (a revenge murder of a would-be father-in-law), he devotes his whole life to the cause of Polish liberation, no longer concerned with his private life. Another work by Mickiewicz, the poetic drama *Forefathers' Eve, Part Three,* presents a hero named Gustaw who at first is a self-centered person and later changes into the faithful patriot Konrad. Or to take another well known "case" from a later work, Henryk Sienkiewicz's *The Deluge,* the transformation of the brawling soldier Kmicic into a model patriot ready to give his life for his country is again the same motif.

Conrad expresses the subdued hatred of the Russian tyrant whose sentence was that of "deferred death." The prince survives, however, and returns from exile, totally deaf. But although he is separated from his people by a wall of silence, he no longer lives in isolation. He has attained the rare redemption given to Conrad's protagonists, in real rather than ironic terms.

The literary echoes in the story are also apparent in its narrative method, obviously similar to the Polish *gawęda* ("yarn"), in which a narrator recalls a personal tale in an informal fashion. In another sense, the story also suggests the customary Polish genre of *żywot* ("life"). Conrad's father, Apollo Korzeniowski, was the author of such a work: *The Life of General Kolyshko,* a hero of the 1831 rising. Conrad's uncle, Tadeusz Bobrowski, was the author of *Memoirs* from which the novelist drew entire passages and used them almost without changes in "Prince Roman". Two examples are the scene in which the prince makes his gesture, and the marginal note of the emperor, practically quoted verbatim.

Another interesting manifestation of Conrad's reliance on the Polish literary sources is the use of Latin phrases in the story. This was a frequent custom in Polish memoirs or yarns, and it was called the "macaronic" style.

The Polish literary motifs in the story are significant for they emphasize Conrad's deepest feelings. When Conrad describes the condition of Prince Roman before his trial he utters quite a few patriotic sentiments:

How much remained in that *sense of duty,* revealed to him in sorrow? How much of his awakened love for his native country? That country which demands to be loved as no other country has ever been loved . . . with *unextinguishable fire of a hopeless passion* which only a living, breathing, *warm ideal* can kindle in our breasts for our pride, for our weariness, for our exultation *for our undoing.*

There is something monstrous in the thought of such an exaction till it stands before us embodied in the shape of a *fidelity without fear and without reproach.* (144–45)

And earlier Conrad refers to the ferocity and fanaticism of extreme patriotism:

There is ferocity in every passion, even in love itself. *The religion of undying hope* resembles the mad cult of despair, *of death, of annihilation.* The difference lies in the moral motive springing from the *secret needs* and the unexpressed aspiration of the believers. (136)

There is little doubt that for Conrad Poland was primarily this "religion of undying hope."

Chapter Six

The Destructive Element

The Eternal Constancy: *Lord Jim*

Betrayal is the keynote of *Lord Jim* (1900), which began, like "Youth" and *Heart of Darkness,* as a short story and only later developed into a full-size novel. Similarly, the theme and the plot of the novel are not far removed from the other two tales. Like Kurtz and young Marlow, Jim begins his career with the notion of an idealistic and romantic achievement but ends his life (after the descent into the dark sea and into the wilderness of Patusan) as an apparent failure. As in the other two works, Conrad fills *Lord Jim* with an abundance of light and dark imagery.

But *Lord Jim* goes far beyond the two shorter works in structure and in the complexity of its main declared theme: the consciousness of lost honor. For while the other works were inspired by Conrad's own experiences, they do not reflect Conrad's preoccupation with betrayal and guilt, as this novel does. Conrad wrote *Lord Jim* at a time of great personal troubles—financial, medical, and artistic. This was the period during which he elaborated his ideas on fiction, and in *Lord Jim* he used most of the devices for which he became known.

Initially, the novel was conceived as a story called "Jim: a Sketch." Later on, Conrad added the word "Tuan" before "Jim," meaning the Malay equivalent of "lord." Since Jim is not of noble extraction (as Brown is no gentleman), the very coupling of the common "Jim" with "lord" establishes an ironic intent.[1] Jim is not the fictional representation of one man but rather a composite, in very broad terms, of at least three men: Jim Lingard, James Brooke, and Augustine Podmore Williams. The first was a nephew of Captain Tom Lingard (who appears in *Almayer's Folly, An Outcast of the Islands,* and *The Rescue),* whom the natives called "Tuan Jim" and who served aboard the ship *Vidar* along with Conrad in 1887–88. The officers of the ship referred to him as

"Lord Jim" in mock recognition of his haughty manner. The second was an English sailor who traded in northern Borneo, joined the cause of the natives struggling against pirates and potentates, and ultimately became the Rajah of Sarawak in 1841 and a legendary character. He died as Sir James Brooke in 1868. The third man was involved in the "pilgrim ship scandal" which served as the core of Conrad's plot. A 993-ton steamer, the *Jeddah*, with about 900 Moslem pilgrims aboard, sailed from Singapore for Jeddah, which was the port of Mecca, in 1880. On August 7 all the white officers except one abandoned the ship during a storm. When the ship did not sink and was towed to Aden there was an inquiry which showed that there was an attempt by the ship's owners and her captain in collusion with a Singapore Arab to benefit from an insurance policy they had bought before the voyage.[2]

These sources are of great interest to the biographer and the student of Conrad's style and narrative technique, for they reveal how an artist uses his material; how the novelist has created a different order of reality by subtly altering the historical events of the *Jeddah* episode and his conception of "Tuan Jim." Though once again Conrad has a Marlow pursuing the fortunes of a man lost in a moral wilderness, there is a basic change. In *Heart of Darkness* Marlow overshadows Kurtz; in *Lord Jim,* the opposite occurs. Though Marlow tells the story, it is Jim who is constantly the center of our attention. Everything, in fact, revolves around Jim, whose betrayal of his code of honor leads to his ultimate destruction.

Marlow is horrified by the contrast between Jim's appearance and his performance in the moment of danger. The trouble with Jim, Marlow patiently explains, is the man's swift and forestalling imagination, which, in Conrad's view, is "the enemy of men, the father of all terrors . . ." (11). It is imagination, among other things, that separates Jim from the rest of mankind and his fellow mariners, allowing him to live in the dream of romantic achievement, as real to him as the windmills were to Don Quixote.

The ordinary sailor regards the ship as a place where he and the rest of the crew earn their living. Jim sees it as a carrier into the lands of his dreams, a mere platform from which he will sally forth in romantic exploits and reveal what he imagines to be his many-sided courage.

This young son of an obscure parson is the chief mate on the *Patna,* an Eastern steamer carrying 800 Moslem pilgrims. Jim and the other four men live amidships in isolation from their human cargo, but Jim has nothing in common with these men. The sea means to him (as it did to young Marlow of "Youth") glamour and romance. The dreams, more real than the actual monotony of an uneventful passage, breed in him an exaggerated self-confidence. All men could flinch in a moment of danger, but—he felt sure—he alone would know how to deal with the spurious menace of wind and sea. Perhaps he could have become the hero he wished to be had he not taken the post of the chief mate of the *Patna without* ever having been tested by a longer period of service or by a single case of crisis. This lack of experience, coupled with Jim's exuberant imagination, constitutes the crux of his dilemma. The disparity between his idealized vision of himself and the humiliating defeat brought about by reality is intolerable.

The isolating and destructive influence of his imagination shows first when he fails to respond quickly in an emergency. Instead of rushing to the rescue of a man who had fallen overboard, Jim *watches* the accident as if confounded, and remains rooted to the spot. Only a little while ago he saw himself saving people from disaster. In his own vision he appeared as a solitary castaway, struggling for survival. He fought savages on tropical shores and quelled mutinies on the high seas; he cheered up his men when they were cast adrift in a small boat, always setting the example of devotion to duty. But when the *real* chance to show his unflinching heroism came, he lost it. He was too late. He did *not* jump overboard to save the drowning man. He experienced the first shock of defeat.

It was himself that he saw in all those exploits. What appealed to him was applause, a desire to be admired as a hero and not the actual saving of people in distress or performing the arduous task of steering a ship to safety. Conrad defines this egotism as a sort of sublimated, idealized selfishness. Jim's egocentric feeling reached such a degree that when the major crisis of his life occurred and he failed again, it assumed tragic proportions. The precious world of his dreams was blown to bits the moment he *did* leap from the *Patna.* Only this time he should *not* have jumped. From this moment he was "a solitary man confronted by his fate" (340). What happened was tragicomic. On a dark night, several days after leaving port, the *Patna* strikes an unidentified submerged object and tilts bow down. The chief engineer is convinced that the ship is sinking. The captain and the other officers prepare to abandon ship without waking the pilgrims or getting them into lifeboats. In any case, there aren't enough lifeboats for all the passengers. Jim refuses to help in the launching of the boat for the captain and the officers. When the third engineer has a heart attack and fails to respond to the shouts of "Jump" from below, Jim suddenly leaps off the ship. But he cannot go back to the ship. Narrating the incident to Marlow, he cries: "It was as if I had jumped into a well—into an everlasting deep hole. . ." (111).

The *Patna* does not sink but is towed into port; her officers run from the city but Jim remains to face the Official Inquiry and is duly deprived of his license. Marlow is a spectator at the inquiry, and as he pursued the developments of Kurtz in *Heart of Darkness,* he now identifies himself with the plight of the young man. Jim is an outcast—a sailor in exile from the sea. He yearns for rehabilitation but, like Almayer, he cannot forget. The memory of the ghastly night torments him. And worse than the memory is the thought that he has missed the great chance of his life. His exalted vanity makes the idea unbearable. He will seek for a way to return to the community as a trusted and honorable man. He will also receive punishment for the heroics of his fancy; he must expiate the transgression of desiring more glamour than he could carry. He is as isolated in his grief and remorse as he was in his dreams of future achievements. In the remote corner of the world, where he attempts to regain his honor (with Marlow's help), "he was protected by *his isolation,* alone of his own *superior kind,* in close touch with Nature, that keeps on such easy terms with her lovers" (176).

The power of imagination, which creates another reality for him, superior to that of physical reality, has deprived him of the moral contact with other people. Overwhelmed by the inexplicable, he is baffled by his own personality, by the irrationality of his own nature and the irrationality of the world about him. Yet he never gives up his dream, nor does he allow the *Patna* incident to lapse into oblivion. The isolation of the romantic dreamer was a not unpleasant burden, if it was a burden at all. But the moral isolation that follows his desertion of the

Patna is extremely hard to endure. He feels cut off from the rest of his kind, like a trapped beast trying to escape from an enclosure of high stakes.

Jim's inner conflict reaches a paradoxical point. In order to retrieve his honor he must lose it in the court. In order to return to the world as an honest man he must first get away from it. But the latter means a total renunciation of his major dream—to win recognition, the applause of the world. The escape into the isolation of Patusan does not even guarantee redemption in his own eyes. A similar antinomy results when Jim attempts to explain to others what is inscrutable about himself. It is a vicious circle. Jim's dispute is with an invisible personality, "an antagonistic and inseparable partner of his existence—another possessor of his soul" (93). Unwilling to admit that he has been betrayed by his own nature, he believes that some mysterious impulse must have driven him to that abject leap from the *Patna*. Only an act of supreme self-sacrifice can assuage his sense of defeat and restore his dignity.

Jim's tormenting self-questioning is paralleled by Marlow's quest and his "probing" attitude toward the young man. Why, it can be asked, is Marlow so preoccupied with the fortunes of Jim? And why is Brierly, the judge who disqualifies Jim? Both are searching for truth. Marlow is fascinated by the mystery of Jim's behavior and the obscure truth of his case appears to him momentous enough to influence mankind's conception of itself. This truth, Marlow observes, may be revealed in a moment of illusion and in a state of "utter solitude" (313). In his attempts to probe the unfathomable, Marlow comes to resemble Jim as he seeks for clues to Jim's personality.

There is in Jim's fate a sort of profound and *terrifying logic* as if it were *our imagination* alone that could set loose upon us the might of an overwhelming destiny. (342)

The logic is terrifying to Marlow, as it is to Brierly, who does not relish the prospect of condemning a white man in public. Because they are endowed with the same vivid imagination that Jim possesses, they become profoundly involved in his life; Jim's indifference to the community, rooted in his "exalted egoism," exasperates them but at the same time turns into an illuminating experience that sheds light upon their own lives. For they too fear entrapment by destiny.

Brierly's verdict in Jim's case discloses to him the hitherto unsuspected weakness of his character—or is it his unsuspected strength? The trial is to him as the wreck over which the *Patna* passed was to Jim—a test of his true courage and integrity. Jim's conviction that he has committed wrong makes him face the Court of Inquiry with a stubbornness that is incomprehensible to the other members of his white community. Similarly, Brierly's conviction that he would not have acted differently had he been in Jim's place on the fateful *Patna* exposes the flimsiness of his professed courage and prowess and destroys his reasons for living. He has identified himself with Jim, and since he punishes the young man for what might have been his own crime, he must also mete out punishment to himself—symbolically jumping into the sea—as Jim did.

Conversely, Jim's attitude of forgiveness toward Gentleman Brown can be explained by his sympathetic identification of himself with the ruffian; he cannot condemn and destroy the outlaw without at the same time condeming himself. Brown is Jim's alter ego, as Jim is the other self of Brierly. And *Lord Jim,* like "The Secret Sharer" and *Under Western Eyes,* is a study of the split personality. In the continuous series of tests Jim is tempted to identify with men whom his idealized standard of conduct commands to shun or to despise: the captain of the *Patna,* whom he joins in the boat, thus becoming an accomplice in the captain's crime; Gentleman Brown, who invades Jim's domain in Patusan and taunts him by using the very words and images to describe his own situation, e.g., "I am sick of my *infernal luck.* . . . There are my men in the same boat—and, by God, I am not the sort to *jump out* of trouble and leave them in a d——d lurch. . . . I am here because *I was afraid once* in my life. . . . I won't ask *you* what scared *you* into this *infernal hole* . . . (382–83).

The encounter with the emissaries of the "civilized" world shatters Jim's hopes for rehabilitation. The "second desperate leap of his life" (380) into Patusan, where he found recognition, trust, and love, only proved to him that he could not get away—from himself. His hesitant handling of Brown suggests to the reader that perhaps Jim is not, after all, "one of us," but rather "one of them"—the social outcasts, the traitors. Instead of trying Brown he is tried by him, as, in effect it was Jim who sentenced Judge Brierly to death by the nature of his response to the accusations. Hence, when Brown "asked Jim whether he had nothing fishy in his life to remember that he was so damnedly hard upon a man trying to get out of a *deadly hole* . . ." (387), he acted the part of the prosecutor who knew very well how to win his case.

And there ran through the rough talk a vein of subtle reference to *their common blood,* an assumption of *common experience*; a sickening suggestion of *common guilt,* of *secret knowledge* that was like *a bond of their minds and of their hearts.* (387)

Common blood, common experience, and common guilt—these are indeed links in a common bond that ties Jim to Brown. The world has caught up with Jim by sending its Nemesis in the person of Brown, to remind him of his initial transgression. Now he will have to compound it by two new offenses: sparing Brown and refusing to spare himself, thereby breaking his promise to be faithful to both Doramin's people and to Jewel.

In Patusan Jim comes close to his dream of rehabilitating himself. He is *tuan,* lord over the natives who trust him and honor him. But he betrays their trust by sparing Brown and his crew. For the second time in his life Jim is cognizant of failure, and once more he insists on "playing the game" in his own, inimitably egotistic manner: he must pass the ordeal of confession and admission of guilt at a public forum before being punished for his transgression. Once again he seems to be fulfilling a deep masochistic need in himself. By being hurt or even being destroyed on his own terms he will be forgiven and will thus escape the loneliness of guilt. Thus, the courtyard of the chief Doramin becomes, in effect, another Court of Inquiry—with one qualifying difference. This time Jim must lose much more than his sailor's license. He has come, very much like the old sailor Whalley, to the end of his tether. That is why he responds to Jewel's desperate cry "Will you fight?" not with action but with a resigned "There is nothing to fight for . . . nothing is lost. . . . There is no escape" (412). Jim has decided to defy his fate. "The *dark powers* should not rob him twice of *his peace*" (409).

With a touch of superb irony Marlow quotes from a letter which Jim's father has written, and muses upon the contrast of the two worlds of his young friend. The good old parson counsels his son to "resolve fixedly never, through any possible motives, to do anything which [you believe] wrong. . . . He goes on equably trusting Providence and the established order of the universe . . ." (341). The old man has been writing his sermons for forty years—"little thoughts about faith and virtue, about the *conduct of life* and *the only proper manner of dying. . .* (341). Marlow repeats the last two phrases, as if to underline their importance. Then he refers to "these placid, colorless forms of men and women peopling that quiet corner of the world as free of danger or strife as *a tomb* . . . and breathing equably the air of *undisturbed rectitude* . . ." (342). Like the Marlow of *Heart of Darkness* upon his return from the Congo, he does not display too much respect for the ordinary, respectable members of the community. He does not reject it, but he allows the reader to choose for himself. It is a hard choice between the safe but tomblike existence of a quiet English community and the romantic world of Lord Jim. In the former, people "would never be *taken unawares,* and never be called upon *to grapple with fate*" (342). In the latter, located on the other side of the earth, Jim tried to put his father's pious maxims to practice as best he could; in this world he *was taken unawares* by fate and fell victim to his imagination, to become "romantic beyond the wildest dreams of his boyhood" (342). Indeed, for a man like Jim there was only *one* conduct of life and *one* manner of death, called for by "his exalted egoism" (416).

In his final comments Marlow reiterates his solidarity with Jim: "He is one of us—and have I not stood up once, like an evoked ghost, to answer for *his eternal constancy?*" (416). He is not sure whether he was wrong, after all. The reality of Jim's existence is ambiguous; it comes to Marlow "with an immense, with an overwhelming force. . . ." But there are also moments "when he passes from [my] eyes like a *disembodied* spirit astray amongst the passions of this earth, ready to surrender himself *faithfully* to the claim of *his own world of shades*" (416).

Conrad's impressionistic method is not a wholly new technical innovation, for it has been used in the mystery tale and in other forms of the novel. The innovation lies in Conrad's intricate fusion of disparate elements, which forces the reader to move in several directions, to piece together a jigsaw puzzle as he fits the various incidents of the narrative in their proper places. This is where the function of Conrad's narrator Marlow proves to be so important. Marlow is both the supplier of the scattered details of the story and an "organizer" of the facts in his own right. He places the seemingly disjointed aspects of Jim's story before the reader, and the latter can perceive the true identity of Jim by way of Marlow's impressions. "He existed for me," says Marlow, "and after all it is only through me that he exists for you" (224).

The result of this impressionistic approach, which bears a great resemblance to Henry James's handling of different points of view, is drama, subtlety, and symbolic density. The changing viewpoints, Jim's, Marlow's, and those of other characters, enrich the psychological tapestry of Conrad's canvas and enhance the moral complexity of the protagonists. For we are not concerned merely with the heroes' reactions to a given situation, but are called upon to judge these reactions, as we are constantly tempted to evaluate Marlow's responses to Jim's behavior. This provides the element of surprise and many psychological contrasts. It also makes it easier for Conrad to hide his own exasperated pities and indignations behind the facade of the indefatigable, prying Marlow.

Marlow stands between the two extremes in this novel, as he stood between the darkness of Kurtz and the civilized world. His mediating role is important both from the purely structural point of view and as a basic device of affording psychological insights into Jim's life. The many-leveled commentary on Jim results in a subtle portrait of a nonheroic hero, so common in today's fiction. In 1900, the year of the book's publication, this treatment of a romantic hero was, if not entirely original in its conception, certainly fresh in the nineteenth-century English novel. This novelty, coupled with the involutions of the narrative, has baffled many a reader not prepared to unravel the psychological contortions of its heroes, or, in other words, to disentangle the complex chronology of the novel. Both are essential to Conrad's method. Marlow provides the psychological distance necessary for the reader that he may admire Jim (as Marlow does) or at least sympathize with him, but also that he may see his basic unworthiness. Jim's story is unfolded by several different speakers, whose opinions are usually reported by Marlow, but also by Jim himself, whose words are often in the nature of a confession.

Marlow's method, like Conrad's in his authorial descriptions of nature and men, is akin to painting.[3] The kaleidoscope of visual impressions keeps on turning, each one progressively more dismal, growing more remote, growing more enigmatic, always presented in a contrasting image of light and dark, to baffle the spectator-reader, to dazzle him with the brilliance of Jim's light, to shock him with the darkness of his irrevocable fate. Marlow complains that he could never see Jim clearly, that Jim was no more than an illusion, "a strange and melancholy illusion, evolved half-consciously like all our illusions . . . visions of remote *unattainable truth, seen dimly*" (323). The last, really last vision of Jim, as Marlow leaves him in Patusan, again reiterates the initial image: the young man all in white against the darkness of the night, an enigmatic figure whose opportunity was still veiled. Here we begin to follow Conrad's narrator as his eye turns into a moving camera, and we perceive Jim from an ever-increasing distance:

The *twilight* was ebbing fast from the sky *above* his head, the strip of sand had sunk already *under* his feet, he himself *appeared* no bigger than a child—then only a speck, a tiny *white speck,* that *seemed* to catch all the *light* left in a *darkened* world. . . . And, suddenly, I lost him. . . . (336)

We must now do what Marlow has done, as he explains it in a letter to "the privileged man": "I put it down here for you as though I had been an *eyewitness.* My information was *fragmentary,* but I've *fitted the pieces together,* and there is enough of them to make *an intelligible picture*" (343). A picture of Jim is what Conrad had in mind, after all. And he has given us a veritable gallery of pictures as well as reels of film, showing fragmentary glimpses, views, and movements of his protagonist and those who came in contact with him. At the end of the novel, he asks every reader to emulate Marlow's example by fitting the fragments together to form his own intelligible picture, though, like Marlow, he may find it to be "the detailed and amazing impression of a dream" (318).

The central painting of the novel is done. The last visual glimpse of the hero is as equivocal as the first one, which is as it should be, for such was the artistic intent of the novelist-painter. The reality of his canvas must present Jim's *shadowy* ideal of conduct *and* his *eternal* constancy: the image of the inscrutable and forgotten Jim yet also the one so well remembered by Marlow; the young man *under a cloud,* but also *one of us*; overwhelmingly real *and* a disembodied spirit. The novel ends on a note of interrogation, as it begins with an inquiry into the perplexing *Patna* case: "Who knows?" It is the final invitation to the reader to embark on yet another investigation of Jim, yet another attempt to piece together all the impressions, views, glimpses conveyed to us by Marlow. If there is still any doubt that Conrad intended those impressions to be *paintings,* perhaps these words might dispel it: ". . . *sight* of the *Patna* . . . like a *picture* created by *fancy on canvas* . . . with its life *arrested* in an *unchanging light* . . . forever suspended in their expression . . . I am certain of them. They exist as if under an enchanter's wand."

Yes, they do. As if by magic, the "mere images" have been symbolically marshaled to do battle, to challenge first our sight then our faculties of analysis, turning our fleeting impressions into a more permanent synthesis—the final portrait of Jim.

As in *The Nigger,* the subtitle, "A Tale," suggests the fabulous. "The conquest of love, honor, men's confidence—the pride of it, the power of it, are fit materials for a *heroic tale,*" Marlow observes at the beginning of chapter twenty-two, the beginning of his last promised *few* words about Jim, which turn out to be another 191 pages. Indeed, the second half of the novel reads like a romance spun by an enchanter who resembles Shakespeare in making this tale not so much heroic as tragic. [4]

While Jim's dream of being a hero is romantic, his inaction aboard the *Patna* can be contrasted with the non-romantic Malay who steers the ship calmly or with the little fellow Bob Stanton of the *Sephora,* who loses his life in an attempt to save a lady passenger. He jumps, too, but *heroically.* Similarly, the French lieutenant does not cut a romantic or heroic figure, but he *does* what Jim dreamed of doing. As Hamlet's purpose is blunted by his hesitation so Jim's dream is tarnished by contact with reality. Jim's Hamletian self-interrogation, however, does not dwell on the terrible breach of human solidarity in the *Patna* case—the abandonment of 800 pilgrims aboard the ship. But in a most painfully ironic reversal, his final decision not to kill Brown can also be regarded as testimony of his moral sense. For though he cannot kill Brown (as Hamlet cannot kill Claudius) because he is his double, it is also possible to argue that Jim is reluctant to kill anyone and will not kill with premeditation, thereby once more evoking the Christian precepts of his parson father. Lord Jim and Lord Hamlet face the same question, and suffer from a similar dilemma—the execution of a father's wish, the choice of the right way of living and the right way of dying. The question, Marlow says, "is not how to get cured but how to live" (212). Stein agrees, recalling Hamlet's soliloquy: "*Ja! Ja!* In general, adapting the motto of your great poet: That is the question. . . . How to be! *Ach!* How to be!" (213). Stein's diagnosis of Jim's condition has puzzled many a reader:

Yes! Very funny this terrible thing is. A man that is born falls into a dream like a man who falls into the sea. If he tries to climb out into the air as inexperienced people endeavor to do, he drowns—*nicht wahr?* . . . No! I tell you! The way is to the destructive element submit yourself, and with the exertions of your hands and feet in the water make the deep, deep sea keep you up. So if you ask me—How to be? (214)

Stein's metaphor is symbolically uttered in a subdued light apparently because it is meant to be, like Jim's wedding with a shadowy ideal of conduct—a *shadowy* philosophy that entails a contradiction. Man is born only to find himself facing a destructive element of dream, whose rejection can be as deadly as any attempt to climb out of the water. The ambiguity of Stein's advice and diagnosis is underlined by the visual dimension: "The whisper of his conviction seemed to open before me a vast and *uncertain* expanse, as of a crepuscular horizon on a plain at dawn—or was it, *perchance,* at the coming of *night?* One had not the courage to decide; but it was a charming, and *deceptive light, light,* throwing the *impalpable* poesy of its *dimness* over pitfalls—over graves . . ." (215). Charming, deceptive, impalpable dimness—the intellectual sense of Stein's words is enhanced by the visual, painterly coloration, and the word "perchance," drawn from Hamlet's soliloquy.

Unlike the magnificent butterfly, man does not accept reality; in Stein's words he wants to be a saint and he wants to be a devil—he is a thinking and a dreaming animal. Jim's shame has turned him into an outcast, as Hamlet's loss of the throne and his realization that his mother is "stained" and that he has failed to avenge his father's murder causes Hamlet's great loneliness and despair. Each man must die in the defense of his own code of honor. Both end on a note of quiet desperation. Hamlet's cryptic and moving last words, "The rest is silence" (V, ii, 369), are imitated, in a sense, by Jim's final gesture, as he sends *his* last "proud and unflinching glance. Then with his *hand over his lips* he fell forward, dead" (416). For him, too, the rest is now silence. He has said enough. He will speak no more. He will act no more. He will suffer no more. The rest is up to the audience and to the readers.

The impressionistic form of the novel has enabled many of the latter to arrive at sometimes diametrically opposed interpretations of Jim, as critics have differed over the view of Hamlet. The Polish aspects of this non-Polish book are particularly fascinating to those who see the novel as Conrad's sublimated confession of guilt. Gustav Morf was the first to equate Jim's leap from the ship with Conrad's "jump" or his desertion from the sinking ship of Poland.[5] *Lord Jim,* he wrote, "was more than a psychological novel; it was a psychological novel written before psychoanalysis was founded."[6] It shed more light on Conrad's personality than any other book, for it expressed Conrad's own fears and guilt complex. Morf draws a parallel between Conrad's fear of having forfeited his honor by the desertion of his native land and Jim's betrayal of his duty. By killing Jim Conrad overcomes his guilt-complex. Morf finds Jim's death to be the only satisfactory closing note, since now his honor will be unstained.

The "neat" psychoanalytical explanation will not do. In his anxiety to attain the only possible victory left to him which, in existentialist terms, means the choice of his commitment, Jim remains the incurable romantic egotist. By turning the sole arbiter of his freedom, his right to live or to die, by turning away from the reality of life with Jewel, the native woman who loves him, Jim illustrates the "either-or" quality of his existence. In a truly Sartrean manner Jim is preoccupied with his own cowardice, his inadequacy, and the final discovery is followed by his quest of death as a means of moral redemption, but also as means of self-assertion—a final act of free will. The punishment for the crime is the final epiphany to Jim (and to other characters of Conrad, e.g., Razumov), for it reveals to him the essence of living—the moral truth. It is Jim's spiritual regeneration, his ultimate redemption.

But it is, essentially, an ironic redemption, for it achieves nothing beyond an affirmation of an ideal of conduct which Marlow defines as *shadowy.* Jim's triumph is yet another manifestation of his paradoxical condition: in order to be *faithful* to his ideal code of honor, to pay his debt to Doramin and Dain Waris, he must commit another betrayal— of Jewel; moreover, it is a destructive victory since it ruins the lives of the survivors and wipes out with one stroke the reputation he has earned by his *faithful* devotion and courage.

Conrad appeals to the Polish reader[7] because of his preoccupation with fidelity, the same reason that made Almayer attractive to the novelist. Conrad wrote: "What made you [Almayer] so real to me was that you held this lofty theory with some force of conviction and with an admirable consistency."[8] This is exactly the fascination of Jim for Marlow, who tells us: "The whisper of his conviction seemed to open before me a vast and uncertain expanse. . . . His life had begun in sacrifice, in enthusiasm for generous ideas . . . no one could be more romantic than himself" (52). And in Lingard's actions (in *The Rescue*), "performed simply, from conviction, what may be called the romantic side of the man's nature came out; that responsive sensitiveness to the shadowy appeals made by life and death which is the groundwork of a chivalrous character" (74).

It is Jim's redemption, ironic or otherwise, and his exalted romantic credo, summed up by Stein in his now-famous "To follow the dream and again to follow the dream—and so *ewig—usque ad finem* . . ." that the Poles found so attractive in the dark days of World War II. Today they still admire Conrad the Romantic, but several critics also notice the affinity he has with the movement of Positivism and its emphasis on hard work, suffering, and devotion to duty. The mentorial, stern severity of Tadeusz Bobrowski's guidance must have had an effect upon Conrad. There is little doubt that the Positivist philosophy of Uncle Tadeusz is partly responsible for the development of Conrad's manly character and his high moral standards of honor. It is not surprising to find this phrase, *usque ad finem*, in one of Bobrowski's letters to Conrad:

I have been through a great deal, I suffered over my own fate, the fate of my family and my Nation and perhaps it is because of these sufferings and disappointments that I developed in myself that calm view of life's task, whose motto, I dare assert, was, is, and will be *usque ad finem*: the love of duty, perceived more narrowly or widely, depending on given circumstances, and therein my practical creed. . . .[9]

This emphatic statement of Conrad's mentor is echoed in the novelist's own pronouncement of his intimate views in *A Personal Record*: "Those who read me know my conviction that the world, the temporal world, rests on a few very simple ideas; so simple that they must be as old as the hills. It rests, notably, on the idea of Fidelity" (xxi).

Yet, as Zdzisław Najder observed, "hopeless fidelity was the essence of Conrad's feeling for Poland, but that made him not closer to but, on the contrary, more estranged from other Poles."[10] Hopeless fidelity to his fatherland was one of the major reasons why Conrad could not write about Poland. Moreover, he did not know too much about Poland and its life, having left the country when he was only a boy, and having spent twenty years aboard ships. When he did, finally, begin to write about Poland, it was not as a novelist but as a journalist, after his visit to Poland in 1914. His attitude toward Poland always remained somewhat ambiguous, for he could never quite overcome the feeling of guilt.

It is possible, therefore, that in *Lord Jim* Conrad "confessed" his innermost feelings about his fatherland. "The significance of crime," Marlow observes during the Court of Inquiry, "is in its being a *breach of faith with the community of mankind,* and from that point of view he was *no mean traitor . . .*" (157). He wonders somewhat indignantly that there is "no awe-stricken multitude to be horrified at *his guilt* and be moved to tears at his fate . . ." (157). In his Author's Note, dated June 1917, Conrad expresses his surprise at a lady who did not like the book because, she said, "it is all so morbid." Conrad waxes indignant, wondering whether she was European at all. "In any case," he concludes," no Latin temperament would have perceived anything morbid in the acute consciousness of lost honor" (ix). Jim, he assures us, "is not the product of coldly perverted thinking. He's not a figure of Northern Mists either" (ix). Perhaps when Conrad saw "his form pass by—appealing—significant—under a cloud—perfectly silent" (ix), *he* was moved to tears. Perhaps he was thinking of his own youth.

The Consuming Mine: *Nostromo*

Although fidelity and betrayal are also the central motif of *Nostromo,* the novelist's prime concern is not with the plight of a single hero whose dilemma he dramatizes. Before this novel Conrad's main themes dealt with the individual isolated from the community by his dream, his transgressions, or a solitary seaman battling the elements and human frailty. *Nostromo,* however, is a sprawling political novel, the story of a whole country—Conrad's *War and Peace.* The principal action of the novel takes place within only three days, but its span of time and space has epic breadth. Conrad unfolds before us a panoramic view of Costaguana, a republic in South America. The fortunes of numerous and varied protagonists are told against the background of Costaguana's tortuous history, notably its civil war, and the financial machinations of big capital. Costaguana comes alive not as an authentic, photographic recreation of the artist's memory but as a mythical land; and the silver mine of San Tomé, like the majestic white head of the Higuerota mountain, is one of the several major symbols of the novel that underline the universality of its themes.

Despite his initial doubts about the novel, Conrad came to realize the scope of his achievement when he wrote about the novel in his Author's Note to *The Secret Agent*: ". . . an intense creative effort on what I suppose will always remain *my largest canvas* . . ." (ix). *Nostromo* is the author's most ambitious book, by his own admission, "the most anxiously meditated of the longer novels" (Author's Note, p. vii). It is also one of his most carefully revised books, which occupied him for some twenty months (1903–1904), a period marred by poor health and serious financial troubles.

As Conrad was laboring to create his republic of Costaguana, he complained: "All my memories of Central America seem to slip away. I just had a glimpse twenty-five years ago."[11] In her book *The Sea Years of Joseph Conrad*[12] Jerry Allen shows that Conrad's memory was, his contention notwithstanding, remarkably accurate. Thus, for example, she suggests that Costaguana was really the "coast of Guiana" described by the Elizabethan adventurer, Sir Walter Raleigh. The latter's imaginary San Thomé mine became in Conrad's novel the corrupting silver mine of San Tomé. Conrad's voyage to Colombia in 1877 produced a rich store of information. A year earlier the country had undergone a disastrous civil war. When Conrad saw the country it was once again in throes of a revolution. *Nostromo* reveals many geographical and historical details of Colombia, and the fictional Sulaco is a fairly faithful rendering of Cartagena, a Colombian port. There are also references to

Panama, but not to Venezuela, which (because of his letter to Richard Curle) was mistakenly assumed to have been Conrad's source.[13]

On one level, the novel deals with the story of a man who stole a lighter full of silver. Conrad borrowed this tale from Frederick Benton Williams's (pseudonym of Herbert Elliot Hamblen) *On Many Seas*.[14] He also read Frederick Masterman's *Seven Eventful Years in Paraguay* (1869) and Edward B. Eastwick's *Venezuela: or Sketches of Life in a South American Republic*. Many details, including the names of the principal characters, were taken from Masterman (Decoud, Gould, Mitchell, Corbelàn, Fidenza, Monygham, and Barrios). Conrad's story is considerably expanded. The San Tomé silver mine, financed by American millionaire Holroyd and owned by Charles Gould, dominates the life of the Occidental Province of Costaguana. The mine is a corrupting agent that causes moral and political trouble, and it symbolizes "material interests." Lured by the prospect of enrichment, rebels from the interior start a revolution. During the conflict Nostromo, an "incorruptible" people's leader, is entrusted with a lighter loaded with the bars of the San Tomé silver, which he is to hide. Accompanied by Martin Decoud, a skeptical journalist, he sets out for a desert island in the Placid Gulf. At night Nostromo and Decoud discover Hirsch, a merchant from Esmeralda, hiding on their boat. The lighter collides with a ship manned by the rebels, and as a result of a freakish accident Hirsch is carried onto the troopship and arrested by Colonel Sotillo. He is questioned about the silver, but when he tells the truth nobody believes him. He is tortured and shot by Sotillo. The lighter is thought to have been sunk. Nostromo, however, has managed to bury the silver bars on the island, and he leaves Decoud alone on it. Overpowered by a sense of solitude and his own skepticism, Decoud commits suicide, having weighted himself with four of the silver bars before shooting himself in a boat and drowning. Nostromo comes back to the island and, since he cannot account for the missing ingots of silver, he cannot admit that the silver has been saved. Later, disappointed by the lack of appreciation shown him by his masters, he decides to keep the treasure for himself. He goes to the island periodically for silver. But a lighthouse is built on the island, and it is kept by one Georgio Viola, whose two daughters, Linda and Giselle, love Nostromo. One night Nostromo, who is secretly courting Giselle though he is betrothed to Linda, is mistaken by the demented Viola for a rejected suitor of Giselle, and is shot.

The corrupting nature of silver is hinted by Conrad's epigraph to the novel, taken from Shakespeare's *King John*: "So foul a sky clears not without a storm" (IV, ii, 108). Not only the foul sky of war and revolution is evoked by the play, but also the bastard's cynical philosophy of life in terms which at once recall the prime motif of *Nostromo*— the corrupting metal:

Bell, book, and candle shall not drive me back,
When *gold* and *silver* becks me to come on.   (III, iii, 12)

This same bastard is sent by the king to "skae the bags/Of hoarding abbots" (III, iii, 7), the kind of anticlerical pronouncement which Conrad often sounds in the novel.

Silver corrupts individual men and whole bodies of men; they undermine the foundations of the republic because men like Holroyd and Charles Gould become so powerful that they are in effect the undisputed rulers of the mine and the country. Both the heroes and the villains of *Nostromo* submit to the blandishments of the corrupting metal. Nostromo turns traitor; Gould lavishes affection on the mine rather than on Emilia; Sotillo is driven to murderous fury. In Conrad's own words: "Silver is the pivot of the moral and material events, affecting the lives of everybody in the tale . . . this was my deliberate purpose. . . . The word 'silver' occurs almost at the very beginning of the story proper, and I took care to introduce it in the very last paragraph."[15]

The revolutionary groups and the legitimate governments alike are doomed to ultimate failure. Even though the province of Sulaco manages to secede from Costaguana, and the San Tomé mine is functioning again, Conrad does not give us the impression of any future peace and stability. On the contrary, he intimates further social and political upheavals, and a continuing vicious circle of violence. Perhaps this is so because no single set of political platitudes, no ideology or religious creed can be crowned with success. Any progress in society is, like the ironic victories of Conrad's protagonists, merely an illusion. The only reality (except for people like Decoud) is man's struggle to preserve or to establish his own identity. Nostromo attempts to defend his image of incorruptible fidelity. Antonia is the very model of fidelity which Nostromo must lose. (Although Antonia is drawn after Conrad's recollection of his first love, this young woman is rather vaguely sketched in the novel.) Hirsch, who trusts the social institutions and is betrayed by them, must come to the ultimate assertion of his status as a social scapegoat. Emilia Gould and Georgio Viola maintain their pursuit of an emotional and political allegiance. Father Beron and Sotillo live in the relentless exercise of power, and so do Holroyd and Charles Gould.

As in his essay "Autocracy and War" (published in 1905), in which he assails Tsarist Russia and offers some prophetic insights, Conrad does not present any clear-cut political panacea in *Nostromo*. Yet he was, in the words of his collaborator, "above all things else, . . . a student of politics, without prescription, without dogma, and, as a Papist, with a profound disbelief in the perfectibility of human institutions.[16] Thus, Conrad criticizes Anglo-Saxon imperialism in *Nostromo*, as he berated the Belgian and Dutch imperialism in his earlier works. But he does not preach or condemn life itself.

. . . though there is much in *Nostromo* that is frightening and on the face of it pessimistic, the net effect of its politics and its morals is strangely exhilarating. It makes you want to share in life not less but more vigorously; and that is just what most modern fiction fails to do.[17]

This statement by E. M. W. Tillyard implies that *Nostromo* is considerably more than a dramatized discussion of a political theme. Tillyard noticed the elements of the fairy-tale, for example, in the sinister figure of General Montero, "the malicious fairy, slighted, resentful, and bent on mischief, at the christening feast of the infant railway."[18] Similarly, Mrs. Gould appears as the good fairy, Charles Gould as the exiled prince, and later the "king of Sulaco." As in other works, Conrad frequently refers to ghosts and magic.

But it is the characters, no less than the vivid descriptions of mythical Costaguana, that are responsible for the dramatic intensity of the novel. Conrad chose the name of one character as the title but later on wavered in his estimate of Nostromo's importance.

In a letter to Ernst Bendz, a Swedish professor, Conrad claimed that "Nostromo had never been intended for the hero of "Tale of the Seaboard."[19] And in response to Cumminghame Graham's critical remarks, Conrad wrote: "I don't defend Nostromo himself. Fact is he

does not take my fancy either. . . . But truly N. is nothing at all,—a
fiction, embodied vanity of the sailor kind,—a romantic mouthpiece of
the 'people' which (I mean 'the people') frequently experience the very
feelings to which he gives utterance. I do not defend him as a creation."[20] Conrad's later note to the novel, however, contradicts these
apologetic statements, indicating that Conrad owes his conception of
Nostromo as both hero and villain to Dominic Cervoni, the Genoese
friend of his early maritime exploits; that, furthermore, he regards
Nostromo as "that central figure" (xi) and devotes more than two full
pages to the discussion of this character out of a total eight (three of
which are also taken up with the description of the "vagrant anecdote,"
the source to Nostromo's theft of the lighter).

At the beginning of the book Conrad draws the reader's attention to
the man's name. "This is our Nostromo!" Signora Teresa laughs omi-
nously. "What a name! What is that? Nostromo?" (23). The Italian
nostromo ("boatswain"), or *nostromo del porto* ("boss of the stevedores"), is
the Spanish *capataz de cargadores*. Nostromo is also *nostro uomo*—our
man; Gian' Battista Fidenza—faithful John the Baptist. Costaguana,
incidentally, means the coast of *guano*, the bird excrement used in
making explosives; it can also mean the land of palms.

Nostromo is an enigmatic figure who can be admired, pitied, or
censured. Conrad observed that he had "no particular interest in crime
qua crime" (Author's Note, p. viii); it is natural that he wanted to
explore Nostromo's "faithful devotion" and his "moral ruin" (xii–xiii).
The ambiguity of Nostromo's character is reinforced by the frequent
play of light and darkness. He does not steal the silver out of greed alone
and, therefore, cannot be regarded as an ordinary thief. The silver mine
which turns into an obsession for Charles Gould and destroys him as it
had destroyed his father, is clearly an agent in Nostromo's moral
disintegration. It is only after Decoud has removed four ingots of the
treasure that Nostromo's reputation of incorruptibility is threatened
and he becomes a thief so that the world might still regard him as an
honest man. It is a typical Conradian choice: A betrayal must be
committed for the sake of fidelity or inner truth, but the act of betrayal
makes attainment of the aim (fidelity) impossible.

Martin Decoud, the skeptical journalist, perhaps most closely pat-
terned on Conrad's own experience, is reluctantly drawn into the affairs

of Sulaco and its silver mine; he is finally driven to suicide by his lack of a moral identity. Decoud is yet another example of the terrible Conradian contradiction: his very materialism makes it impossible for him to survive when he is left alone on an island for ten days. He is "swallowed up easily in this great unbroken solitude of waiting without faith" (498). Faith, Conrad shows us again and again, is illusory, but it is also a necessity. Thus, the novel abounds in paradoxical situations and devastating ironies. It is a masterful web of politics and psychology, a most prophetic view of revolution and counter revolution, replete with the horrors of civil war, torture, indiscriminate killing, cynical exploitation of the masses against the background of individual tragedies—told with stirring realism.

Nostromo finds himself in a situation which proves intolerable for a man who thrives on the exercise of his vanity. Having acquired his fortune by stealth, the proud Nostromo cannot display it openly. Having lost his former identity as Nostromo, the incomparable Capataz de Cargadores, becomes like Decoud, questioning everything, doubting his very existence, bitter and skeptical. Before he is set free from his anguish by old Giorgio Viola's bullet (ironically, it is Nostromo himself who suggested that old Giorgio ought to be the keeper of the Great Isabel, thereby, as it were, appointing his own executioner), Nostromo commits one more act of betrayal—of Linda, to whom he was betrothed. The vicious circle of falsehood is broken only with his confession to Doña Emilia before his death. " 'I die betrayed—betrayed by—'/But he did not say by whom or by what he was dying betrayed" (559). Nostromo, the faithful, blames the silver for his fate and wants to reveal the hiding place of the treasure. But Mrs. Gould, whom he calls "Shining! Incorruptible!" (560)—the very epithets applied to silver, hates the accursed metal as much as he does. She stops Nostromo from telling her where the silver is; she does not reveal his secret to Dr. Monygham, who accepts her denial

like an inexplicable fatality *affirming the victory* of Nostromo's genius over his own. Even before that woman, whom he loved with secret devotion, he had been defeated by the magnificent Capataz de Cargadores, the man who had lived his own life on the assumption of *unbroken fidelity, rectitude, and courage*! (561)

Mrs. Gould's lie, like the white man's lie in "Karain," or Marlow's in *Heart of Darkness,* is an act of compassion toward Dr. Monygham, whom she prevents from lapsing into his former, cynical bitterness. But it is also her own act of defiance, her mute protest against the inhumanity of "material interests." She alone (and the reader) knows that Nostromo's is a hollow victory. She alone understands the real nature of the silver mine. To her Charles Gould's success is not different from that of Nostromo—an ironic victory. She saw the San Tomé mine "possessing, consuming, burning up the life of the last of the Costaguana Goulds"(522). Her wealth and the respect in which she is held by all bring no happiness. "The mine represents a perverted, political doctrine: *'First seek ye material interests and the Kingdom of God shall be added unto you'* "[21] The silver mine is the church and Charles Gould is its missionary, who is alienated from her and anything not connected with his mine. And she herself ends up "considered lovely, respected, honored, and as solitary as any human being had ever been, perhaps on this earth" (555).

This solitariness envelops the minor as well as the major characters of this novel. One of them is of special interest because he reflects some of Conrad's prejudices and his literary borrowings. Hirsch, "the hide merchant of Esmeralda," is the second archetypal Jew in his fiction, the other being the idealized Yankel of "Prince Roman"; the sharp caricature of his initial appearance can be related to Dickens's portrayal of Fagin in *Oliver Twist*.[22] At the same time, however the transformation of "the little hooknosed man from Esmeralda" from a pitiful and comic figure into a betrayed man (like Nostromo), capable of a desperate act of defiance, resembles that of Shylock in Shakespeare's *The Merchant of Venice*. As Hirsch is put through his paces, one cannot help wondering, Irving Howe observed, whether Conrad does not indulge in this instance "in the Elizabethan game of having his Jew sweat." Hirsch, like Shylock, is represented as an *alien,* endowed with the negative traits of a Shylock; he cringes in fear; he is supposed to be cunning; he is insulted by everybody; he is "a pitiful wretch" or "a luckless wretch," "a wretched man"—epithets used by *various* speakers, including Conrad, the storyteller.

In addition to Shakespearean motifs, there was another influence on Conrad when he composed the novel: that of Polish patriotism. As

mentioned above, Conrad modeled Antonia Avellanos on a Polish girl
he loved (Janina Taube or Ophelia Buszczyńska), and whose strength of
faith he hero-worshipped: "She had perhaps more glow and less serenity
in her soul than Antonia, but she was *an uncompromising Puritan of
patriotism,* with no taint of the slightest worldliness in her thoughts"
(Author's Note, xiv). Antonia's power of conviction differs from Nostromo's "faithful *devotion*" which contains something despairing as well
as desperate in its impulses (xii). Holroyd, too, had an overwhelming
"*faith* in his destiny" (77). Charles Gould's "*faith* in the mine was
contagious . . . Charles Gould, in his unshaken assurance, was obsti-
nately *convincing*" (p. 75); the chief engineer had "*unbounded devotion* to
the task . . ." (41).

Having confessed the Polish origin of Antonia Avellanos, Conrad
goes one step further and identifies himself with Decoud: " . . . it was I
who had to hear oftenest her [the girl who served as a model for
Antonia] scathing criticism of my levities—*very much like poor Decoud
. . .* (Author's Note, xiv). Conrad could have been referring to himself
when he described Decoud as "the adopted child of Western Europe"
(156), and similarly, he might have been thinking of Poland when he
put the following words in Decoud's mouth:

There is a curse of futility upon our character: Don Quixote and Sancho Panza
chivalry and materialism, high sounding sentiments and a supine morality,
violent efforts for an idea and a sullen acquiescing in every form of corruption. . . . (171)

Conrad himself had been called "an incorrigible, hopeless Don
Quixote . . ." (*A Personal Record,* 44). And it was probably Decoud-
Conrad who uttered the familiar Polish expression: "Pro Patria" (158).
This theme of patriotism is harped upon throughout the novel: e.g.,
Don José: "If all other provinces show only half as much patriotism as
we occidentals . . ." (190). Gustav Morf suggests that Costaguana
represents Conrad's native land, and offers several ingenious analogies
between the author's own guilt feelings and the similar torments of his
fictional heroes.[23] Yet *Nostromo* is not "Polish" in the sense that, for
example, "Prince Roman" is, in terms of direct historical and cultural
background, except, perhaps, in the description of Sulaco, which, as
Tillyard argued,[24] indicated the Polish city of Cracow, where young

Conrad lived for a while. The rich gallery of political figures, cut-throats, adventurers, the dramatic scenes of action, the patriarchal scenes from Casa Gould—all these (and many other details) recall the tradition of the Polish historical novel, especially Henry Sienkiewicz's famous *Trilogy*.

Costaguana is not merely a typical country in South America; its turbulent history could be that of any West European country, or that of Poland, which, like Costaguana, went through a transition from feudalism to capitalism. Conrad's "material interests" represent his view of a perverted political doctrine and of the havoc wrought by industrialization. Conrad's skeptical view of any political ideology may be attributed to his disillusionment as a Pole whose country had been partitioned.[25]

Perhaps that is why he has created Decoud. Decoud does not embrace any religious, moral, or political dogma. Like Ivan Karamazov, he is destroyed by his own skepticism: As his name suggests, Decoud is "unsewn." Unlike Dostoevsky, Conrad does not fully develop the psychological motivation for his suicide. He presents a rather sudden collapse of a man who comes face to face with his own emptiness. By drowning and shooting himself Decoud "solves" his moral dilemma, but taking the four ingots of silver from the treasure (to weight his body) he provides an insoluble moral problem for Nostromo. Decoud's exit, Conrad would have us believe, is merely a confirmation of his spiritual death.

Unlike Decoud, Charles Gould does not lack faith, but he too manifests a weakness of character. *His* fatal flaw is a total enslavement to the San Tomé mine, and he, rather than Nostromo, can be regarded as the tragic hero of the novel. His character is enhanced by three foils: Nostromo, the chief engineer, and Emilia Gould. Nostromo's excessive vanity is contrasted with Charles Gould's idealistic self-deception. The chief engineer's practical idealism makes Gould's dream possible. He resembles Conrad's stoic captains who rarely engage in rhetoric but confine themselves to the steadfast task of steering their ships and a safe delivery of their cargoes. The chief engineer has a boundless devotion to his duty—another kind of fidelity. Being a practical man, however, he knows that "we can't move mountains" (157). Gould believed that material interests contained an intrinsic value which would promote the welfare of all. Thus, his notion of progress is not based on a romantic dream of achievement but rather on a fairly prosaic credo of making things pay. The third foil to Gould, his wife, is perhaps the novel's most vividly drawn figure. In a sense, she complements the chief engineer's practical wisdom, yet she is utterly opposed to her husband's materialism. When she decides to marry Charles Gould she is momentarily touched by his boyish passion for the exotic Costaguana and his fierce determination to redeem it. She is literally swept off her feet, and resigns herself to her destiny—to become one of the San Tomé mine's victims.

Mrs. Gould overshadows the other women in the novel. Antonia, Linda, Giselle, and Teresa Viola are somewhat limited portraits. Yet Conrad's range of characterization is extensive. Emilia Gould's love for Charles is quie different from Antonia's for Decoud or the two Viola girls' for Nostromo. The male protagonists of the novel show a similar variety. Nostromo and Captain Mitchell are presented as simple men (the latter with a humorous touch); Dr. Monygham and Decoud as most complex.

Complex, too, is Conrad's narrative manner which is no longer the traditional nineteenth-century practice of building up a hero. Conrad's heroes or, more accurately, nonheroes remind us of the protagonists of Kafka, Sartre, and Camus—the alienated, tortured, at times semicomic or absurd sufferers of the twentieth-century novel.

The narrative manner, too, anticipates the twentieth-century practice of defying the usual time sequence (although, of course, there have been a few precedents in the past, e.g., Laurence Sterne's *Tristram Shandy*). Although the story is generally told in the omniscient third person, Conrad again uses the device of the narrator, not, to be sure, anyone like Marlow. He makes Captain Mitchell relate some incidents and tells others through Decoud's letter. On a few occasions Conrad addresses the reader directly or, possibly forgetting himself, employs the intimate "I" or "we." As in *Lord Jim,* the author *reflects* the personalities of some protagonists through the elaborate and lengthy accounts of others; for example, Nostromo comes alive in the reactions to him by Decoud and Monygham.

The novel has been criticized for its length, repetitiousness and the melodramatic ending, but it has also been praised for its display of narrative versatility. The time shifts in the novel produce the effect of irony but they tend to irritate the impatient reader or the one who dislikes any break in the continuity of action. Yet it is the intricate narrative technique that enables the author to combine scenes of great scope and variety with astute, often profound, reflections on society, politics and the unpredictable vagaries of man's behavior.

It is true, however, that the end of the novel suffers from a certain shortcoming. In Chapter 11 (Part Three, The Lighthouse) Dr. Monygham and Mrs. Gould review the events of the novel—the solution—and for a moment the reader may get the impression that Conrad has resorted to the typical "neat" ending of a Victorian novel, with heroes properly rewarded, and villains duly punished. The Sulaco revolution is over; Dr. Monygham feels he has had some rewards. As they reminisce and indulge in social talk, Antonia shatters the mood by raising the specter of another revolution.

The tragic realism of the novel is somewhat lessened when Conrad returns to the story of "Our great Nostromo" (as Dr. Monygham refers to him now) and ends the book with a melodramatic account of his death and the reaction of the two Giorgio girls. Yet Conrad did not carelessly lapse into this development. It was dictated by the very conception of the novel. Thus, when Doña Emilia again asks the pessimistic question: "Is it this we have worked for, then?" he changes the subject. "It is about Nostromo that I wanted to talk to you. Ah! that fellow has some *continuity and force. Nothing will put an end to him*" (512).

Soon, however, it becomes evident that these words are as untrue as the exalted views of the Sulaco revolution. Yet Conrad may well have intended to soften the stark vision of Costaguana by a small measure of affirmation. Dr. Monygham keeps his self-respect; the chief engineer maintains his practical and stoic posture; old Viola preserves his honor though he kills the wrong man; Mrs. Gould guards Nostromo's secret and remains stalwart and uncorrupted by the mine; Linda Viola, betrayed by Nostromo, avers her fidelity. "It's I who loved you . . . I! Only I! . . . I cannot understand. I cannot understand. But I shall never forget thee. Never!" (566). The exclamation of Linda's *"fidelity, her pain, bewilderment, and despair"* (566), rings over the dark gulf and is heard by Dr. Monygham as "another of Nostromo's *triumphs,* the greatest, the most enviable, the most sinister of all" (566). Conrad's final emphasis is on "his conquests of treasure and love" (566). Like the triumph of Lord Jim, these conquests are profoundly ironic. Love endures but it appears dreamlike and rather absurd.

Linda's not too convincing outcry is also symptomatic of the novel's main faults: the occasional overwriting, the exaggerated solemnity of some descriptive and analytical passages (especially those dealing with the mind of Nostromo and Decoud), the too frequent repetition of symbols like "material interests," "silver," "darkness," and, finally, the artificiality of his love scenes—a characteristic of many other works of Conrad.

But these faults do not lessen the total impact of the novel. Conrad's account of the social and political upheavals in Costaguana reads like a contemporary rendition of recent wars and revolutions—not merely in South America. The evil rampant in Costaguana, symbolically presented as silver, is timeless. The sentimental idealism of the American millionaire Holroyd is no less hollow than that of Charles Gould, and both are of *our* time as well as of Conrad's turbulent republic. Holroyd's credo is not different in essence from that enunciated in words or practice by today's giant corporations:

. . . Time itself has got to wait on the greatest country in the whole of God's Universe. We shall be giving the word for everything: industry, trade, law, journalism, art, politics, and religion, from Cape Horn clear over to Smith's Sound, and beyond, too, if anything worth taking hold of turns up at the North Pole. And then we shall have the leisure to take in hand the outlying islands and continents of the earth. We shall run the world's business whether the world likes it or not. The world can't help it—and neither can we. . . . (77)

Arrogance of power? Conrad knew, as he understood "The cruel futility of things . . . the cruel futility of lives and deaths thrown away in the endeavor to attain an enduring solution of the problem" (364). He did not offer *any* solutions. But his *Nostromo* revealed the corruption of power or wealth as well as the moral dilemmas they pose. As Charles Gould is consumed by the mine so Nostromo is affected by his new condition of being a thief. "A transgression, a crime, entering a man's existence, eats it up like a malignant growth, consumes it like a fever" (523). The contemporaneity of the novel is further attested to by a remarkably prophetic insight—the description of the "refinement of cruelty" (374) inflicted upon Dr. Monygham, whose subjugation by the inquisitional Father "had been very crushing and very complete" (373).

Nostromo is one of the first "difficult" modern novels. In some ways it is a more difficult and baffling novel than *Lord Jim,* for its chronology is disrupted and the distoritons of emphasis are bewildering. But the breath of its canvas and the richness of its characters have convinced another novelist, Robert Penn Warren, of its importance. He justly calls the novel "one of the few mastering visions of our historical moment and our human lot."[26] Indeed, *Nostromo* is one of Conrad's masterpieces, if not *the* masterpiece. Like *Lord Jim,* it is a story of betrayal, or several betrayals, an account of the destructive influence of isolation upon human beings. But it is much more. It is a great, massive symbol of his total vision of mankind. The republic of Costaguana is Conrad's view of the world, a profound study of the forces of deception and self-deception in human affairs.

Chapter Seven

The Desperate Shape of Betrayal: An Intimate Alliance of Contradictions

The Secret Agent: Alone in London

Conrad's interest in moral and political anarchism goes back to his early work, notably to Kurtz's Nietzschean vision of the overman or super-man whose exercise of ruthless power culminates in the negation of his original idealism.

Some of the paradoxical utterances by anarchists in *The Secret Agent* (1907) echo the cry of horror by Kurtz. The fanatical Professor is scornful of Michaelis's thesis of a world in which the strong are to nurse the weak. He, the Professor, considers the weak (in a mock reversal of the biblical augury) to be the source of all evil. "They are our sinister masters—the weak, the flabby, the silly, the cowardly, the faint of heart, and the slavish of mind. They have power, they are the mul-titude. Theirs is the kingdom of the earth. Exterminate, exterminate! That is the only way of progress. It is!" (303).

The novel focuses on that shape of betrayal which is caused by and causes an alliance of inner contradictions in the breasts of feeling and passionate men and women. Conrad explains in his Note how a casual perusal of a book by Anderson, the Assistant Police Commissioner in London, triggered an almost chemical reaction in his mind, a disturb-ing mental change which evoked a bizarre vision of

an enormous town . . . a *monstrous* town more populous than some conti-nents . . . a cruel *devourer* of the world's light. There was room enough there to place any story, depth enough there for any passion, variety enough there for any setting, *darkness* enough to bury five millions of lives. (xii)

The fictional canvas of *The Secret Agent* has thus been reduced from the epic vastness of a South American continent "of crude sunshine and brutal revolutions" (xii) to the perimeter of the city. The complex, multiple plot of *Nostromo* has been replaced with one of compact, dramatic concentration on three principal actors—Verloc, his wife, Winnie, and her half-witted brother, Stevie. There is, of course, an entire assembly of minor characters representing the English police, the Foreign (Russian) Embassy, and the anarchist variety—many of them created with great verisimilitude. But it is the Verloc family that holds the reader's attention, and the fortunes of these three people are central to all that happens in the story.

Nostromo's romantic and heroic incorruptibility gives way to the comic, ironically conceived, "incorruptible Professor"; Gould's grandiose dreams and his passion for the silver mine; Dr. Monygham's intellectual and emotional intensity, Decoud's despair and masochistic self-analysis—such as these are not to be found in *The Secret Agent*. It shows a world of little, mediocre men and women, an uncouth and flabby double agent selling unsavory goods in his shop; his wife, Winnie, content to be ignorant of everything, basking in the state of superficial respectability; overfed revolutionaries and dignitaries of the state. A tale, in Conrad's own words, "of sordid surroundings and moral squalor" (vii). Conrad's mocking eye scans the urban scene whose debased humanity is savagely exposed and denigrated.

The main dramatic event on which the novel is based is the bombing of the Greenwich Observatory, considered a spectacular outrage by the press in 1894, when it occurred while Conrad was living in London, working on *Almayer's Folly*. In this incident, an anarchist, Martial Bourdin, was carrying explosives when he was blown to pieces at Greenwich. Today it would be merely another, rather minor statistical item in a continued global phenomenon of politically or criminally inspired bombings, kidnappings, highjackings, blackmail, robbery, and plain murder. Yet one is impressed even today with Conrad's astute political judgment on the subject of political terrorism; he calls the attempt to blow up the Observatory "a blood-stained inanity of so fatuous a kind that it was impossible to fathom its origin by any reasonable or even unreasonable process of thought. For *perverse unreason* has its own logical process" (x).

It is the ability to perceive political action in terms of unreason or madness that makes Conrad so modern. The apocalyptic events of the last two World Wars have provided many an incident corroborating Conrad's dark vision of humanity in this novel. Re-reading his novel in 1920, Conrad concludes in his "Author's Note" that the book "makes a grisly skeleton. But still [I] will submit that telling Winnie Verloc's story to its anarchistic end of *utter desolation, madness and despair* . . . I have not intended to commit a gratuitous outrage on the feelings of mankind" (xv).

The somewhat deranged Professor repeats these words almost verbatim when he declares, "*Madness and despair*! Give me that for a lever, and I'll move the world" (309).[1] The omniscient narrator, too, uses the same words to describe Winnie's sad end: "The suicide of a lady—*this act of madness and despair*" (310).[2] Later on, the phrase becomes the obsession of Comrade Ossipon, whose betrayal of Winnie finally triggers her suicide, but it also plants the seed of destruction in himself.

The dedication and the subtitle of the novel are interesting. The former reads: "TO H. G. WELLS / THE CHRONICLER OF MR. LEWISHAM'S LOVE / THE BIOGRAPHER OF KIPPS AND THE / HISTORIAN OF THE AGES TO COME / THIS SIMPLE TALE OF THE XIX CENTURY / IS AFFECTIONATELY OFFERED." The latter is "A Simple Tale." Simple? Well, not quite. The main aspect of this novel is precisely that nothing in it is as it appears to be; nothing is simple, not even people like Winnie Verloc, who, in intellectual terms at any rate, is exceedingly limited, almost stupid in her determination not to know unpleasant things. But she is not simple in psychological terms, nor is Conrad's view of people and things simple or simplistic. A bitter, lacerating irony—the kind Swift uses in his *Gulliver's Travels,* turns this novel into part farce, part tragedy. If it is comedy, it is macabre or black comedy. The view of London is Dickensian, that is the London of *Bleak House,* shrouded in fog and legal iniquity—indeed, a city without light, an "enormous town slumbering *monstrously* on a carpet of mud under a veil of raw *mist* . . . its interminable straight perspectives of *shadowy* houses bordering empty roadways lined by strings of gaslamps . . . monotonous streets with unknown names where the dust of humanity settles *inert* and *hopeless* out of the stream of life" (300). Monstrous, misty, inert and hopeless—these are the guidelines, as it were, of Conrad's darkly ironic vision in *The Secret Agent.*

The title itself implies an ironic ambivalence. Taken literally, it means a double agent; in its metaphorical sense, a secret agent is not unlike Conrad's "secret sharer," one's double, suggesting a great deal of psychological complexity. Thus, a secret agent, in the political sense, is a person whose loyalty towards the state is divided. He is trying to preserve the social and political structure while also secretly desiring its destruction, or—"an alliance of contradictions."

As a political refugee, Conrad's own position was sensitive and ambivalent. He could not and would not attack his adopted country. Hence he would try to be as circumspect as possible in presenting a thorny political issue in England. Conrad's tale of anarchism in the heart of London is not, therefore, an attempt to show any threat to the stability of English political life. In fact, none of the anarchists is English.

Verloc is a double agent, working for the Russian Embassy and for the English police. Ostensibly, he is the owner of a little shop in Soho, where he peddles pornographic literature, and where he meets his anarchist friends. He lives with his wife, her invalid mother, and her idiot brother. The very nature of a secret agent's profession is deception, or, to use a more specific term—betrayal. For Verloc deception (or betrayal) must begin at his home. It is one of the principal themes in the story, and one of the main factors that bring most characters in contact with one another.

In Conrad's description of the novel's gestation, "Winnie Verloc stood out complete from the days of her childhood to the end. . . . This book is that story, reduced to manageable proportions, its whole course suggested and centered round the *absurd cruelty* of the Greenwich Park explosion" (xii). One must always be a bit wary of Conrad's evaluations of his own work or of his authorial disclaimers. The passivity, the ignorance, and, in a sense, innocence of Winnie cannot make *her* the prime *agent* of the book's action which is generated by Verloc, the secret agent, and *his* decision to send Stevie on his last errand. Yet Conrad's explanation does strike a profoundly revealing note: not only the explosion and Stevie's violent disintegration smack of absurdity. Even more absurd is Winnie's betrayal of herself which must inevitably lead to her betrayal of Mr. Verloc.

Thus, as Jim degrades himself in a public forum in order to redeem his own sense of honor, to manifest a faithfulness to his idealized romantic conception of himself, so Winnie gives up her butcher lover for Verloc, whose "barque seemed a roomy craft" and who always had some money in his pockets. But "there was *no sparkle* of any kind on the lazy stream of *his* life. It flowed through *secret* places" (243). In effect, then, Winnie has sold herself to Verloc not to affirm any romantic notions of honor but in an act of perverse fidelity to her mother and brother. She thus betrays the ideal conception of herself for "*a life without grace or charm,* and *almost without decency*" but of an "exalted *faithfulness* of purpose even unto murder" (298). The memory of her romance with the young butcher "survived, tenacious, like the image of a *glimpsed ideal* in that *heart* . . ." (275). When she learns of Stevie's macabre death, she has a vision of her husband and brother walking up Brett Street, "the last scene of an existence created by Mrs. Verloc's genius; an existence *foreign to all grace and charm*, without beauty and *almost without decency,* but *admirable* in the continuity of feeling and tenacity of purpose" (244; note how Conrad repeats the same words in two different scenes).

This vision of Verloc and her half-witted brother being a father and son is Winnie's "supreme illusion" (244) which offers no consolation, as did the Intended's illusory view of Kurtz; nor is there anything triumphant about it as in Jim's last unflinching glance. No, Winnie's moral disintegration is complete, paralleling her brother's physical annihilation. His innocent, childlike altruism and goodness appear more solid than her protective maternal passion for him. His death merely emphasizes how rare such innocence is and how vulnerable, while her first independent action, the murder of her husband, plunges her into a state of moral darkness and corruption. Her professed respectability is sham; her understanding of Verloc, shared by her self-sacrificing mother, totally false; her sense of safety and security, illusory; her readiness to be kept in the dark, an indication of her inner void. Thence the road leads to "madness and despair." Her ultimate betrayal of her husband has brought her to the condition of utter desolation: "The vast world created for the glory of man was only a vast *blank* to Mrs. Verloc. . . . She had nothing. She was the *most lonely* of murderers that ever struck a mortal blow. She was *alone in London*: and the whole town of *marvels* and *mud,* with its *maze* of streets and its *mass* of lights, was *sunk* in a hopeless *night,* rested at the *bottom* of a *black abyss* . . ." (270–71).

But Winnie is not the only character to live in darkness and ignorance. The plot of the novel advances through a series of confrontations,[3] usually between two chracters at a time, who are often doubles. These meetings dramatize their apartness and isolation, and the difficulty or the impossibility of communication. Since only the reader is informed as to what each of the characters thinks and what he or she knows, a great deal of suspense and dramatic irony is produced, amply spiced by Conrad's sardonic humor.

Thus, in three of such confrontations between husband and wife there are both irony and a foreshadowing of things to come. In the first, Mrs. Verloc reports Stevie's passionate response to a newspaper story about a German soldier "tearing half-off the ear of a recruit. 'I had to take the *carving knife* from the boy' Mrs. Verloc continued. . . . He would have *stuck* that officer *like a pig* if he had seen him then' " (60). In the second, Verloc complains to Winnie about an encounter with the First Secretary of a great Embassy: "A silly, jeering, dangerous brute, with no more sense than . . . you didn't know. Quite right, too. What's the good of telling you that I stood the risk of *having a knife stuck into me* any time these seven years we've been married? I am not a chap to worry a *woman that's fond of me*" (238). Not only is Winnie not fond of her husband. She, rather than the anarchists, will stick a carving knife into Verloc. Whereupon she will complain to Comrade Ossipon what a good wife she has been: "I loved him [the butcher boy not Verloc] dearly . . . seven years—seven years a good wife to him, the kind, the good, the generous, the—seven years. Seven years a wife to him . . . He was a devil!" (276). In the third confrontation, Verloc, his cover blown by the discovery of Stevie's identity, now swears revenge:

It was a very appropriate revenge. It was in harmony with the promptings of Mr. Verloc's genius. It had also the advantage of being within the range of his *powers* and of adjusting itself easily to the *practice of his life,* which had consisted precisely in *betraying* the *secret* and unlawful proceedings of his *fellow men.* Anarchists or diplomats were all one to him. Mr. Verloc was temperamentally no respecter of persons." (245)

Winnie remains silent and preserves a statuesque immobility as Conrad informs us that "Mr. Verloc was inclined to put his *trust* in any woman who had given herself to him. Therefore he *trusted his wife*" (245). Winnie feels like screaming but she chooses to keep her tongue as her husband rambles on; now she becomes possessed of a fixed idea which, ironically, was planted in her mind by Verloc himself—that of revenge upon "the man *whom she had trusted*" and who "took the boy away to kill him" (249).

As Verloc goes on, full of self-pity and once more referring to "a knock on the head or a *stab* in the back" (248) at the hands of the comrades, he suddenly feels very hungry. Here Conrad gives one of the mastefully comic scenes on the theme of cannibalism, suggested early by the notion of the city of London *devouring* its populace. Verloc falls upon "the piece of roast beef; laid out in the likeness of *funereal meats* for Stevie's obsequies. . . . He partook *ravenously, without restraint* and *decency,* cutting thick slices with the sharp *carving knife* . . . (253). He lays down the carving knife, listening to the sounds from the bedroom above. A few moments later Winnie's disconnected wits begin to consider her options. "She could scratch, kick, and bite—and *stab,* too; but for stabbing she wanted a *knife*" (256). And in a few moments she will come down, snatch the carving knife from the side of the *dish,* and with leisurely movements she will plunge it into Verloc's breast.

Winnie has not planned her revenge. She is too stunned by her brother's death; like Jim, she is immobilized not by fear or excessive imagination but by the pain of loss, the bewilderment, the shock at her husband's betrayal, his destruction of what she loved most. Her murder of Verloc with the carving knife used to cut the meat he is enjoying is her response to his amorous advances made to her after he has satisfied his hunger. This is *her* way of making love to him at this particular moment. She has submitted to him out of her love for her brother and mother. She has barely tolerated him. Now, all the pent-up frustrations, all the bitterness of her emotional slavery, well up within her and explode into murderous violence.

Yet she exhibits no tortured conscience like Jim, Nostromo, or Decoud; no profound moral awareness, merely subsequent fear of the consequences of her action. Her suicide, thus, unlike that of other "symbolic" suicides in Conrad's fiction, is merely pathetic. This is why Conrad turns Winnie into Stevie's double in the moment of her murderous action in a manner reminiscent of Ansky's *The Dybbuk*: "As if the homeless soul of Stevie had flown for shelter straight to the breast of his sister, guardian and protector, the *resemblance* of her face *with that of her brother* grew at every step, even to the droop of the lower lips, even to the slight divergence of the eyes" (262). The irony of this doubling of brother and sister lies, of course, in the contrast between Stevie's kindness and Winnie's murderous rage. She avenges Stevie's death by killing her husband, but it is also her final act of self-destruction. When she places her trust in Ossipon after the murder, as she had trusted Verloc before, she once again demonstrates her poor judgment no less than her moral shabbiness. She even suggests to him that they don't have to get married, while reminding him of her former respectability. This fine comic touch is further enhanced by Conrad's repeated use of a phrase from *Othello,* "Put out the light." Chapters 3 and 9 end with Winnie solicitously asking her husband whether she ought to put out the light and getting his gruff response (60, 181). Unlike Othello, Winnie will not hesitate to kill her spouse. Nor will she become aware of the ironic meaning of her frantic pleas to her next lover (and victim), the robust anarchist Ossipon, to put out the light in the parlor, where her slain husband is lying on the couch: "Look. The light—the light in the parlor. . . . Go in and put it out—or I'll go mad" (283). As he tries to draw away from her in fear and disgust, she keeps urging him on: "Quick! Put it out! . . . Go in! (284) . . . Go in and put that light out, Tom. It will drive me crazy" (287).

She cannot see Ossipon's aversion to her any more than she could penetrate the mask of Verloc's outward equanimity. She has lived by his side, refraining "from going to the bottom of facts and motives" (245). He deceives her about his comings and goings, and is deceived by her into thinking she is fond of him. Their relationship is not based on genuine affection or understanding but on a *blind trust.* But then, Conrad suggests, the whole world of this London is *blind* because men and women cannot see themselves or others as they really are. *Trust* is one of Conrad's key words, repeated again and again to underline the brittleness and shallowness of human relationships.

When Winnie asks Verloc, "Where have you been today?" he replies, "Nowhere! The *insufficiency* and *uncandidness* of his answer became pointedly apparent in the *dead silence* of the room" (192). Indeed, *insufficient* and *uncandid* pointedly describe all men and women in the novel whose lives are deadened by their lack of communication, which is a kind of silence. All but one, the idiot boy, Stevie whose altruistic concern for humanity is unheeded by others. He resembles Myshkin of Dostoevsky's *The Idiot,* whose moral sensitivity is scorned by the unfeeling world. Stevie's body disintegrates in the physical sense, but his spirit and his presence are felt after his death—a dubious immortality that causes more violence and destruction in its wake. Stevie's impact, however, is felt when he is alive, too, since his strange "art" gives the novel its basic form and a central symbolic metaphor.

He draws "innumerable circles, concentric, eccentric, a coruscating whirl of circles that by their tangled multitude of repeated curves, uniformity of form and confusion of intersected lines suggested a rendering of *cosmic chaos,* the *symbolism of a mad art* attempting the inconceivable" (45). This strange occupation suggests another thing, too, the circular method of the novel: its flashbacks, its iteration of images and words. It could also draw the reader's attention to other possible allusions: the Shakespearean wheel of fortune and the Wheel of Fire, and the perfect sense of order that this geometric line conveys, so unlike the disorder of life in *The Secret Agent.* Stevie indeed attempts the inconceivable in ironic terms, namely, the practice of charity. His compassion for the whipped horse, a familiar evocation of a similar scene from Dostoevsky's *Crime and Punishment,* his feeling for the poor and the downtrodden stand in dramatic contrast to the callous disregard for life and humanity exhibited by the police, the political conservatives, and the political radicals alike. The poor cabman justifies his attitude by pleading for himself. Whipping is hard but he, too, is whipped by life. "I've got my missus and four kids at 'ome" (166).

Moreover, in a profoundly ironic manner, the idiot boy is the one who asks probing questions, not his sister or her husband. Winnie's determination that "things do not stand looking into" suggests a moral flimsiness. Mrs. Verloc "wasted no portion of this transient life in seeking for fundamental information. . . . Obviously it may be good for one not to know too much" (169). But Stevie, though of a most imperfect mind, *is* curious and inquisitive: "Unlike his sister, who puts her *trust* in *face values,* he wished to go to *the bottom of the matter*" (173).

Perhaps, like the meaningless circles of the moronic Stevie, man's destiny is cyclic: its curves lead nowhere; the tangled multitude of these curves stands for the chaotic human existence. But Conrad uses the circle in another way, too. He introduces symbolic circular images which are invested with a magical connotation of power (as the ring which Stein gives to Jim, the seal of Seraphina in *Romance,* or the coin in "Karain"). The round object usually signifies fidelity and a close social or familiar bond. The sea, so omnipresent in Conrad's fiction, when viewed from the deck of a ship, is a perfect circle. In this novel, Conrad employs circularity both in specific references to round or cyclic objects, or in an intricate pattern of linguistic curves, so to speak, by the frequent iteration of selected words or phrases, or by the reiteration of his basic themes of betrayal and fidelity, knowledge and ignorance, true and false morality.

Like Mr. Vladimir's wit, Conrad's own method appears to be "discogering droll connections between incongruous ideas" (19). Though the irrational attempt to obliterate time itself (by destroying the Greenwhich Observatory) fails, the basic irrationality of life is emphasized. This London is both Dickensian and Kafkaesque: its people are grotesque; its streets are not numbered consistently. The urban landscape defies logic and common sense, but so does the whole strange tug of war between the anarchists and the defenders of the established order.

The cyclical, tightly organized structure of the plot, the authorial control and stylistic confidence, are unmatched in other novels. Perhaps it is this very quality of deliberateness, without providing any relief of romantic or sentimental affirmation, that accounts for the unique quality of the novel. It is filled with images of darkness, drabness, and ferocity, often steeped in gallows humor, which has aroused an unprecedented critical interest. It is easy to find fault with the novel which some critics have labeled as being too cold, too overwritten; even Conrad himself considered it a bit too symbolic. The image of the ponderous Verloc is the chief metaphor of this narrative, no matter what interpretation the readers choose, "his intense meditation, like a sort of Chinese wall, *isolated* him *completely* from the phenomena of this world of *vain* effort and *illusory appearances*" (154). The betrayers of *The Secret Agent* are all punished, along with the innocent Stevie; yet, except for Ossipon, there is little or no conscious self-punishment such as we observe in Conrad's early work. This will come to the fore again in his next novel of treason and fidelity, *Under Western Eyes*. Still, Conrad has managed to dramatize[4] his paradoxical view of humanity with clarity, precision, and savage irony, as he portrays the proximity (in moral terms) of criminals and the police; of the revolutionaries to the materialistic middle class; of the protective love to murderous hate; of scientific reason to anarchist unreason; of imbecility to logic; of despair and madness to sanity. The grim chilliness of Conrad's comic view of London, wrapped in lacerating ironies, is unrelieved except, perhaps, by its indirect "messages": the betrayal of one's ideal conception of self is deadly; the betrayal of human solidarity is deadly, and, finally, the absence of love and communication among human beings is also deadly.

Under Western Eyes:
Alone in St. Petersburg and Geneva

Under Western Eyes (1911) is also a political novel dealing primarily with betrayal, but it is a very different book. Here are a few of the main points of difference. First, though the subject of Russian politics appears in *The Secret Agent* with the satirical portrayal of Mr. Vladimir and the other members of the Embassy, it is only in this novel that we have Conrad's truly "Russian" story. Second, it is, in Albert Guerard's words, "a great tragic novel,"[5] and *The Secret Agent* is essentially a comic one. Third, the latter is told from the omniscient point of view, while the former employs the detached, Marlovian teacher of foreign languages as the narrator. Well, perhaps not quite Marlovian, except in the most general sense; the Marlows of *Lord Jim*, "Youth," and *Heart of Darkness* are all active men of the sea, concerned with a quest for self-knowledge in their respective commitment to Jim, a younger romantic self and Kurtz, a commitment largely dictated by a fondness. The language teacher, on the other hand, does not pursue any occupation. His own life is uneventful and dull, his outlook on life that of a conventional Englishman of a liberal political persuasion who rather dislikes and resents Razumov, whom he professes not to understand. Fourth, the nature of betrayal and punishment therefore is different in each of the novels. Though Verloc and Winnie both die and Comrade Ossipon suffers a delayed shock at his betrayal of Winnie, there is no real moral conflict in them or in any other characters, and no real questioning of one's own conscience. In *Under Western Eyes*, however, Conrad returns to his early interest in the "destructive element" of a man's moral sensibility which, as we have seen in Jim's case, may also be his redemption from guilt.

Once again Conrad has selected a young man to be his hero; he is Kirylo Sidorovitch Razumov, a student at the University of St. Petersburg, and the illegitimate son of Prince K——. Like Jim, Razumov is put through an unexpected test which will reveal his character and his moral nature. One day Victor Haldin, a revolutionist who has just killed a hated Minister of State, comes to his room, seeking shelter and assistance. Razumov's dilemma cannot really be solved satisfactorily. He does not sympathize with the revolution and is preoccupied with the writing of a prize essay in order to gain a silver medal. Haldin has been merely a casual acquaintance who mistakenly assumes that Razumov shares his views and will offer him full support. Razumov, it is reiterated a number of times, inspires confidence in people. Having locked Haldin in his room, Razumov goes to the peasant Ziemianitch to make arrangements for Haldin's escape; he finds him in a drunken stupor and beats him mercilessly. Then, walking the streets, he is beset by doubts. He is overwhelmed by a sense of helplessness: "I am being crushed—and I can't even run away. . . . He had nothing. He had not even a moral refuge—the refuge of confidence. To whom could he go with this tale—in all this great, great land?" (32).

Razumov takes his tale to Prince K——, who does not quite acknowledge him as a son yet indicates a measure of recognition by secretly pressing his hand. The Prince's carriage brings them to the house of General T——, where Razumov again tells his story without, however, mentioning his visit to Ziemianitch. While he is being praised for the moral soundness of his action, Razumov begins to feel great revulsion for the General. Now that he has betrayed Haldin, he begins to identify with him, to imagine him lying in his room, waiting to be arrested. He returns to his room and after a lengthy discussion leaves Haldin alone once more. He then waits for the clock to strike twelve, his mind hovering "on the borders of delirium. He heard himself suddenly saying, 'I confess,' as a person might do on the rack. 'I am on the rack,' he thought . . ." (65).

Haldin is tortured and hanged. Razumov is sent to Geneva to spy on Russian revolutionaries there. He falls in love with Nathalie Haldin,

Victor's sister who is living in exile with her mother. She believes Razumov to be a fellow revolutionary who worked with Victor. Like Jim, Razumov must be the agent of his own humiliation. He confesses the whole truth to Miss Haldin and later on to a group of the revolutionists. Nikita Necator, a fellow revolutionary but also a double agent for the Russian police, punishes him in a symbolic fashion: he shatters Razumov's eardrums, plunging him to a world of silence for the rest of his life. Later on, Razumov is run over by a tramcar. He must live out his days in Russia, nursed by Tekla, a humble woman who has served Peter Ivanovitch, the self-styled feminist revolutionary. When Nathalie's mother dies, she too goes back to Russia to live in obscurity as a charitable helper of the poor and the convicts.

Initially, Conrad began the novel as a story called *Razumov,* as he had started the first draft of *The Secret Agent* under the title *Verloc.* In a letter to John Galsworthy in 1908, the author promised to render "the very soul of things Russian." In the first version Razumov marries Haldin's sister and only after their child begins to look like the betrayed revolutionist does Razumov reveal the truth to his wife. Conrad puts the emphasis on the psychological problem of the young man rather than on the political theme. The finished product, however, is a remarkable novel about Russia, remarkable because of Conrad's anti-Russian sentiments.

As one could surmise from the caricatural treatment of the Russians in *The Secret Agent,* Conrad regarded them as basically inscrutable and cynical or corrupt people, savoring of Slavo-Tartar Byzantine barbarism, incapable of any form of government except despotism. Conrad's Russophobia, however, has not prevented him from creating an essentially sympathetic hero, though there are satirical and caricatural presentations as well. The successful depiction of Russians in this novel is achieved despite Conrad's often professed ignorance of Russia (like that of the teacher-narrator) and his reluctance to deal with them.

That is why it is worthwhile to examine the correspondence between *Under Western Eyes* and *Crime and Punishment.* Dostoevsky's student-killer is Raskolnikov (*rasskol* means split, dissent), whose best friend and alter ego is Razumikhin (*razum* means reason, intelligence). Razumov and Raskolnikov are both fatherless students who consider themselves superior to ordinary mortals. Having committed a major transgression, they attempt to analyze it and then to explain it away. Each will be surprised at the discovery that he has a conventional conscience; each will suffer terrible pangs of remorse; each will go through a period of hallucination, dreamlike sequences, and masochistic self-torment; each will engage in a psychological duel with a fatherlike superior, representing the authorities; each will demonstrate the necessity for a moral purification to be obtained only by means of a public confession; each must remain totally alone and isolated; each ultimately finds his redemption through a young woman's sympathy, faith, and devotion. In both novels, there is a mother and daughter; both mothers go mad. Razumov's encounters with Councillor Mikulin and General T——parallel the meetings of Porfiry with Raskolnikov; in each case, the older interviewers are father figures. The faithful Tekla of Conrad reminds us of the humble Sonia; both, moreover, serve as doubles to the men under their care. Nathalie recalls Dunya. Sophia Antonovna shares her first name with Sonia, a diminutive of Sophia. The latter, though a prostitute and not, like Sophia Antonovna, a revolutionary reformer, is actually the principal reformer of the young sinner.

A startling similarity lies in the conclusion reached by the two student-transgressors. Raskolnikov asks, "Was it the old hag I killed? No, I killed *myself* and not the old hag."[6] Razumov, too, identifies with his victim: "It's *myself* whom I have given up to destruction . . ." (341). "In giving Victor Haldin up, it was *myself*, after all, whom I have betrayed most basely" (361). There are other similarities, such as the doubling of characters, the accusation of an innocent man, and the surge of people toward the confessor. But perhaps the most telling correspondence is the devastating realization of the young heroes that they are trapped, that they have nowhere to go. Raskolnikov recalls Marmeladov's question' "Do you realize, do you realize, sir, what it means when you have nowhere to go . . . For every man must have at least somewhere to go."[7] When Mikulin's questioning becomes intolerable to Razumov, he declares his intention to retire and is stopped dead by the dramatic though softly spoken challenge of the bureaucrat: "Where to?" (99). Later on, Razumov will explain to Nathalie why he came to her: "It is simply because there is no one anywhere in the whole great world I could go to. Do you understand what I say. No one to go to. Do you conceive the desolation of the thought—no-one-to-go-to?" (354).

Such similarities do not imply a slavish imitation of *Crime and Punishment*. What might have begun as a parody of the Russian book eventually developed into an original Conradian psychological novel. The influence of other writers upon Conrad does not detract from his fictional achievement; on the contrary, the literary allusiveness broadens the fictional scope (at least for those readers who can recognize the conscious or unconscious sources) by enriching the texture of the narrative. Thus, one can find echoes from Adam Mickiewicz's *Forefathers' Eve* in Conrad's description of Russia as "monstrous blank page" (33)[8]

There are also pronounced echoes from Shakespeare, especially from *Macbeth* and *Julius Caesar*, two tragedies of betrayal. The common dramatic and psychological situation of the novel and of *Macbeth* is the betrayal of a trusting guest. As Macbeth's reputation of nobility and valor is established before his deed, so, too, Razumov's trustworthiness is reiterated. Haldin explains to the bewildered Razumov why he has come to him in one word: "Confidence" (19). The phrase "He inspires confidence" is repeated in several variants until it becomes almost comic when Razumov thinks dully and irascibly: "They all, it seems, have confidence in me . . ." (52). Like Verloc's, however, Razumov's trustworthiness is deceptive. He too will become a spy, a secret agent. As in the two Shakespearean tragedies, there is the evocation of symbolic darkness; there is the problem of living a shamed life, and there are the supernatural phenomena accompanying severe guilt.[9]

It is this interest of Conrad in the problem of living a shameful existence that links *Under Western Eyes* with *Lord Jim* and *Nostromo*; for both Jim and Decoud share with Razumov his desperate longing for moral support; both have experienced the terror of loneliness. Razumov "was as lonely in the world as a man swimming in the deep sea. The word Razumov was the mere label of a solitary individual" (10). And Razumov feels that "No human being could bear a steady view of moral solitude without going mad" (39).

Despite his "Western detachment" the professor manages to put together a story of great passion and great moral complexity, as he unfolds, quite sympathetically, it must be noted, the tale of Razumov's woes. But though he has assured the reader that he is merely presenting documentary evidence, the actual manner in which the story is told is, in effect, that of an omniscient narrator whose attention to dramatic and gory details (as in the account of the assassination of Minister de R., the President of the notorious Repressive Commission) recalls Conrad's "objective" description of Stevie's death in *The Secret Agent.*

As the action develops, it becomes apparent that we actually have two basic stories fused together by the omniscient narrator: the professor's and Razumov's diary. To attain an even greater degree of detachment, Conrad introduces additional points of view. Thus, for instance, Razumov's confession, perhaps the most dramatic event of the novel, is thrice removed from Conrad: the teacher's narrative provides two accounts of the confession, one by Julius Laspara and the other by Sophia Antonovna. She, incidentally, reports that her story comes from Razumov himself. The narrator fills in all the missing details from Razumov's diary.

The involuted time sequence and the multiple points of view, gathered by a principal "objective" narrator, result in a story of considerable dramatic potential that is, however, not fully realized because the sheer multiplicity of views at the end of the novel lessens the impact of Razumov's confession. While the symbolic and ironic density of the text indicates that Conrad still possessed great creative vigor and the clarity of vision, some readers may question the need for such involved treatment of what could have been a single, central dramatic pivot in a psychological drama. The narrator's function in this novel is that of a chorus and an intermediary between the reader and the several sources of information. One the other hand, it can be argued that the very indirectness and the interposition of the narrator in the story enable Conrad to provide a selection of events, arranged to achieve the maximal ironic thrust.

A satirical stance is evident in the portrayal of some of the "international conspirators," the Dickensian exaggeration of *The Secret Agent* turning into a more subtle parody of Dostoevsky, as in the admirable piece of caricature in the person of Peter Ivanovitch. Like the murderous Nikita, he is burly, a man who had "one of those bearded Russian faces without shape, a mere appearance of flesh and hair with not a single feature having any sort of character" (120). Conrad pokes fun at this pretentious fugitive from Russian justice, whose exploits were celebrated in a story of his life "written by himself and translated into seven or more languages" (120). He goes on ridiculing Peter Ivanovitch and his strident feminism, for he is actually an exploiter of women and, to use a contemporary "classification," a "male chauvinist."

Nathalie, however, is not a woman to be exploited, for she has her own mind. She believes that reform "is impossible. There is nothing to reform. There's no legality; there are no institutions. There are only arbitrary decrees. There is only a handful of cruel—perhaps blind—officials against a nation" (133). This view has a contemporary ring; it could have come from the pen of Alexandr Solzhenitsyn in his frequent condemnations of Soviet tyranny. Her discussion with the teacher turns to the subject of a violent revolution and its aftermath. The revolution is started by the unselfish and the intelligent, the teacher argues, "but it passes away from them. They are not the leaders of a revolution. They are its victims: the victims of disgust, of disenchantment—often of remorse. Hopes *grotesquely betrayed,* ideals caricatured—that is the definition of revolutionary success" (134–35). The charitable old gentleman, who is truly fond of beautiful Nathalie, does not want her to become a victim, but she refuses to think of herself and cries out for liberty "from any hand" (135).

Nathalie Haldin is Conrad's favorite, too, for he has chosen her words to serve as an epigraph to the novel though he usually drew on a great variety of sources for this purpose. The epigraph reads: "I would take liberty from any hand as a hungry man would snatch a piece of bread . . ." (135). Suppose, however, that the liberty she longs for comes from the hand of a Razumov, a betrayer? Her conviction that "the right men are already amongst us," the men her brother's letter described as "unstained, lofty, and *solitary existences*" strikes a hollow note since we know that the man Haldin mentions, carrying the letter of introduction from Father Zosim, is Razumov, the very person responsible for her brother's arrest and execution. Her strange notion of a "concord" to be enacted in Russia is an echo of Conrad's own words, "an alliance of contradictions." The narrator knows her scorn for all the practical forms of "political liberty known in the Western world." He is puzzled by what he calls "Russian simplicity, a terrible corroding simplicity in which mystic phrases clothe a naive and hopeless cynicism" (104). Nathalie naively hopes that antagonistic ideas shall be reconciled. When the narrator protests with some irritation that such concord is inconceivable, she retorts: "Everything is inconceivable. . . . The whole world is inconceivable to the strict logic of ideas. And yet the world exists to our senses, and we exist in it. . . . We Russians shall find some better form of national freedom than an artificial conflict of parties—which is wrong because it is a conflict and contemptible because it is artificial. It is left for us Russians to discover a better way" (106).

This utopian vision defies and insults the narrator's western sense of rationality. Nathalie's mystic and logically misty ideas smack of cynicism which will not admit the truth. The teacher sums up the difference between them thus: "I think sometimes that the psychological secret of the profound difference of that people consists in this, that they detest life, the irremediable life of the earth as it is, whereas we westerners cherish it with perhaps an equal exaggeration of its sentimental value" (104). Razumov's political ideas are the very opposite of Nathalie's—at least in his initial stage as a student. He is calm and logical. Haldin refers to his "frigid English manner" (16) and to his being "Collected—cool as a cucumber. A regular Englishman" (22). He is politically conservative and he wants to rise in the ranks of society. He enunciates his philosophy in five lines, scribbled in a large hand which becomes "unsteady, almost childish": "History not Theory. / Patriotism not Internationalism. / Evolution not Revolution. / Direction not Destruction. / Unity not Disruption" (66). Symbolically, he stabs the paper with his penknife to the wall. This political credo is penned after the deed of betrayal is done, and he feels he is on a rack, and even says to himself, "I confess." He then goes to sleep and wakes several times that night, "shivering from a dream of walking through drifts of snow in a Russia where he was as *completely alone* as any *betrayed* autocrat could be . . ." (66). Much later, however, in a verbal duel with Peter Ivanovitch, Razumov rejects the notion that he is an extraordinary person. Peter Ivanovitch senses some affinity with Razumov: "You are a man out of the common. . . . This taciturnity . . . this something inflexible and *secret* in you. . . . There is something of a Brutus . . ." (208). Brutus, of course, is a man who betrays his Caesar. Peter Ivanovitch adds, "But you, at any rate, are *one of us*" (Conrad's italics). This echo from *Lord Jim* is painfully ironic because the *us* here does not represent any tradition of loyalty and trust but its very opposite. Both men stand for a degree of fraud, moral and intellectual. Razumov refuses to accept Peter Ivanovitch's notion that he aims at stoicism: "That's a pose of the Greeks and the Romans. Let's leave it to them. We are Russians, that is *children;* that is—*sincere;* that is—*cynical,* if you like" (207). The *us* means, therefore, us, the Russians.

This exchange is no longer in the manner of caricature. Rather, the narrator reveals the philosophical and psychological contradictions of the protagonists. His own reservations about Nathalie's views, despite his obvious affection for her, his skeptical assessment of the revolutionist's aim and practice; his caustic view of the Swiss; his disclaimers about his ignorance of the Russians while making pejorative statements about them[10]—all these also add to "the alliance of contradictions" which seems to render the elderly teacher an unreliable narrator. But it is precisely because his motives and his veracity may be suspect that this method achieves its most telling effect: the reader is forced to take sides, as in *Lord Jim.* The reader, in fact, is forced to identify not only with Nathalie, who is the language teacher's "pet," but also, and perhaps to an even greater extent, with Razumov and the revolutionists as well.

It is, indeed, difficult not to feel a sense of profound sympathy for Razumov and also for the revolutionists whose cause Conrad rejects but whose proponents by and large have not been reduced to caricature, as in *The Secret Agent.* The understanding and pity some of them show to the crippled young man enhance their humanity and thereby their psychological verisimilitude. As Conrad points out in his "Author's Note," his greatest anxiety was "to strike and sustain the note of scrupulous impartiality" (viii). There is little doubt that the "obligation of absolute fairness" imposed upon him "historically and hereditarily" was adhered to. Conrad avers that he "had never been called before to a greater effort of *detachment:* detachment from all passions, prejudices and even from personal memories." He is gratified that the book "had found recognition in Russia and had been re-published there in many editions" (viii). This effort of detachment was most taxing for Conrad, for he suffered a nervous breakdown after the completion of the novel, as if the identification with Russia was more than his mind and heart could stand. As if, moreover, he had seen a dark vision of the future.

For in no other political novel of Conrad do we find such profound and prophetic insights into the nature of men and women living under an autocratic regime and rebelling aginst it; especially insights into the men practicing political violence. Take, for example, his comment on Nikita, whom he calls "the perfect flower of the terroristic wilderness." What troubled Conrad most in dealing with him "was not his monstrosity but his *banality.*" How remarkably familiar this sounds today when we think of Hannah Arendt's book about Adolph Eichmann, entitled *The Banality of Evil.* The most terrifying reflection, Conrad concludes in his Author's Note, speaking for himself and possibly for our age, "is that all these people are not the product of the exceptional but of the general—of the normality of their place, and time, and race." Writing this in 1920, Conrad was able to predict the futility of revolutionary action to alter human nature. His words carry an uncanny contemporary resonance:

The ferocity and imbecility of an autocratic rule rejecting all legality and in fact basing itself upon complete moral anarchism provokes the no less imbecile and atrocious answer of a purely Utopian revolutionism encompassing destruction by the first means' to hand, in the *strange conviction* that a fundamental change of hearts must follow the downfall of any human institutions. These people are unable to see that all they can effect is merely a change of names. The oppressors and the oppressed are all Russians together, and the world is brought once more face to face with the truth of the saying that the tiger cannot change his stripes nor the leopard his spots. (ix–x)

As mentioned before, Conrad dedicated *The Secret Agent* to "H. G. Wells . . . The Biographer of Kipps and the Historian of the Ages to Come." Perhaps this dedication reveals the underlying philosophical intent in both *The Secret Agent* and in *Under Western Eyes,* two novels which span the comic and the tragic views of mankind. Though Conrad and Wells were good friends at one time, the latter's views on social utopia were anathema to Conrad, as Chernyshevsky's *What Is to Be Done?* had been to Dostoevsky. "You don't care for humanity," Conrad wrote to Wells, "but think they are to be improved. I love humanity, but know they are not."[11]

A Set of Six: Simply Entertaining

The stories in *A Set of Six* (1908) date to the period when Conrad was writing *The Secret Agent,* the result, as Conrad put it in his Author's Note of 1920, "of some three or four years of occasional work" (vii). The stories are of uneven literary quality and the collection was not meant to show any particular thematic unity. Strangely enough, however, they all deal with different aspects of Conrad's familiar themes: betrayal and fidelity and cases of double life; they reflect, in a lower key, the psychological and political preoccupations of the author in the preceding two novels. Except for the first story, "Gaspar Ruiz," the tales are subtitled, as if Conrad wanted to make sure that the reader's interpretation was properly guided.

"Gaspar Ruiz" (*Pall Mall Magazine,* July–October 1906) was written or at any rate begun, as Conrad recalls, "within a month of finishing *Nostromo*" (viii), but the author does not think the story and the novel are similar in mood, intention or style. Indeed not, for it is a very slight story—an offshoot of his reading for *Nostromo,* and once more set in a South American country, in Chile. The melodramatic plot unfolds through the narration of an officer but the point of view is not consistently maintained. Accused of desertion by the republicans, sentenced to death, the acquiescent Gaspar is "stirred now to a sort of dim revolt by his dislike to die the death of a traitor. *He was not a traitor*" (7). After his escape, he marries an aristocratic girl who bears him a daughter. Her Royalist sentiments demand revenge upon the republicans against whom she incites her husband, and eventually he ends up fighting them. As a result of treachery, his wife and child are imprisoned, and Gaspar perishes in his attempt to free them in a dramatic scene where he offers his own back as a gun-carriage. The cannon is fired but it breaks the giant's back. His wife now repents, protests her love for Gaspar. The child survives and is adopted by the officer whose life Gaspar has once saved. She is a simple soul, like her father, "the strong man who perished through his own strength: the strength of his body, of his simplicity—of his love" (70).

"The Informer—An Ironic Tale" (*Harper's Magazine,* December 1906) is brought to the reader indirectly. A Mr. X, whose revolutionist exploits and scandalous writings dear to the middle classes have made him rich, meets the narrator with whom he shares an interest in Chinese porcelain and gourmet food. Mr. X tells the narrator the strange story of Sevrin, the anarchist who is also a double agent, a *"genius among betrayers"* (93), and Horne, an artist turned revolutionary who also "led a double life" (83). There is also, as in *The Secret Agent,* a former science student, a comrade nicknamed Professor who, surrounded by tins of

Stories' Dried Soup, is engaged in perfecting new detonators. He is described in ironic terms: "His was the true spirit of an extreme revolutionist. Explosives were his faith, his hope, his weapon, and his shield. He perished a couple of years afterwards in a secret laboratory . . ." (88).

Recalling the themes of professional betrayal in *The Secret Agent* and *Under Western Eyes,* Comrade Sevrin "was accustomed to arrange the last scenes of *his betrayals* with a deep, subtle art which left his reputation untouched" (93). The punch line of the story, which will be used by Conrad in "Prince Roman" (written in 1910), is the phrase "From conviction," which is repeated again and again. Sevrin, it appears, was the craftiest of informers who poisons himself when his true identity is revealed, but not before he declares his credo to Horne: "I have been thwarting, deceiving, and *betraying* you—*from conviction*" (97). The subtitle of the story is best illustrated in the scene of Sevrin's disclosure and the distress of the Lady Amateur of anarchism, whose pretense of making love to an anarchist was elevated into an art; also in the psychologically complex relationship between the placid, detached narrator and the tempestuous and monstrous Mr. X.

"An Anarchist—A Desperate Tale" (*Harper's Monthly,* August 1906), actually written before "The Informer," is a kind of a dry run for the full performance of *The Secret Agent*. After a French mechanic called Paul gets drunk one evening and yells, *"Vive l'anarchie!* Death to the capitalists" (147) in a fit of sentimental stupor, he is locked up on a charge of "assault, seditious cries, and anarchist propaganda" (147). The young Socialist lawyer who defends him ignores Paul's pleas of innocence and his total ignorance of things anarchistic. Instead, he presents his client as "the victim of society and his drunken shoutings as the expression of infinite suffering. The young lawyer had his way to make . . ." (147–48). As the lawyer's speech for the defense was magnificent, Paul got the maximum sentence. When he is released he finds himself at the mercy of the anarchists, who use him and finally get him sent to the penal colony at Cayenne. He escapes with two anarchists in a boat and forces them to row the boat at gunpoint until they are exhausted. He then shoots both of them in cold blood. After his escape Paul is once more being exploited on a cattle estate, which is also an island, where he lives in total isolation. He tells his story to a lepidopterist, who is Conrad's narrator.

With cutting irony, the lepidopterist, who has come to the island in quest of rare butterflies, points out that this island is "like a sort of penal settlement for condemned cattle," and the lowing of herds is "a deep and distressing sound . . . rising like a monstrous protest of prisoners condemned to death" (137). The convict, whom the French manager persists in calling "Anarchiste de Barcelona," though he is French, too, finishes his tale in great agitation. The lepidopterist stays up with him "in the name of humanity." He ponders this strange case of social injustice and sums up his ideas: ". . . he was very much like many other anarchists. Warm heart and weak head—that is the word of the riddle; and it is a fact that the *bitterest contradictions* and the *deadliest* conflicts of the world are carried on in every individual breast capable of feeling and passion" (161). The narrator leaves us with a vision of "the anarchist slave of the Marañon estate waiting with resignation for that sleep which 'fled' from him, as he used to say, in such an unaccountable manner" (161). Indeed, it is a tale of desperation.

"The Brute—An Indignant Tale" (*Daily Chronicle,* December 5, 1906) is a very slight thing, describing with proper indignation, to be sure, what is perhaps the only case of an unfaithful ship in Conrad's fiction. The ship, called the *Apse Family,* is brutish in two ways: she is (from Conrad's point of vantage) unusually large, thus demanding more toil from her crew; and she has a supernatural knack of killing at least one person on every voyage.

The fuss that was made while that ship was building! Let's have this a little stronger, and that a little heavier; and hadn't that other thing better be changed for something a little thicker . . . there she was, growing into the clumsiest, heaviest ship of her size before all their eyes . . . She was to be 2,000 tons register, or a little over; no less on any account. But see what happens. When they came to measure her she turned out 1,999 tons and a fraction. General consternation! And they say old Mr. Apse was so annoyed when they told him that he took to his bed and died. (111)

She was unaccountable. If she wasn't mad, then she was the most evil-minded, underhand, savage brute that ever went afloat. (112)

The reputation of the "Brute" is coupled with another danger—the presence of two women aboard the ship, the captain's wife and his niece, who falls in love with the chief mate. The "Brute" lives up to her nasty reputation, for the niece is killed in a freak accident as she is flung overboard by the iron arm of the anchor. The ship herself, too, is finally wrecked in what appears to be a providential act of poetic justice. Once again the presence of a woman suggests an ill omen, for the ship herself is betrayed by the second mate, who is flirting with a woman passenger, having deserted his watch and thus driving the ship ashore.

Gerald Morgan claims that one of Conrad's own ships was most likely the killer ship, the *Falconhurst*. He also suggests that this mad ship "belongs with the mad sea of "The Secret Sharer" and the mad cosmos of *The Shadow Line*. Both of these tales are set in the China Sea, where the bereaved chief mate of the "brute" ends up commanding a steamer.[12] Conrad's fondness of the word shows up in *Under Western Eyes:* before his liberation, Peter Ivanovitch appears as "a dumb and despairing *brute*" (124). Tekla's poor Andrei is killed "by these official *brutes*" (236); Ziemianitch is called by Razumov "a *brute*, a drunken *brute*" (352); and, finally, the murderous Nikita is called "that brute" (380).

Though "The Duel—A Military Tale" (it appeared as "A Point of Honor" in *Pall Mall Magazine,* January–May 1908) is of novella length (100 pages), it is really a delightfully comic anecdote of a feud between two Napoleonic hussars, told dramatically and with an unmatched lightness of touch. Feraud, a fierce Gascon, and his fellow officer in Napoleon's army, D'Hubert, who is rather meek and soft-hearted, are engaged in a series of duels during a period of fifteen years. The utterly unreasonable, quixotic nature of their encounters is enhanced by the fact that no one knows why these two men keep fighting, and whatever the initial insult Feraud imagined to have received from D'Hubert, it is never mentioned or actually remembered.

In contrast to the "anarchist" tales, the mood of this story is sunny, and Conrad's irony is gentle rather than savagely lacerating. The absurdity of the extended duel reveals the paradoxical Conradian truth: the enmity between the two dueling Frenchmen was due to an illusory cause, yet it gave both warriors a sense of meaning and purpose in life. For the first time in his life D'Hubert falls in love (with a girl called Adèle), and he now realizes that life has become more precious to him. His desire to free himself from Feraud once and for all borders on desperation. But it is the menacing presence of Feraud that gives his life its special meaning. When D'Hubert finally wins the last duel and chooses to hold his antagonist's life at his disposal, he feels "an inordinate tenderness towards his old adversary and appreciated emotionally the murderous absurdity their encounters had introduced into his life. It was like an additional pinch of spice in a hot dish. He would never taste it again. It was all over" (223). Thus, their relationship had become "an intimate connection of a nature which makes it a point of honor" for D'Hubert to assume full responsibility for the life of his erstwhile adversary, protecting him from the wrath of army command. General Feraud, for his part, is crestfallen when he is retired from the army. "He felt suddenly strange to the earth, like *a disembodied spirit*" (230), the very words Marlow uses to describe Jim's utter estrangement from mankind. Ironically, that is the way D'Hubert feels when he asserts his victory over Feraud, whose life he now claims: "I can't really discuss this question with a man who, as far as I am concerned, does not exist" (258). Here is the rub. General D'Hubert's triumph is ironic for he has not gained anything thereby. On the contrary. When he risked his life in the final duel, in order to free himself from Feraud and to "win a girl's love," he had known moments when by a marvelous illusion, this love seemed to be already his, and this threatened life a still more magnificent opportunity of devotion" (259).

Once more Conrad shows his fondness for the word "brute"; Feraud growls, "You take the nearest *brute*, Colonel D'Hubert . . ." (213), this one being a Russian cossack. D'Hubert understands, finally, that his Adèle loves him, for she rushes to the site of the duel, running two miles. " 'I owe it all to this stupid *brute*,' he thought" (264). But, of course, he does not hate the "stupid brute." He writes to him, formally returning to him his forfeited life, but Feraud will not be reconciled. " 'We must take care of him, secretly, to the end of his days,' D'Hubert declares to his wife. 'Don't I owe him the most ecstatic moment of my life?' " (266).

The last duel between the two officers is thus the ironic trigger which allows D'Hubert to make the most important discovery of his life—the love Adèle has for him. "But for his [Feraud's] stupid ferocity, it would have taken me years to find you out," he says to his wife, adding, "It's extraordinary how . . . this man has managed to fasten himself on my deeper feelings" (266). D'Hubert and Feraud have become secret sharers.

"The Duel" is not really a tale about militarism, though Conrad was fascinated by the Napoleonic legend, and he used the subject again in "The Warrior's Soul" and in the final unfinished novel *Suspense*. This story, more than any of the other five, proved the point Conrad made to his publisher, namely that "they are just stories in which [I've] tried [my] best to be *simply entertaining.*"[13] Little wonder, then, that the quality of entertainment expressed best by the form of a simple, straightforward narrative no less than the light comedic approach appealed to the contemporary filmmakers. The recent (1978) release by Paramount Pictures of *The Duellists* is one of the more successful cinematic adaptations of a Conradian story, starring Harvey Keitel as Feraud and Keith Carradine as D'Hubert and directed by Ridley Scott. The film won the 1977 Cannes Film Festival award as the best first film by Scott. Though most critics praised the production and considered it, on the whole, quite faithful to Conrad's text, one dissenting voice claimed that the charm and irony of the story were lost in the process of cinemation. Juliet McLauchlan points out that a subtle falsification is introduced by the change in the title and the importation of a second love-interest into the story.[14]

"Il Conde—A Pathetic Tale" (*Cassell's Magazine,* August 1908), the final story in the collection, has generated diametrical opposites in the critical assessment of its appeal and quality. For example, Jocelyn Baines views it as "an excellently told but very short and unimportant story. . . ."[15] Frederick R. Karl, on the other hand, maintains that "Il Conde" "is surely one of his *finest* stories and looks ahead to his last major novel, *Victory.*[16] The subject of the story was suggested to him by Count Szembek, a Polish friend of the Conrads during their stay in Capri. It concerns a very refined Count living in Naples. When he is assaulted in the park by an aristocratic *Cavaliere,* a member of a group called *Camorra,* the old man's sense of security and order collapses. The threat of the *Cavaliere*'s knife shocks *Il Conde*, whose dignity is outraged by being held up unceremoniously at the point of a long knife. He hands over his wallet containing only 340 or 360 lire, a very insignificant amount, and the cheap watch he happens to wear that evening, having left his valuable gold half-chronometer at a watchmaker's for cleaning. When the *Cavaliere* demands his rings as well, the Count refuses, closing his eyes and expecting a fatal push of the long blade which was resting against his stomach. But he is left alone and he then remembers his gold twenty-franc piece which he has hidden "as a sort of reserve in case of an accident" (285). The Count, still reeling in shock after this "abominable adventure," goes for some refreshments to the

Cafe Umberto, his tranquility "wantonly desecrated. His lifelong, kindly nicety of outlook had been defaced" (284). As the Count pays the waiter with his reserve gold piece, he is observed by the *Cavaliere*, who again approaches him and insults him with the contemptuous "Ah! So you had some gold on you—you old liar—you old *birba*—you *furfante*! But you are not done with me yet" (288).

The poor trembling *Il Conde* tells this entire episode to the narrator, who is both appalled and amused. He cannot refrain from a caustic observation: "I am sure that if he had been not too refined to do such a blatantly vulgar thing as dying from apoplexy in a café, he would have had a fatal stroke there and then" (288). But, as he continues, "all irony apart," he perceives *Il Conde*'s difficulty though he cannot persuade him to stay. The Count's case is a case of honor, as in "The Duel"—"His delicate conception of his dignity was defiled by a degrading experience. He couldn't stand that. . . . To go home really amounted to suicide for the poor Count" (289)—both on account of his health and his wounded sensibility, the kind Jim exhibited.

But the Count's appearance may be as misleading as that of Jim, for it may well be that he is (to echo the story's subtitle) merely a pathetic pederast involved in a rather sordid adventure which the narrator himself terms "a deucedly *queer* story" (281). Douglas A. Hughes points out that *birba* means scoundrel and it is the feminine gender, while *furfante* means rogue. Both words can be affectionate epithets rather than insults between strangers.[17] The Count's loss of dignity cannot be compared to Jim's loss of honor, and it is hard to see how an outside act of violence can thus undermine one's sense of worth, unless it is coupled with an awareness of one's own dishonorable action or conduct. Clearly, the Count feels guilty because he has been driven into a public recognition of his secret self.

Another interpretation may be offered by an analogy between *Il Conde* and Heyst,[18] whose serenity is also shattered by the rude invasion of the diabolical trio of bandits. Frederick Karl suggests that there is an allegorical intent in the story, suggesting that the Count's sheltered existence is symbolic of Europe on the eve of the First World War. The Count's retreat and Heyst's Samburan are in reality no worldly paradises. They are places from which both heroes must be expelled and sent to their ultimate destruction.

The epigraph to the story is *"Vedi Napoli e poi mori,"* which means "See Naples and then die!" It is, the narrator concludes, a saying of excessive vanity, yet the Count, who shunned immoderation and excess, actually behaved "with singular *fidelity* to its conceited spirit" (289). He is too sensitive, too weak and vulnerable to face the physical threat of a political terrorist, as Heyst is too indolent and disarmed by his crippling philosophy of life to lift a hand in his own defense.

Chapter Eight

How to Love

Chance and *Victory*: Knights and Damsels

Though critics are divided in their appraisals of the relative merits of
Chance (1913) and *Victory* (1915), some preferring the former and others
the latter, they generally agree that both suggest a decline in Conrad's
powers as a novelist. Betrayal, the leitmotiv of *The Secret Agent* and
Under Western Eyes, still looms large in these two novels, but they are,
like most of Conrad's late fiction, devoted primarily to the exploration
of the flawed human heart. They are about love but also about sex or, as
in the case of poor Captain Anthony, the abstinence thereof with his
wife, Flora. "All of it," said Conrad, is "about a girl and with a steady
run of references to women in general all along. . . . It ought to go
down."[1] Well, it did. *Chance* is Conrad's first financial success which is
due to a number of factors: its serialization in the *New York Herald*; a
clever and energetic promotion by Alfred Knopf, newly arrived at
Doubleday; a simple and popular title, catchy headings for chapters
(not used before or again) and the two parts; an ample dose of
sentimentality and pseudophilosophy, mostly on the subject of women;
and, of course, mere chance.

The titles of the novel's two parts imply that Conrad treated the story
as a kind of fairy-tale, for Part I is called "The Damsel" and Part II "The
Knight." In the past, Conrad subtitles usually suggested the author's
intent, but here the subtitle "A Tale in Two Parts" is rather per-
functory; at best, it invites the reader's caustic response that only one of
the two parts (the first) is any good. The epigraph by Sir Thomas
Browne alludes to all things being governed by Fortune, thus echoing
the title, *Chance:* "Those that hold that all things are governed by
Fortune had not erred, had they not persisted there."

The plots of both novels stress the impact of blind chance and the helplessness of the protagonists overtaken by it. Indeed, Flora de Barral, the damsel in distress of *Chance*, is the victim of blind fate. Without a mother, the only child of a gullible swindler who preys on others' gullibility, she attempts suicide after her father's bankruptcy. She is betrayed and insulted by an evil governess and she languishes in a state of a profound, moral shock and isolation. Like Lena in *Victory*, who is pinched by Mrs. Zangiacomo and hounded by the gross Teutonic hotelkeeper Schomberg, she is also pursued by the head of a German household. She is completely alone, at the mercy of the world. Fate (or chance) brings a "knight" to rescue the forlorn maiden, and each proves to be a hermitlike man who has withdrawn from a wicked world, and who is emotionally crippled. Both "knights" are offspring of literary men: Anthony is the son of a "delicate" poet, and Heyst is the son of a pessimistic philosopher. Like Conrad's literary father, Apollo Korzeniowski, these fathers have exercised a most damaging influence upon their sons by contributing to their sons' pain and inflicting psychic wounds upon their minds. Anthony's father gave him an overrefined sense of delicacy, so much in contrast to his sister's feminist toughness; Heyst's philosopher father, the author of *Storm and Dust*, has bequeathed to *his* son a deadly creed of doubt which results in a Hamletian paralysis of will, and the inability to act or to be committed to anyone or anything.

Another basic similarity in the two novels is Conrad's interest in sensuality, more specifically of the homosexual variety. Thus, in *Chance*, the aggressively feminist Mrs. Fyne exhibits all the traits of a lesbian. Flora's elopement with Roderick provokes her wrath. Although she herself is married, she does not want women to be women; she believes that women should "turn themselves into unscrupulous sexless nuisances." The effeminate, pistol-packing Jones is described by his "secretary" Ricardo as a *freakish* gentleman who hates women: "Yes, the governor funks facing women" (161). Eventually, the "governor" will shoot Ricardo for his involvement with a woman.

The plot of *Chance* centers on the plight of Flora, whose father is sentenced to a seven-year term in jail. Abominably treated by her governess and relatives, she finds a haven with the Fynes; Mrs. Fynes's brother, Captain Anthony, falls in love with Flora after she attempts to throw herself over a precipice. Ironically, Mrs. Fyne now turns against Flora and tries to prevent her marriage to Roderick. Under her influence Flora writes a letter to her in which she states that she does not love Roderick but will marry him for convenience. Roderick, however, will not give her up since he wants to shield Flora. He takes her and her father, who has been released from prison, on a voyage on the *Ferndale* which he commands. Marlow is right when he doubts that the isolation of the sea would help the young couple. For the ex-convict de Barral the ship is another jail, and he regards Captain Anthony not as a charitable soul but as another jailer. As in *Nostromo,* Conrad isolates these three people on a ship. All three are torn by conflicting emotions of love or hate.

Anthony refuses to have sex with his wife in the belief that she does not love him; Flora, on the other hand, thinks that Roderick has married her merely out of pity. "But who would have suspected Anthony of being a heroic creature" (328), Marlow wonders, exasperated by his sublime delicacy. "That's your poet. He demands too much from others. The inarticulate son had set up a standard for himself with that need for embodying in his conduct the dreams, the passions, the impulses the poet puts into arrangement of verses" (328). Lord Jim dies celebrating a wedding with a shadowy ideal of conduct. Captain Anthony's conduct, like Jim's, tears him away from the arms of a woman who loves him, and whom he also loves. His inarticulateness does not permit him to break through the barrier of estrangement between himself and Flora. "Chance had thrown that girl in his way . . . this eager appropriation was truly the act of a man of *solitude* and *desire* . . . a man of long and ardent reveries wherein the faculty of sincere passion matures slowly in the *unexplored recesses of the heart*" (328–29).

In *An Outcast of the Islands* Conrad first explored the destructive impact of the untrammeled sexual passion on Willems. Here, though he defines Roderick's passion as "dominating or tyrannical," and being close to "folly and madness" (329), he does bring the lovers together after a prolonged period of mental and, presumably physical, agony. Anthony, unlike Willems, is not destroyed by his lover. On the second voyage of the trio, de Barral, driven by jealousy, attempts to poison Anthony. Upon being discovered, he takes his own life. At this point, the lovers finally overcome their estrangement. Yet, though Conrad avowedly begins the story as a kind of fairy-tale, there is no "happily ever-after" for Flora and Roderick. Anthony drowns, but at least young Powell gets his Flora.

A lively critical debate has been waged for decades as to whether *Chance* (and for that matter, *Victory*) is a lesser novel because of Conrad's difficulty to deal adequately with love. Perhaps Conrad was reluctant or unable to deal with intimate details of sex; unable to present sexual complications as vividly as some of the novelists of the 1960s or 1970s have done. Still, he managed to convey some fairly convincing portraits of men and women, especially women: Flora, her governess, and Mrs. Fyne. The latter, to be true, is somewhat "overdone" in Marlow's zeal to define her feminism.

Similarly, the resolution of the novel suggests a weakening of Conrad's customary concern with verisimilitude. The mysterious disappearance of a carving knife from the mess-room of the *Ferndale*, the poison which de Barral unaccountably brings to the ship, and, finally, the presentation of Powell as a cardboard prince—these suggest indeed the melodramatic or romantic stuff of a fairy-tale. Conrad himself defines this aspect of the book: "I suppose that to him [Mr. Powell] life . . . was something still in the nature of a fairy-tale with a 'they lived happily ever after' termination. . . . Powell felt in that way because the captain of a ship at sea is a *remote, inaccessible* creature, something like a *prince of a fairy-tale,* alone of his kind . . ." (288).

Moreover, Conrad is only partially successful in his narrative method. The story is told by Marlow to the nameless author of the novel who argues with him about his opinions and impressions. Marlow's story draws upon the information of the Fynes, Powell, and Flora, who in turn convey their impressions of things and people. Conrad's return to Marlow as a narrator is less felicitous since it is a different Marlow, somewhat misogynous, garrulous, and, frankly, a bore. Unlike Dowell, the pathetic narrator in Ford Madox Ford's *The Good Soldier,* whose dullness serves a distinctly ironic purpose since he tells us more than he knows or understands himself, this Marlow is one of the three speakers in the novel, the other two being the "I" and young Powell. Neverthe-

less, the narrative method of *Chance* is often regarded as Conrad's most
Jamesian work, and a good example of his innovative approaches to
fiction by presenting his story without the conventional limitations of
chronology.

The principal narrator rambles on, and instead of telling us what
actually happened, he tells what he *imagines* to have happened: "And we
may conjecture what we like. I have no difficulty in imagining that the
woman . . . must have raged at large." The narrator is thus deeply
interested in the tale, but, given his temperament, he can maintain an
ironic distance from what he is reporting on.[2]

The sense of unreality in *Chance* reappears with a vengeance in
Victory. The word which Conrad uses to describe Schomberg's psychology, "grotesque" (in a Note to the First Edition), constitutes a key to
the novel's tonality. *Victory* is not merely a melodramatic novel of
Conrad's decline, as critic after critic suggested. While not an artistic
tour de force, it is still an effective novel whose highly allusive literary
frame, rich texture, and comic invention have been largely ignored
hitherto. Conrad's preoccupation with Calderón's *La Vida es Sueño* [Life
is a Dream], translated into Polish by Conrad's favorite Romantic poet,
Juliusz Słowacki, is one of the central elements in Conrad's often
contradictory and paradoxical statements about the human existence. It
appears in many of his works but it is in *Victory* that it reaches its
climax, as Heyst, immobilized by his crippling philosophy, is fascinated by Jones, "this skeleton in a *gay* dressing-gown, jerkily agitated
like a grotesque toy on the end of an invisible string"; Heyst is
bewildered and it seems to him "that all this was *an incomprehensible
dream*" (389). In fact, for Heyst life becomes a grotesque dream or, more
accurately, a terrifying nightmare. Camille R. La Bossière suggests that
Conrad's view of life comes both from Calderón and from Cusa's
principle of *coincidentia oppositorum,* or an allegorical conflict of opposing
forces, "a circular logic of contraries. . . . Conrad struggles to *see* the
'Inconceivable' by the light of this synthetic logic and to translate into
verbal analogies the 'unspeakable' truth of man and universe. The truth
eludes surface logic and the language of affirmation."[3]

Indeed, *Victory* is based on this allegorical conflict of opposing
forces, with Conrad once again delving into the problem of human
alienation. As we follow the fortunes of the two lovers isolated on their

island of Samburan, the physical nature of their universe has shrunk yet it contains the whole gamut of human passions. The moral problems of the protagonists are no less complex than their love-making and, ultimately, survival. Even the villains have a certain kind of morality, and they assume the stance of the devil's disciple. For example, Ricardo keeps harping on the alleged betrayal by Heyst of his friend Morrison. Until Lena comes along, Ricardo displays a certain loyalty to his master, the "governor." As in other novels, only the extreme, the final existential test, can reveal the meaning of life to the hero, and by that time it is too late.

Heyst skims the surface of the world. He is not fully alive; though he has a chance to defend himself against the villains who are about to take Lena from him, and even his own life, he will do nothing until the very last moment. Only when everything is lost does he begin to understand the true nature of his own life and emotions. Only when Lena is dying does he understand finally that he has been in love with her. He is not merely disgusted with the world, he is disgusted with himself. And that, as in the case of Hamlet, makes it impossible for him to act.

Heyst believes that a man is lost if he forms a tie. He is a man of universal scorn and *unbelief*, "the most detached of creatures in this earthly captivity, the veriest *tramp* of this earth, an *indifferent stroller* going through the world's bustle" (199). Yet he is essentially a rather naive and a good man who is suspected of foul play against his associate Morrison when, in fact, he has proved most charitable toward him. Ironically, echoing Jim's ambivalence at the Court of Inquiry, Heyst's action, when he does choose to act, will prove him both right and wrong. His voluntary commitment to Lena's welfare—or the forming of a tie—will prove his undoing; on the other hand, his distrust of life and his fatalism make him impotent and thereby nullify his genuine concern with Lena's safety. He cannot and will not fight back.

The original name Conrad chose for this man was "Berg" (or mountain in German), which, like Kurtz in *Heart of Darkness,* was to be symbolic, suggesting perhaps a man larger than life, a strong, towering personality. In the final version, however, Heyst won. But this name is closer to *heist* or *theft*. Is it too farfetched to assume that Conrad did not notice the correspondence, for, after all, Heyst does steal his little Lena (Magdalen[4] and Alma) from the lecherous Schomberg? The trace of the original conception remains, to some extent, since Heyst is of noble parentage and is referred to as "a puffect g'n'lman . . . but he's a ut-uto-utopist" (8) or a dreamer living in a state of unreality.

As in *Chance,* this sense of unreality pervades the novel and estranges the two lovers from each other. "The girl was to him like a script in an unknown language, or even more simply mysterious, like any writing to the illiterate" (222). In *Chance*, we have "psychological wilderness" and Marlow becomes an expert in it; here we face the wilderness of a god-forsaken island along with the cultural and moral gap between the two lovers. In *Chance* Flora suffers from a "mystic wound"; in *Victory* Heyst is the victim of this injury, both intellectual and psychic. Lena is a mystery to Heyst, who in turn is a mystery to her. She knows him so little that she, too, like his enemies, is at first convinced that he may have murdered poor Morrison; and when she decides to save her lover and obtain Ricardo's knife, she stoops to deception and becomes so intoxicated with her dream of self-sacrifice that, in effect, she is partially responsible for the final catastrophe. Thus, in each case, we see an extreme form of solipsism, not too far removed from Jim's "exalted egoism" in psychological terms.

But while Lena is granted the triumphal gesture of self-sacrifice, Heyst is left in despair. The unpredictable decree of destiny (chance) has caught up with him and exposed the utter futility of his unbelief. Even a short moment before her death, Heyst was capable of believing her infidelity as if "paying her back for her doubts about him. She speaks to him "in accents of wild joy," but he looks at her "with a *black, horror*-struck curiosity." In this final melodramatic scene, Lena resembles Jewel who is trying to hold on to her lover and also to send him away, to save him: "I have done it! . . . Never get it back. Oh, my beloved!" (403). Whereupon the refined Heyst bows his head gravely and speaks in his polite Heystian tone: "No doubt you acted from instinct. Women have been provided with their own weapon. I was a *disarmed man.* I have been a *disarmed man* all my life, as I see it now. You may glory in your resourcefulness—your profound knowledge of yourself; but I may say that the other attitude, suggestive of *shame,* had its charm. For you are full of charm!" (404).

I suppose one can say that Conrad fails here stylistically. Would any man speak like this to his dying lover? But the point is that Heyst cannot *see* the truth because he is too wrapped up in his own detached view of things to be able to *see anything.* He even turns his back on her as her enchanting voice cuts deep into his heart. Only when her voice begins to falter does he spin around and finally go to her, snatching her up bodily out of her chair and becoming aware of her limpness as the knife drops to the floor with a metallic clatter. Like Othello in the moment when he perceives that he has killed an innocent Desdemona, Heyst cannot utter a word, but must "let out a groan . . . the heavy plaint of a man who falls clubbed in the dark" (405). The melodramatic and, unfortunately, somewhat sentimental scene between the lovers reaches its climax, yet it contains the familiar ring of Conrad's bitter irony.

" 'Oh my beloved,' " she cried weakly, 'I've saved you! Why don't you take me into your arms and carry me *out of this lonely place?*" (406). But Heyst is now afraid to touch her as he bends low over her, "cursing his fastidious soul, which even at that moment kept the true cry of love from his lips in its *infernal mistrust* of all life" (406). Heyst has brought Lena to the illusory paradise in Samburan with the intent of saving her from a menacing world. But it has proven both lonely and destructive. Lena breathes "her last, triumphant, seeking for his glance in the shades of death" (407). *His* last words indicate a measure of enlightenment: ". . . woe to the man whose heart has not learned while young to hope, to love—and to put its trust in life!" (410).

Heyst's suicide by means of the purifying *Flammentod* ("death by fire") and Lena's death from Jones's bullet both symbolize their respective failures and ironic triumphs. The thunderous and melodramatic ending of the novel (seen by some critics as a typically Victorian tying-up of loose ends) is also Shakespearean. It recalls the storms of the major tragedies like *King Lear, Macbeth,* and *Julius Caesar* and the romance *The Tempest.* [5] The upheaval of nature mirrors the storm within men's souls. As the violent struggle on the island of Samburan comes to its pathetic close, the thunder over it ceases "to growl at last" (406). All the principal combatants are dead: Ricardo, appropriately "shot neatly through the *heart*" (411); Pedro, the Caliban-like servant, shot by Wang, the unfaithful servant of Heyst, with the revolver he has stolen from his master; Jones, the strange alter ego of Heyst, tumbles into the water and drowns in what may be another "purifying" death in the novel. The story is over, and Heyst's assessment of his unreal situation on the island has been confirmed by the events. When he was held prisoner by Jones he had a feeling that it was all "an elaborate *other-world joke,* contrived by that *specter* in a gorgeous dressing gown" (389). As the story opens with Heyst's *enchantment* with the islands, with Lena's voice, so the enchantment develops gradually into a macabre nightmare, a grotesque vision of human existence.

Although Conrad's epigraph for *Victory* is drawn from Milton's *Comus,* the subtitle "An Island Tale," the apparent parallel with Villiers de L'Isle Adam's *Axël,* the numerous Shakespearean echoes, and the main allegorical thrust all point to an analogy with *The Tempest.* The islands of Prospero the enchanter, and Axel Heyst, the Enchanted, are invaded by sinister people who are vanquished in the end, but each of the elder men, the real and the surrogate father, must sustain the loss of his young ward, and be left in a mood of despair.

In some ways Conrad goes back to *Lord Jim* in his presentation of Heyst as a *"thoroughly white man"* (14), always immaculately attired in white apparel, even wearing white shoes. His appearance, like that of Jim, is misleading. Heyst *seems* virile and strong and cuts a martial figure with his flaming red moustaches and glowing cigar. Yet there is that same infernal alloy in his metal. Neither man's mother appears to have played any part in the shaping of Heyst's or Jim's personalities, while each of the two fathers exercised a profound and lasting influence. And as Jim fails in his confrontation with Gentlemen Brown, so Heyst is taunted by "Gentleman" Jones (as he is called by Ricardo), who explains the meaning of his being a *reckoning*: "I, my dear Sir . . . I am the world itself come to pay you a visit. In another sense I am an *outcast*—almost an *outlaw.* If you prefer a less materialistic view, I am a sort of *fate*—the *retribution* that waits its time" (379). Both men are outcasts *and* doubles.

Despite its flaws, *Victory,* in my view, is not a simple pseudo-Victorian novel; nor does it signify a complete decline of Conrad's artistic powers, as suggested by Albert Guerard or Thomas Moser. Upon closer scrutiny, the novel reveals an impressive tonal richness: from black comedy to sentimental melodrama; from philosophical meditation to romantic twaddle; from static descriptions to scenes of brutal violence; from delicate, almost prudish depictions of sexuality to riotously comic aspects of fetishism and voyeurism.[6]

For all the stylistic lapses, Conrad's conception of Jones and Ricardo justifies their language. The latter's utterance, according to Guerard, is too effeminate. But Ricardo, with his knife strapped to his leg and frequently exhibited, *is* effeminate *and* a fetishist to boot, whose central passion, it appears, is focused on Lena's foot: " 'Give your *foot*,' he begged in a *timid* murmur. . . . She advanced *her foot* forward a little from under the hem of her skirt; and *he threw himself on it greedily.* She was not even aware of him" (400). This is not awkward prose; it makes excellent comedy. Conrad continues with a straight face: "Ricardo, *clasping her ankle,* pressed his *lips* time after time to the *instep, muttering gasping* words that were like *sobs,* making *little noises* that resembled the *sounds of grief and distress*" (401).

Lest one consider this unintentionally humorous or an expression of Conrad's own subconscious sexual patterns, one must note the somewhat caustic authorial comment on the psychological condition of Jones, which also anticipates Ricardo's own strange tastes. When Ricardo explains his governor's rabid hatred of women, "he paused to reflect on this psychological phenomenon, and as no philosopher was at hand to tell him there is no strong sentiment without some terror, as there is no real religion without *a little fetichism,* he *emitted* his own conclusion" (161).

Well, there is more than a little fetishism and voyeurism in *Victory* and, as Dr. Bernard Meyer repeatedly observed,[7] a tendency to blur the distinctions between the masculine and the feminine, and to endow women with phalluslike characteristics of solidity, hardness, and the power of thrust and penetration: "Suddenly Ricardo felt himself *spurned* by the *foot* he had been *cherishing*—spurned with a *push* of such *violence* into the very *hollow* of his throat that it swung him back into an upright position *on his knees.* He read his danger in the *stony* eyes of the girl" (401). There is a great deal of comic-serious business with Ricardo's slipper, as it is missed, found, tossed out the window by Lena, then triumphantly retrieved by Ricardo. "As soon as it *passed the opening,* it was out of her sight. . . . It had gone clear."[8] She stood "as if turned into *stone*" (302–303). Lena reels forward and momentarily finds support in yet another fetishist object by "embracing with both arms one of the tall, *roughly carved posts* holding the mosquito net above the *bed,*" thereby saving herself "from *a fall*." She clings to it for a long time, her forehead leaning against the wood. Her sarong slips and reveals part of her naked body, the long brown tresses falling in lank wisps. "Her *uncovered flank,* damp with the *sweat of anguish* and *fatigue* gleamed *coldly* with the *immobility* of polished *marble*" (304–305).

I offer these examples of prose that is neither sentimental nor awkward. Perhaps there *are* passages of pure melodrama in *Victory*, as there are in Dickens's *Bleak House,* beloved of Conrad. But as the death of little Jo works despite the overwhelming sentimentality of the scene, so does the scene of Lena's death. It is not surprising that Conrad's American audience was moved to tears when he read it aloud. *Victory* is, thus, its alleged and real flaws notwithstanding, a novel of allegorical and tragic dimensions. Its treatment of sexuality, of women in general, is in my view, more complex than in the early works such as *Lord Jim* or *Heart of Darkness.*

It has been suggested that *both* Jones and Heyst are homosexuals and that the "powerful theme" of the novel is "that homosexuals, who represent a withdrawal from normal relations and a denial of life, are doomed and damned beyond redemption."[9] If one accepts this thesis, it is possible to argue that Jones's bullet, intended for Ricardo to punish him for his betrayal, reaches Lena's breast because Jones now acts on Heyst's behalf. He must rid himself of Lena so that he can have Heyst, his alter ego, to himself. Ironically, Lena saves Ricardo by kicking him in his throat, in a sense justifying his faith in her. Only he thought she would kill *Heyst.* One wonders whether with her final gesture in handing Ricardo's phallic knife (the symbol of his manhood) to Heyst she thereby unwittingly delivers his death sentence. Indirectly, she does drive Heyst to his death with her own act of sacrifice.

On another level, the novel is a microcosm reflecting the less than perfect society of prewar Europe. Its title, tagged on, as it were, after its completion (the book appeared in 1915), represents not merely Lena's ambivalent victory but also the dubious victory scored by the Allies in World War I. Peace was imposed on the smoldering volcano of the European continent. The smoking volcano is a constant reminder of the ironically paradisiac island of Samburan. The volcano's glow is compared to the end of a gigantic cigar, and the reader does not fail to make the connection between the cigar-puffing Heyst of martial appearance and the dormant volcano. The safety offered by the island and Heyst's looks are as deceptive as the deck of the *Patna* and Jim's impressive mien. The unexpected strikes with murderous fury as the unholy trio of bandits lands on the island. There is no security in this strange Eden. There is only the inevitable disaster, the terrible, meaningless, and absurd carnage at the end, no more absurd, however, than the carnage of the battlefields of France that erupted in 1914. Davidson sums up the story by a reference to warfare: "there are more dead in this affair . . . than have been killed in many of the battles of the last Achin war" (408).

But though Davidson echoes Marlow's question at the end of *Lord Jim,* "Who knows?" (411), the ending of *Victory* is in some ways more poignant and effective than that of *Lord Jim.* Let us examine the final word of the novel, "Nothing," a word which has been used repeatedly to create a sense of dramatic irony, reminiscent of King Lear's shock at Cordelia's "Nothing." The word-frequency table of the concordance to *Victory* indicates that not counting auxiliary words and proper names, *nothing* is one of the most often used words (160 times) after *man* (293 times) and *eyes* (233 times). Could one draw a corollary from this that man is *nothing?* Perhaps, but with some qualifications. Heyst repeats the word, thereby underlining the illusory quality of his and Lena's retreat. His assurances ring hollow: "Is your mind turning towards the future . . . because if it is so there is *nothing* easier than to dismiss it. In our future, as in what people call the other life, there is *nothing* to be afraid of" (222). "*Nothing* can break in on us here" (223). "*Nothing* whatever was to be *seen* between the point and the jetty" (226). "*Nothing* was to be *seen.* . . . The civilization of the tropics could have *nothing* to do with it" (227).

The frequency of Shakespearean allusions in the novel leaves no doubt of the final word's connotation. Lear's "*Nothing* can be made of *nothing,*" is not unlike the elder Heyst's skeptical philosophy. The point of *King Lear* is, in my view, that everything comes from *nothing.* Lear gives his two evil daughters everything in the material sense—but he gets nothing in return. Cordelia gives him a word, "Nothing," and gets *nothing* in return. Lear gives Cordelia nothing but actually gets everything from her. Love is not to be measured by words of flattery or by real estate. It is spiritual; it is not quantitative at all. That is why it comes from *nothing* material. Heyst's resolution to do *nothing* in this world is a transgression not different from Jim's egotistic *"Nothing* can touch me" (325). Heyst has broken Conrad's code of human solidarity. He must learn, as other Conradian heroes have, that no man is an island unto himself.

Heyst's exit from the turbulent stage[10] of Samburan implies that though he has negated the world, the world has not negated him. If there is any logic in his suicide after Lena's passionate affirmation of her love for him, it is his paradoxical acceptance of himself as a responsible man in the real world of men and women. Yes, Heyst has learned, too painfully, perhaps, the lesson that man must put his trust in life. So now he finally decides to act, to acknowledge Lena's life and his responsibility therefor, while denying life itself. Once more, as in Conrad's view of anarchistic violence in *The Secret Agent,* it is the logic of perverse unreason. It is absurd.

Chapter Nine

Rite of Passage

"The Secret Sharer" and *The Shadow-Line:*
Two Tales of Initiation

"The Secret Sharer" (1910) and *The Shadow-Line* (1917) are seven years apart, yet both return to Conrad's early preoccupation with the themes of initiation and the exploration of self, which are, in a sense, the same thing, for no apprenticeship can succeed without the attainment of self-knowledge. The road toward self-cognition is complex and painful, for it passes through the undiscovered country of one's subconscious; it is a descent into one's darker self, which must be acknowledged. Only then can each of the young captains in the two stories emerge, like the Marlow of "Youth" and of *Heart of Darkness,* a wiser and a sadder man, a man steeled by the experience of having passed the supreme test of his life.

Moreover, both tales are told from the first-person point of view, narrated in a fairly chronological manner. "The Secret Sharer," as the subtitle tells us, is a personal account of "An Episode From the Coast"; *The Shadow-Line* is "A Confession." In the Author's Note to the former, Conrad claims that "The Secret Sharer" and a companion story, "A Smile of Fortune" (which appeared in the volume *'Twixt Land and Sea,* 1912, along with a third story, "Freya of the Seven Isles"), "notwithstanding their autobiographical form . . . are not the record of personal experience" (ix). Perhaps not, in the literal sense, but rather in a way in which he acknowledges *The Shadow Line* (originally titled "First Command") to be "a personal experience seen in perspective," whose effect in memory "is to make things loom large" (ix). One of those things that stand out is Conrad's recollection of the ship's company who were "complete strangers to their new captain" (x).

"The Secret Sharer" opens with a new captain aboard a ship, to which he is a total stranger. The very first paragraph describing the young captain's view of the coast from the deck of his vessel suggests the main thematic emphasis of the story: "On my right hand there were lines of fishing stakes resembling a *mysterious* system of *half-submerged* bamboo fences, *incomprehensible* . . . and *crazy of aspect* as if *abandoned forever* . . ." (91). As in the beginning of *Lord Jim,* the young captain is alone with his ship which is floating in "an immense stillness," while he is aware of being "the only stranger on board" and, what is more important, "a stranger to [myself], since except for the second mate, he is the youngest man on the ship "and untried as yet by a position of the fullest responsibility" (93). Jim dreams of romantic adventures, feeling certain he will not flinch in times of stress and danger. This young captain, however, is insecure. He wonders to what extent he will be faithful to "that *ideal conception* of one's personality every man sets up for himself *secretly*" (94).

The test of this conception comes soon enough in the person of Leggatt, a fugitive sailor from the *Sephora,* whose naked body appears like a headless corpse to the captain bending over the side of his ship. He discovers Leggatt's presence after a peremptory and highly unorthodox if not irresponsible dismissal of his officers from duty, an act which "prevented the anchor-watch being formally set and things properly attended to" (97). The alter ego theme is thus set from the very first moment of their encounter, since the captain as it were superimposes his own head upon Leggatt's body: together they form one entity, one man. Their strange conversation, conducted in a whisper, establishes "a mysterious communication" between the young captain and the fugitive, who is guilty of having killed an insubordinate sailor during a storm but who is also responsible for saving his ship. Thus, of the two young men, one is an untried captain, insecure in his first command, and the other a killer without a ship, yet confident and resolute despite his plight. They speak the same language, come from similar backgrounds, went to the same training school. But the most important bond between them is the invisible bond, the almost total psychic identification of the young captain with Leggatt's condition.

In what is a complete reversal of Razumov's betrayal of Haldin, we now witness a manifestation of incredible trust. Only now the trustworthiness is not deceptive. The "good voice" and the self-possession of Leggatt induce a corresponding state of mind in the captain, who takes the naked stranger aboard, dresses him in his own

sleeping-suit, "just right for his size," listens to his story sympathetically, almost in the avuncular, Marlovian fashion. In a sense, Leggatt's
predicament resembles Jim's, but it is also substantially different.
Twice he repeats the information that his father (like Jim's) is a parson.
To be true, Jim does not want to go back to his father, whose pious
prescription for the right way of living and dying he has taken so
seriously. But Jim voluntarily goes to the Inquiry Board to face the
music, while Leggatt is determined to keep running: "My *double* gave
me an inkling of his thoughts by saying: 'My father's a parson in
Norfolk. Do you see me before a judge and jury on that charge?'" (101).

The plot of the story is very simple but it is a surface simplicity at
best. The young captain tries to fulfill his responsibility to the ship and
her crew, while Leggatt is trying to evade the consequences of his
breach of maritime discipline. By hiding a person fleeing from justice,
the young captain may reveal his charitable disposition: he has a fine
sense of humanity; yet, at the same time, he violates the code of his
community and, furthermore, in his reckless attempt to set Leggatt
ashore, he endangers the ship and the entire crew and risks his own life
as well. This act of folly, however, is precisely the final test of his
manhood and of his ability to command the ship.

The story is a strange mixture of suspense and comedy, especially in
scenes with the old captain of the *Sephora,* who is ridiculed. Yet it is
Leggatt's captain who upholds the law while the young captain breaks
it. The old captain performs a painful duty though he also resents the
chief mate who is a Conway boy, not like himself, who has risen
through the ranks. The young captain does not seem to be bothered by
the fact that Leggatt is a killer. Though he, like old Captain Archbold,
represents the law aboard *his* ship, he chooses not to enforce it; he
chooses, moreover, the path of duplicity, deceiving his whole crew and
Captain Archbold, thereby becoming Leggatt's accomplice. By iden-
tifying with Leggatt so thoroughly, the captain becomes a potential
killer himself, as his irrational handling of the ship implies. His
impulsive gesture of trying to ram his floppy hat on his other self is
fended off at first, but then Leggatt understands and accepts it. The hat,
floating in the water, saves the captain's ship from running aground.

At this moment, the captain is in full command of the ship for the
first time. He has attained a perfect communion with that command.
But *how*—that's a question every reader must ask and answer for

himself. When he gave the hat to Leggatt he was thinking of protecting him from sunshine, not of providing his ship with a saving marker, to spot the coast. Was it right, therefore, to take such chances? On the other hand, how does one *test* oneself or the ship without passing through or even inviting a *crisis*, a dangerous situation which one then overcomes by dint of one's skill and courage? Conrad does not resolve the captain's moral dilemma. He merely suggests its varied aspects.

Leggatt's crime is given biblical connotations by references to "the Cain and Abel business," wherein Leggatt is portrayed as a marked man, a vagabond doomed to wander over the face of the earth. The captain saves him and proves his own navigational skills, but for what kind of fate has he preserved his "secret sharer"? Leggatt is set free, "a proud swimmer striking out for a new destiny" (143). Having refused to accept the punishment of law, he must endure the punishment of exile and the perils of an unknown future. Unlike Jim or Razumov, he has not shown any pangs of conscience; on the contrary, he is rather insolent and a bit priggish in his self-certitude.

Thus, once again, as in *Lord Jim* and *Under Western Eyes,* Conrad has dramatized the conflict between the individual moral sense and a social obligation to the group, represented by the crew of a ship. By not giving us any clear, unequivocal answer, the novelist creates an ambiguity. The captain's actions reflect his basic kinship with the criminality of Leggatt—or a darker side of himself. Only by an act of total psychic identification with Leggatt can the captain free himself of evil and thus ascend the path of professional rectitude. Like Marlow, the captain must reach self-knowledge by entering the depths of his *submerged* self, before he can be initiated into the life of manhood.

The story is a rich mine for critics of the Freudian persuasion.[1] In no other work has Conrad so belabored this psychic division of self. The frequent iteration of images, both obvious and concealed, of the other or secret self tends to be tiresome at times. Yet the total impact of the story's aural and visual effects is overpowering. And, the obviousness of its symbolism notwithstanding, it leaves the reader with a haunting existential question: "How would *I* have acted under similar circumstances?" Can anyone be certain?

The Shadow Line (written in 1915), like "The Secret Sharer," is also concerned with the hero's first command which will prove a most taxing experience and the acceptance of which will be his initiation conferring upon him manhood and professional competence. As in the other story, the mastery of first command must be synonymous with full self-control, which means knowing oneself. The deceased commander becomes the new captain's secret sharer because the young man, unsure of himself, fears the malevolence of a supernatural power. Again we shall see a conflict between a commitment to professional duty and a mysterious irrationality lurking in the captain's soul.

To begin with, the protagonist gives up a good job, seemingly without any reason; almost misses getting his new command through an intrigue; he, too, is a stranger aboard the ship, resented by the first mate, who expected the captaincy himself. The ship is becalmed and almost the entire crew felled by disease. The last captain had sold the quinine and replaced it with worthless powder. Only the cook, Ransome, who has a heart condition, and the captain remain on their feet. After an ordeal of his passage from Bangkok to Singapore, the new captain brings his ship to port.

As in "The Secret Sharer," nothing is really simple. The captain's main problem is again self-doubt. The assumption of command places a sense of intolerable burden on his shoulders: "My first command. Now I understand that strange sense of insecurity in my past. I always suspected that I might be no good . . ." (106–107). His position as captain totally isolates him: "I was already the man in command. My sensations could not be like those of any other man aboard. In that community I stood, like a king in his country, in a class by myself" (62). The specter of the wicked captain hovers over the ship supernaturally, and the young captain feels a "semi-mystical *bond* with the *dead*" (62). He is profoundly shocked by the old captain's treachery because of the realization of their affinity: "That man had been in all essentials but his age *just another man as myself.* Yet the end of his life was a *complete act of treason,* the *betrayal of a tradition* which seemed to me as *imperative* as any guide on earth could be" (62).

Conrad chose as an epigraph to the novella, a quotation from the text itself, "Worthy of my undying regard," which, he explains in his Author's Note of 1920, should refer not to the ship but to its crew, "the ship's company: complete strangers to their new captain and who yet stood by him so well during those twenty days . . ." (x). He also placed another motto on the first page, from Baudelaire, " . . . *D'autres fois calme plat, grand mirroir / De mon désespoir.*"

It is not, however, the French poet of despair and evil who colors the allusive texture of the story; it is Shakespeare. The verbal echoes from *The Tempest* and *Hamlet*[2] in the opening passages are not fortuitous because the captain's dilemma is truly Hamletian. His mysterious melancholy, his disenchantment with the world, and his self-deprecatory tone suggest the melancholy Dane, as the "enchanted garden" of his boyishness and the Prospero-like Captain Ellis bring to mind the world of *The Tempest*. Like Prospero, the young captain inhabits the disparate world of magic (dream) and of reality, the twin world of natural and supernatural experience. "The green sickness of late youth", an oft-iterated phrase, synonymous with "the shadow-line" between youth and manhood, is also drawn from Shakespeare (*2, Henry IV*, 4.3.10; *Romeo and Juliet*, 3.5.157; *Antony and Cleopatra*, 3.2.6). The shadow-line thus defines the gap between untested inexperience of the young captain and the initiation into true manhood and maturity, by dint of an almost ritualistic ordeal. Conrad dedicated the novella to his son Borys, whose military service in France during World War I was *his* supreme ordeal, and "all others who like himself have crossed in early youth the shadow-line of their generation."

Although this short novel lacks the dramatic suspense of "The Secret Sharer," it does have a sustained mood of irony, culminating with the encounter between the benevolent Captain Giles (who appears to have been drawn from Conrad's recollection of his uncle, Tadeusz Bobrowski) and the young captain, now thoroughly transformed from a rather irresponsible youth into a seasoned professional, pleading old age: ". . . I'll tell you, Captain Giles, how I feel. I feel old. And I must be. All of you on shore look to me just a lot of skittish youngsters that have never known a care in the world" (131). Captain Giles is a wise man. He does not smile. In fact, he looks "insufferably exemplary," as he advises his protégé "not to make too much of anything in life." One thinks of Marlow in *Heart of Darkness,* sulking in a Swiftian rejection of mankind. The affirmation of this story is mildly ironic at best.

The narrator quotes from his own diary, revealing a sensitivity and maturity which somewhat contradict his conduct at the beginning of the story, viewed by Conrad with great ironic detachment. The effect of this, as Conrad himself observes, is a certain quality of exaggeration, of making things loom large, which tends to lessen the story's realism.

Norman Sherry's careful study of the novel's sources (in *Conrad's Eastern World*) shows to what extent *The Shadow-Line* is not exact autobiography but rather a subtle manipulation of fact and fiction.[3] Conrad based the story on his own appointment as master of the *Otago* in 1888, using several names from his own experiences, e.g., Master Attendant, Henry Ellis of the S.S. *Melita,* aboard which Conrad journeyed from Singapore to Bangkok; changing, selecting, or exaggerating events to suit his dramatic purpose.[4]

Ransome, the valiant cook suffering from a weak heart, proves to be one of the strangest men aboard. Though he lives in mortal fear, he passes the test of courage superbly. He is the faithful Ariel to the captain's Prospero. Like the great magician, the captain, chastened by his ordeal, accepts the responsibility of his newfound manhood, refusing Captain Giles's playful suggestion to live at half-speed. He has demonstrated Giles's virtuous injunction that "a man should stand up to his bad luck, to his mistakes, to his conscience, and all that sort of thing. Why—what else would you have to fight against?" (131–32). His response to Giles's mock challenge, "Why you aren't faint-hearted?" is the mature, "God only knows." But we, the readers, know it, too. He has passed the test. Yet, wiser and sadder though the captain has grown, his last thought echoes Prospero's mood, for it is of death, "our common enemy," which was Ransome's hard fate, "to carry consciously within his faithful breast" (133).

The Mirror of the Sea: A Very Intimate Revelation

This is how Conrad describes the volume of autobiographical essays, dealing with the manifold faces of the sea, and subtitled "Memoirs and Impressions" (1906). It is a moving testimony to Conrad's passion for the sea and his love of seamanship, often related to his other craftsmanship—that of an artist. The initiation into one was, in a sense, a prelude to the apprenticeship in the other, for he brought the same dedication to both. The mirror of the title is a composite symbolist image which blends the reflections of the sea and the writer's self. Conrad sees the ship masters as artists who are also men of action. He writes lovingly of the ships and seamen he knew, of the nature of seamanship, reaching the pitch of rhapsodic praise for ships and crews in "Initiation." But here he also writes of "the cynical indifference of the sea to the merits of human suffering and courage" (141) and of the elation of doing a job well and earning praise from a master, which "completed the cycle of [my] initiation" (147).

This essay is central in Conrad's altered vision of the sea. The youngster's conception of "its magnanimous greatness" is replaced with a darker picture of what now appears to be "the *true* sea" which, ironically, is not true because it is not faithful, "the sea that plays with men till their hearts are broken, and wears stout ships to death. Nothing can touch the brooding bitterness of its soul" (148). But in "The Tremolino," based on his youthful, adventurous days in Marseilles, Conrad's tone is different. It suggests the mood of romantic exaltation of "Youth," and its characters appear again in *The Arrow of Gold.* The *Tremolino,* like all of Conrad's ships except the *Brute,* is "ever guiltless of the sins, transgressions and follies of her men" (161). The treachery of Dominic Cervoni's nephew served as an early model for Conrad's future fictional traitors.

Like the two tales of Initiation, these essays are essentially a literary confession—eloquent, often moving, and, in Conrad's own words, "the best tribute [my] piety can offer to the ultimate shapers of [my] character, convictions, and, in a sense, destiny—to the imperishable sea, to the ships that are no more, and to the simple men who have had their day" (x).

Conrad as Essayist and Critic: The Novelist Stands Confessed

According to Ford Madox Ford, with whom Conrad collaborated on three novels, *The Mirror of the Sea* and *A Personal Record* were mostly written by his hand from Conrad's dictation.[5] There is no doubt that the discussion of the two writers on literary theory and the probing and prodding questions of Ford helped Conrad to capture the magic of the past in what can be loosely called autobiography. Until 1916, the book was published in England as *Some Reminiscences* and thereafter the title of the American edition (Harper's in 1912), *A Personal Record,* became the standard reference. It also became an early source of information for Conrad's Polish background, his dramatic transformation from seaman to writer, and his alleged choice of English as the language of his art.

A Personal Record, like *The Shadow-Line,* is not exact autobiography, and certainly not the conventional account of events in the subject's life, placed in a chronological sequence. Rather, it starts in *medias res,* with the author musing on the vicissitudes of writing a novel aboard the steamer called the *Adowa,* where the tenth chapter of *Almayer's Folly* was begun. This account is interspersed with observations on Flaubert, the novel-in-progress, recollections of London, and a vision of himself as a child, romantically dreaming of a journey to the mysterious continent of darkest Africa. The writer goes on, in a rambling fashion, to tell about his trip to Poland, meetings with his uncle Bobrowski, anecdotes about his family—in other words, a jumbled record of "these formative impressions" (24). One of the most revealing episodes (and the book is revealing to a much greater extent than the reserved and detached Conrad imagined it would be) is the story of Conrad's first encounter with his "unforgettable Englishman, clad in a knickerbocker suit and marching with the mien of an ardent and fearless traveller" (40). This fleeting meeting (very reminiscent, incidentally, of Aschenbach's similar view of *his* mysterious traveler in *Death in Venice* by Thomas Mann) had a profound impact on the boy. "One does not meet such an Englishman twice in a lifetime" (41).

Conrad's recollections of his Polish past, his adventures in Marseilles, the seafaring years, and his fumbling efforts to become a writer make good reading. But *A Personal Record* is more important in its disclosure of the most secret psychological wounds inflicted upon him in the past: the allegations of betrayal for his "desertion" of Poland, the sense of dread and bereavement; the initiation into a life of seamanship and a life of literary toil. The little book brims over with "quotable" passages on topics of great variety. The language is highly controlled, not plagued by the adjectival excesses of his early fiction, yet never dull.

Conrad stresses his reserve, his reluctance to expose himself, for he firmly believes that he really does not have to reveal everything about himself in order to tell the truth about himself since he has conveyed that truth in his work: ". . . a novelist lives in his work. He stands there, the only *reality* in an invented world, among imaginary things, happenings, and people. Writing about them, *he is only writing about himself*" (xv). But he adds wryly that "the disclosure is not complete. He remains, to a certain extent, a figure behind the veil; a suspected rather than a seen presence—a movement and a voice behind the draperies of

fiction." *A Personal Record* is a record not merely of reminiscences about
his past but also of that "voice behind the draperies." In fact, there are
several inner voices that betray the most intimate emotions experienced
by the novelist.

Though Conrad's opinions about others and himself can and should
be suspect, I believe we must not hesitate to accept his explanation as to
why he wrote in English—often regarded by the critics as a matter of
deliberate choice or adoption. It was neither, declares Conrad. "The
merest idea of choice had never entered my head. And as to
adoption—well, yes, there was adoption; but it was I who was adopted
by the genius of the language . . ." (vii; Author's Note). But though
some readers will refuse to take this or many other autobiographical
statements at their face value, his revelations, no matter how re-
strained, edited, or even contrived, contribute to a better understanding of Conrad the man and Conrad the writer, for they show the many
ups and downs in his three careers; the hesitations, the doubts, the
suicidal moments, and the exaltation of being a seaman and a novelist.

So do his essays, published in 1921, under the title *Notes on Life and
Letters,* which, he shrewdly observed, have to do more with life than
with letters. In the part dealing with letters he put essays about books
and great writers like Henry James, Alphonse Daudet, Guy de Maupassant, Anatole France, Turgenev, and Stephen Crane; in the second part,
ambitiously titled "Life," there are thirteen pieces on a variety of topics
from political essays on autocracy and the Polish problem to essays on
the sea and seamanship, recalling the mood of *The Mirror of the Sea.* The
essays on James and Turgenev, to my mind, are most interesting,
showing Conrad as an accomplished stylist; those about political subjects disclose the extent of Conrad's cultural rather than political
commitment to his native land, and his hatred of autocracy. "Poland
Revisited" is a moving account of his discovery of his older self. "Each of
us," he writes," is a fascinating spectacle to himself, and I had to watch
my own personality returning from another world, as it were to revisit
the glimpses of old moons" (164).

Some of the twenty pieces in *Last Essays* (1926) are also, to an extent,
such glimpses of old moons, most of them written subsequent to the

appearance of *Notes on Life and Letters*. Perhaps the most important contribution in the biographical if not literary sense is the last essay, "The Congo Diary," which Conrad kept in 1890. This final piece echoes the mood of the first essay; both describe the youthful, romantic quest for the unknown that ends with a shocking discovery of human perfidy.

Chapter Ten

In A Minor Key:
"Ease After Warre"

Sleep after toyle, port after stormie seas,
Ease after warre, death after life does greatly please.
—Spenser, *The Faerie Queen*
(Inscription on Conrad's tombstone)

Tales

'Twixt Land and Sea, Tales (1912) contained two more stories in addition
to "The Secret Sharer": "A Smile of Fortune" (*London Magazine*, February 1911) and "Freya of the Seven Isles" (*Metropolitan*, New York,
April 1912), but neither story merits comparison with "The Secret
Sharer" as a successful work of art. The chief critical interest these
stories arouse is in Conrad's treatment of sexual passion and the allegorical motif that will appear in much subtler form in *Chance* and *Victory*.

The four stories of *Within the Tides* (1915) are a collection which
followed *Victory*; they do not live up to Conrad's promise that the
volume is a "deliberate attempt in four different methods of telling a
story,—an essay in craftsmanship."[1] They show Conrad at his weakest
as a storyteller. In fact, the Author's Note of 1920, in which he states
that "the romantic feeling of reality" was in him "an inborn faculty,"
may be of greater interest than the stories themselves. Except, perhaps,
for "The Planter of Malata" (*Metropolitan*, June–July 1914, written in
1913), whose hero elicits this comment: "I resemble Geoffrey Renouard
insofar that when once engaged in an adventure I cannot bear the idea of
turning back" (x). The method used here is that of an omniscient
narrator. The other three stories are "The Partner" (*Harper's Magazine*,
November 1911, written in 1910); "The Inn of the Two Witches"

(*Metropolitan*, May 1913); and "Because of the Dollars" (published under the title "Laughing Anne," *Metropolitan,* September 1914, written in 1912). In "The Partner," the narrator is a writer of stories who solicits a tale from "a statuesque ruffian" and several other persons. "The Inn," subtitled "A Find," is "this tale, episode, experience—call it how you will." The find is a manuscript purchase by the narrator who uses it as the prime source of his story. The narrator in "Because of the Dollars" is also a participant in the plot.

In 1920 Conrad dramatized "Because of the Dollars," which became a two-act play, "Laughing Anne" (published in 1923). Like "One Day More, a Play in One Act," which was a dramatization of Conrad's own story, "To-Morrow" (1902), it was not a success. Neither was his dramatization of *The Secret Agent,* as pointed out above. These were the only dramatic efforts of the novelist, except for his marginal role in the dramatization of *Victory* (see note 9, Chapter 8). He never wrote an original play, though he confessed his wish of being a dramatist: "I greatly desire to write a play myself. It is my *dark* and *secret* ambition"; he nevertheless showed a great ambivalence toward drama, if not downright hostility. For, he continued, "And yet I cannot conceive how a *sane man* can sit down deliberately to write a play and not *go mad* before he has done. The actors appear to me like a lot of *wrongheaded lunatics* pretending to be sane. . . . They are disguised and ugly. To look at them breeds in my melancholy soul thoughts of *murder and suicide*— such is my anger and *my loathing* of their *transparent pretences.*"[2] Conrad's reservations about drama and actors stem, most probably, from his own reluctance to share the creative effort with anyone else, though for a while he managed to collaborate with Ford Madox (Hueffer) Ford. And though he greatly loved and admired Shakespeare, he never quite accepted modern theater as a fitting medium for artistic expression. It is ironic, indeed, for many of his novels and tales reveal a fine sense of drama.

The posthumous *Tales of Hearsay* (1925)[3] gathered four stories: "The Warrior's Soul" (written in 1916); "Prince Roman" (*Oxford and Cambridge Review*, January 1912; also as "The Aristocrat," *Metropolitan,* January 1912); "The Tale" (written in 1916); and "The Black Mate" (Conrad's first story, originally written for a prize competition in *Tid-Bits* in 1886, probably revised).

"The Warrior's Soul" and "The Tale," both minor pieces, share, however, a major Conradian motif: the existential choice under conditions of *situation extrème,* which reveals the moral fiber of the hero. Tomassov, a young Russian officer, yields to the request of a French prisoner, who appeals to the Russian's "warrior's soul," to kill him, for he can no longer bear the indignity of life under the horrendous conditions of defeat. Tomassov finally accedes, but he then becomes the victim himself for having committed a "dark deed." The story has some Polish Romantic flavor without, however, the sincerity and intensity of "Prince Roman."

The Commanding Officer in "The Tale" must also make a difficult if not impossible decision, whether to allow the Northman, who is the captain of a ship that *may* be carrying a contraband cargo or supplying "some infernal submarine or other" to stay or to proceed (193). There is no way in which the Commanding Officer can prove the Northman's duplicity. He finally orders the Northman to leave the coast, giving him a course that would lead "straight on a deadly ledge or rock" (203). The Northman follows it and his ship is lost. He had spoken the truth when he said he did not know where he was. But this does not eliminate the possibility of his having been a spy or a supplier of hostile vessels. The Commanding Officer can never know whether by his decision he has done "stern retribution—or murder" (201). The only thing he can be sure of is that he had done his duty. And his *conviction* (the central word in "Prince Roman") must be ironic at best, as is the nature of Conrad's affirmation.

"The Black Mate," a very slight and rather contrived thing, is a somewhat comic tale of a Mr. Bunter, who sports jet-black hair. He has dyed it in order to conceal his age, and when the bottles of dye get smashed, he pretends to have been knocked down by a ghost, an event during which his hair "turned white, all at once in consequence of a manifestation from beyond the grave." The fairly long (21 pages) preface by R. B. Cunninghame Graham is greater testimony to his friendship with Conrad than to his literary taste, for the four stories do not deserve his lavish praise. Indeed, Conrad, like Shakespeare, "only holds the mirror up to nature for men to see themselves, and draw such moral as they can from their own faces" (28)—but not, regretfully, in these stories of limited virtue.

The Last Novels

Most critics agree that Conrad's last four novels, *The Arrow of Gold* (1919), *The Rescue* (1923), *The Rover* (1923), and *Suspense* (unfinished, 1925), indicate a serious artistic decline though explanations for this decline vary greatly. Whether the artistic deterioration was due to Conrad's ill health and the necessity of dictating or to his choice of romantic subjects which proved beyond his talent or whether it was caused by "the inevitable consequences of the specific psychological defenses adopted by him after his mental illness [in 1910]"[4] or whether it was occasioned by the moral stance of the last period is a matter of critical preference and interpretation.

The Arrow of Gold, A Story Between Two Notes, is a conventional story of two lovers threatened by a wicked rival. It is told, however, in a complicated, unconventional manner, reminiscent of Conrad's earlier impressionistic devices of indirect chronology. In a sense, the novel presents a retrospective glance at his younger self—in the Marseilles days—not unlike the exploration of his first command in *The Shadow-Line.* Here the subject is young love. The gold arrow worn by the heroine, Rita, as a hair pin provides the rule and the central symbol of the novel. Though *The Arrow of Gold* fails in its portrayal of believable characters, it does have occasional flashes of humor and a mastery of fictional devices. The most interesting aspect of the novel is the depiction of young George's isolation as a result of his passion for Rita, which reminds us of Willems's destructive infatuation with Aïssa.

In *The Rescue* Lingard will be similarly afflicted. His romantic dream of Edith Travers must be shattered, leaving this man "of infinite illusions" emotionally and morally crippled. But Mrs. Travers, too, will pay the supreme penalty of "the most complete loneliness"— estranged, isolated no less than the lovers Rita and George. Mills's statement in *The Arrow* applies to both novels: "This world is not a world of lovers, not even for such lovers as you two who have nothing to do with the world as it is" (350).

The mere fact that it took Conrad twenty years to finish *The Rescue* (from 1898 to 1918), suggests that he had serious psychological problems in handling this particular love story. The vacillations of its hero, Lingard, are, in a sense, indicative of the author's own uncertainty about this unwieldy novel. Though it spans two decades of Conrad's writing career, employing many stylistic devices from this long period, the novel lacks dramatic or even stylistic focus. And, as a protagonist, Lingard lacks the complexity of a Jim or the clear-cut conception of a Nostromo or a Heyst.

Perhaps Conrad attempted too much in *The Rescue*. The dichotomy of Lingard is not psychologically convincing, as it is in other cases of Conrad's divided heroes. The language of the novel, no less than its entire conception, is overdone.

The Rover is Conrad's last finished novel, and a sort of a "seaman's return," to use the novelist's own term. The epigraph from Spenser (which appears at the beginning of this chapter) suggests the character of Conrad's last Romantic hero, Peyrol, who is tired of life and is ready to accept "ease after warre" and "death after life." He has been a member of the outlawed Brotherhood of the Coast; he now lives in quiet retirement which, unlike Heyst, he has earned with a life crowded with action. He offers his life as a sacrificial homage to patriotism and to the young lovers (Réal and Arlette). Yet this man of "dark deeds" but of large heart is essentially, like Lingard, a simplistic character, more suited to teenage tastes than to those of the seasoned readers of Conrad. Peyrol is not likely to arouse profound compassion, nor is the morbid anarchist Scevola likely to stir any great political or psychological interest. He is, like Ortega in *The Arrow of Gold*, a "drinker of blood," expressing Conrad's contempt for the blood-drinkers spawned by the revolution. On the other hand, it is possible to view the characterization of Peyrol as having the elements of a fabular figure. Like Tekla in *Under Western Eyes* he has lost his name but he has acquired a new one. The image of a man with a hoard of 70,000 francs sewn into his odd-looking waistcoat reminds us of heroes of Hans Andersen or Alexander Dumas. The problem with such presentation in Conrad is that it is so drastically different from the best portrayals in his fiction that the reader feels somewhat cheated.

Suspense was left unfinished when Conrad died in 1924. It was originally contemplated as a collaboration with Ford Madox Ford, but Conrad decided to work on it by himself. Conceived on a grandiose, Tolstoyan scale, as another Napoleonic novel of war and peace, the book resisted Conrad stubbornly, as did "The Rescuer," the original version of *The Rescue*. Conrad wanted *Suspense* to be his last masterpiece, describing it as "a novel of intrigue with the Mediterranean coast and sea, for the scene."[5] Alas, the 80,000 words of the unfinished novel do not live up to Conrad's expectations, but it is not fair, perhaps, to judge what would have been, undoubtedly, a much meditated and much revised book.

Collaborations with Ford Madox Ford

Some serious critics of Conrad the novelist exclude his collaborations with Ford Madox Ford from their critical appraisal. Albert Guerard, to give one example, only briefly mentions Ford to provide some anecdotal information on Conrad's erratic habits; to relate his "appalling misvaluation"[6] of *The Sisters* and his views on impressionism. But he does not discuss any of the works produced jointly by the two writers. This is a most sensible decision, for though the collaborative novels are usually listed in the canon of his works, they cannot be the subject of a critical scrutiny of Conrad, except as a study of the impact the collaboration had on Conrad's development as a novelist or, for that matter, Conrad's influence on Ford Madox Ford. Each has turned out to be an artist of considerable achievement. Certainly, Ford's *The Good Soldier* is as much of a modern masterpiece as *Lord Jim*. There is not much point, I think, to belabor the question as to who learned more from whom, or even what. Undoubtedly they learned from each other, as they worked together on the theory and practice of the impressionistic novel that could be planned carefully, and making every word and scene count in carrying the story forward. It is this technique of *progression d'effet*, the psychological progression that each of the writers used in his own work, while their collaborative efforts proved to be rather lightweight. I shall, therefore, confine myself to a cursory comment.

The following three novels were written together with Ford Madox Ford: *The Inheritors, An Extravagant Story* (1901), *Romance* (1903), and *The Nature of a Crime* (begun in 1906, published in 1924).

The Inheritors was planned as a satire on contemporary Europe; it was, according to Conrad himself, wholly Ford's idea. *Romance* was an adventure story based on Ford's manuscript of *Seraphina*. It is of greater interest because the work on this novel most certainly affected Conrad's performance in *Nostromo,* which followed the collaborative venture. The attractive Spanish girl Seraphina, the heroine of *Romance,* is the psychological equivalent of the silver treasure of *Nostromo.* There are certain correspondences in the descriptions of fog, especially since in each case a "treasure" is being "saved." But such surface correspondences cannot conceal the fact that *Nostromo* is a great book and *Romance* very rarely merits critical attention. As to the last collaboration, such as it was, Conrad was rather reluctant to acknowledge his part therein in his later life, for it was, after all, as Frederick Karl points out, "a 'joint' effort that was virtually all Ford . . . in many ways a freakish collaboration: a thinly disguised autobiographical memoir by Ford, to which he evidently wanted Conrad to contribute."[7]

Chapter Eleven
Aloof and Apart: Conclusion

. . . there is something exotic about the genius of Mr. Conrad which makes him not so much an influence as an idol, honored and admired, but *aloof and apart.*

—Virginia Woolf[1]

Arthur Symons, a poet whose work Conrad read and admired, wrote a moving tribute after the novelist's death. He likened Conrad's "look into the darkness at the end of the long avenue" to that of Shakespeare, Balzac, and Rodin,[2] thus explaining the nature of his appeal as an artist:

Only great painters have created atmosphere to the extent that Conrad has: and Conrad's is if anything more mysterious, menacing and more troubling to the senses and to the nerves, than theirs; he creates thrilling effects by mere force of suggestion, elusive as some vague mist, full of illusion, of rare magic, which can become poisonous or sorcerous.[3]

Indeed, it is quite easy to draw an analogy between Conrad's art and painting, especially because the visual image is one of the most basic grounds between the novel and painting. And Conrad, from the very first, was concerned with images. In 1899, he wrote to Cunninghame Graham, referring to *Heart of Darkness*: "I don't start with an abstract notion. I start with *definite images* and as their rendering is true some little effect is produced."[4] In 1902, in a letter to William Blackwood, Conrad harped on his novelistic method, ending with this declaration of artistic faith:

I am *modern,* and I would rather recall Wagner the musician and Rodin the sculptor who both had to starve a little in their day—and Whistler the painter who made Ruskin the critic foam at the mouth with scorn and indignation. They too, have arrived. They had to suffer for being "new." . . . My work shall not be an utter failure because it has the solid basis of a definite intention—first: and next because it is not an endless analysis of affected sentiments, but in its essence it is action . . . nothing but action— action *observed,* felt and interpreted with an absolute truth to *my sensations* (which are the basis of art in literature)—action of human beings that bleed to a prick, and are moving in *a visible* world.

This is my creed. Time will show.[5]

He reaffirmed this point in a letter to H. G. Wells in 1905: "But since, O Brother!, I am a novelist I must peak in *images.*"[6]

When Conrad penned his celebrated Preface to *The Nigger of the "Narcissus,"* he singled out the visual as being the most important element of his craft. The task of making the reader hear, feel and, above all, *see* has been used by many a commentator of Conrad as a spring board before taking a leap off his particular critical *Patna.*[7] The Preface has turned into a major tenet of faith for several schools of thought, however, which used it to prove that Conrad was a Romantic, a Realist, a Symbolist, a Romantic-Realist, and, most recently, an Impressionist. The latter school has gained momentum after the critics began linking Conrad with Henry James and Ford Madox Ford. Conrad's connection with the visual arts has been pointed out by a number of critics[8] who agree that there are ample grounds for an analogy between the visual arts and Conrad's imagery. To what extent, however, does Conrad himself consider fiction as being analogous to painting? Or to the eye of the camera? In what sense can his representations of people, nature and things inanimate be seen as verbal paintings, snapshots, or the moving pictures of a roving camera?

Painting was one of the arts Conrad had in mind when stating his artistic credo, in that same Preface to *The Nigger*:

Fiction—if it at all aspires to be art—appeals to temperament. And in truth it must be, *like painting,* like music, like all art. . . . Such an appeal to be effective must be *an impression* conveyed through the senses . . . it must strenuously aspire to the plasticity of sculpture, to *the color of painting,* and to the magic suggestiveness of music—which is the art of arts.[9]

And when Conrad wrote of his favorite Russian author, he clearly showed his preference for *one* of the arts: "I admire Turgeniev but in truth Russia was for him no more than the *canvas for the painter.*"[10]

In most of his works Conrad selects a principal color scheme, often a dramatic contrast between the dark and the light, or focuses our vision upon a dominant image: a snakelike river in the Congo, white ivory, black, impenetrable forests, the immaculately white form of Jim, the shining silver buttons of Nostromo's uniform, or the shining silver ingots. Even some of his nonvisual descriptions of character reinforce the "color scheme" of the intended portrait or draw our attention to the artist's design. Thus, the often excessive use of appositional phrases, no less than his "adjectival style" in descriptions of scenery, produces the result achieved by the painter with a bold stroke of his brush or chalk, often imbued with ironic connotation. Jim is "excessively romantic" and "under a cloud"; Razumov "inspires confidence"; Decoud is "a boulevadier"; Nostromo is the incorruptible "Capataz de Cargadores," "the indispensable man, the tried and trusty Nostromo"; Gould is the king of Sulaco; the darkness of Kurtz is impenetrable and deepening; Ransome has a "faithful breast"; and so on.

Similarly, if the analogy is broadened to include the musical element of a recurring phrase, the frequent leitmotifs like "Pass the bottle," "Do or Die," "his opportunity sat veiled by his side like an Eastern bride" (repeated in *Lord Jim* three times, pp. 243, 336, 416) are like the painter's device of drawing the spectator's eye to a repeated use of a certain color or object in his canvas. In Conrad's verbal portraits there is usually a predominance of one color, either in the literal sense (as with Jim's whiteness or Wait's blackness) or its equivalent—a key word or phrase which defines the character through an instantaneous impression, e.g., Jim's *boyish* aspect, his bull-like pose of aggressiveness, or Singleton's white beard "tucked under the top button of his glistening coat."

As we have seen from the discussion of Conrad's portrayal of Jim, the novelist employed a distinctly *painterly* method of arranging visual impressions as if they were word paintings.

"Mr. Conrad," observed Edwin Muir in 1924, "writes in pictures, for the pictures come, and what he shows us is not action, but a progression of dissolving scenes, continuous and living, which in the end reflect action and give us a true apprehension of it."[11] The final paragraph of Conrad's artistic credo (discussed above in Chapter 3) in his Preface to *The Nigger of the "Narcissus"* once more emphasizes the terms related to the making of pictures, e.g., sight, vision, form, look.

The task of the writer is to arrest the visual aspects of living; when this is done, "all the truth of life is there."[12] Moreover, "one writes only half a book; the other half is with the reader."[13] Conrad's Preface may be rather vague and overwritten, yet he is among those very few writers who have accomplished that task. The artistic lie of his canvases has made us *see* the truth of life.

It was a truth, however, seen through the eyes of a deracinated man, a Pole away from his native land; a sailor away from his ship, engaged in the task of daily scribbling. Conrad had to write in English in order to be an artist yet the very fact of his writing in what was an adopted language caused both an enormous aesthetic increment and a tension peculiar to a writer exiled in a double sense—from his fatherland and from his native form of expression.

Unlike Beckett and Joyce, the two writers who rebelled against their native tradition but remained essentially Irish, Conrad is not a Polish novelist writing in English. However, his modernity and appeal today stem from the psychological awareness of being an émigré writer, even after he had been acknowledged as an English novelist of fame. What makes Conrad such an extraordinary modern writer is his essentially paradoxical vision of the world, and the scope and nature of his novelistic art. On the one hand, he refuses to offer a facile optimistic explanation of man's folly and rapacity, depicting his descent into a spiritual heart of darkness, revealing his absurdity and cruelty, and creating a huge gallery of "displaced persons" engaged in an agonizing quest of their psychic identities. On the one hand, thus, we have a purely spectacular view of the universe in which men and women seem to exist outside of normal national boundaries, their thin veneer of civilized conduct easily pierced by temptation; a universe in which men's moral fiber must be tested as they battle the destructive element within themselves. A universe in which droll destiny destroys romantic dreamers and lovers, where greed, ambition, and lust plague men and women. A world filled with wars, duels, tempests, plots, assassinations, secret agents, counterspies, revolutionaries, anarchists, terrorists, crooks, bandits, generals, heroic or dull captains, and a host of "little people" of varied creed and color. His heroes, nonheroes, and antiheroes stand alone with their choice of nightmares, alone in their attempts to unravel the mystery of their moral isolation; alone to face the horror of the jungle and, much worse, to face the darkness of their own souls.

On the other hand, his fiction also strikes a profound note of affirmation—even in defeat. Directly or indirectly, Conrad advocates the concepts of fidelity, honor, and fortitude. Thus, Marlow gains strength and self-knowledge after his quest of Kurtz in *Heart of Darkness*; thus, Jim's unflinching glance (in *Lord Jim*) as he goes to his death, is, in a sense, a triumphant achievement of mastering his own fate at last; and thus, too, Lena's death in *Victory* is an affirmation of her great love for Heyst, and his symbolic suicide in the flames is the price he must pay for having estranged himself from mankind. His pessimism notwithstanding, Conrad praises human brotherhood, not in the limited political or sociological context, but the kind of brotherhood which is based on human solidarity and the acceptance of basic, ideal human values—his own particular brand of ethical humanism.

Conrad speaks of the artist as the man who must appeal to

the latent feeling of fellowship with all creation—to the subtle but invincible conviction of solidarity that knits together the loneliness of innumerable hearts, to the solidarity in dreams, in joy, in sorrow, in aspirations, in illusions, in hope, in fear, which binds men to each other, which binds together all humanity—the dead to the living and the living to the unborn.[14]

Though the lives of Conrad's characters are invariably catastrophic, they reveal what he has called his main concern: the ideal value of things, events and people. He has always approached the objects of his task "in the spirit of love for mankind and [he has] taken it seriously." Above all, he voyaged into the undiscovered country of the divided man's soul, at war with itself.

His gospel of individualism replaced his lack of belief in deity, but it does not necessarily contradict Conrad's view of human solidarity, since it does not exclude the quest for courage, compassion, honor, fortitude, and fidelity. These values in man must be tested, and therefore most of his protagonists undergo a trial.

Conrad's tales and novels often portray isolated traitors, tormented by guilt and a sense of inadequacy, seeking to atone for their transgressions, seeking for "the grim shadow of self-knowledge."

Theirs is tragic dilemma. The inner, spiritual world must be affirmed but in a paradoxical manner, perhaps not unlike that used by some modern French writers, e.g., Camus or Sartre. The hero discovers a sense of his own worth or reality only when he is faced with self-destruction. Meursault, in *The Stranger,* can become fully alive only when he faces his own execution. Yet Conrad is no nihilist. The sinister forces of nature and destiny may defeat his protagonists, but they do not destroy their humanity.

In 1917 Conrad attempted an assessment of his own position in a letter to Sir Sidney Colvin:

. . . after 22 years of work, I may say that I have not been very well understood. I have been called a writer of the sea, of the tropics, a descriptive writer, a romantic writer—and also a realist. But as a matter of fact all my concern has been with the "ideal" value of things, events and people. That and nothing else. The humorous, the pathetic, the passionate, the sentimental *aspects* came in of themselves—*mais en vérité c'est les valeurs idéales des faits et gestes humains que se sont imposés à mon activité artistique.*

Whatever dramatic and narrative gifts I may have are always, instinctively, used with that object—to get at, to bring forth *les valeurs idéales.* [15]

This basic idealism of Conrad, his lofty conception of the novelist's art, the richness of his style, the freshness and the intensity of his vision—these are only a few aspects of his art that explain his widespread influence on the writers of our century. H. L. Mencken's observation on Conrad still rings true: "There was something almost suggesting the vastness of a natural phenomenon. He transcended all the rules. There have been, perhaps, greater novelists, but I believe that he was incomparably the greatest artist who ever wrote a novel."

Notes and References

Preface

1. See below, Selected Bibliography, Secondary Sources, 2. Biographies.
2. Ibid., 1. Bibliographical Materials.
3. The Institute for Textual Studies, initiated in 1972 at the Texas Tech University, developed a plan to publish all of Conrad's works in critical editions. The general editors are Marion C. Michael, Bruce Harkness and Norman Sherry; the editorial board includes Kenneth Davis, Eugene Eddleman, Adam Gillon, Dahlia Terrell, and Warren Walker. Cambridge University Press will publish the critical editions. See Marion Michael, "The Cambridge Edition of the Complete Works of Joseph Conrad," *Joseph Conrad Today* 4 (October 1978):99.

Chapter One

1. "In sleep all night he grapples with a sail! / But words beyond the life of ships dream on." These two lines conclude a poem, "Joseph Conrad" by Malcolm Lowry, *Canadian Literature* 8 (Spring 1961):24.
2. *A Personal Record,* A Familiar Preface, p. xix.
3. G. Jean-Aubry, *Joseph Conrad: Life and Letters* (London, 1927), 1:81. Hereafter cited as *Life and Letters.* Albert J. Guerard explains that neither the "G" nor the "Georges" nor the "Gérard" used with the name Jean-Aubry is correct. The actual name of the author was Jean Aubry. See Guerard's *Conrad the Novelist* (Cambridge, Mass., 1958), p. 307.
4. *Notes on Life and Letters,* "Poland Revisited," p. 169.
5. Ibid., p. 168. Conrad's own reading list can be found in *A Personal Record,* pp. 70–72. A detailed list, based on Conrad's statements and the memoirs of F. M. Ford, G. Jean-Aubry, and J. Galsworthy, has been compiled by M. F. Mélisson-Dubreil in her book *La Personnalité de Joseph Conrad* (Paris, 1943), pp. 385–86.
6. A great epic poem (1833) by Poland's most outstanding Romantic poet. A prose translation by George Rapall Noyes is available in Everyman's Library (No. 842), 1930. A new verse translation by Watson Kirkconnell was published in 1962 in New York by the Polish Institute of Arts and Sciences in America (distributed by Twayne Publishers, Inc., Boston).

7. *A Personal Record,* p. 124

8. Quoted from a letter to Stefan Buszczyński, Apollo Korzeniowski's friend and his biographer, by Róża Jabłkowska in *Joseph Conrad,* published by the Neo-Philological Committee of the Polish Academy of Sciences, 1961, p. 30.

9. *Last Essays* (Garden City, N.Y., 1926), p. 12.

10. "The Laugh," first manuscript draft of *The Arrow of Gold.* J. Wise Collection, now in the British Museum, London. This passage is quoted in Jean-Aubry's *Sea Dreamer* (Garden City, N.Y., 1957), Appendix, pp. 287–88.

11. *A Personal Record,* p. 44.

12. Tadeusz Bobrowski's *Document,* quoted by Jabłkowska, p. 33.

13. *A Personal Record,* pp. 35–36.

14. Ibid., pp. 120–21.

15. Letter to J. C. Squire, August 21, 1919. In G. Jean-Aubry, *The Sea Dreamer* (New York, 1957), p. 71.

16. *The Arrow of Gold,* p. 256.

17. *The Sea Dreamer,* p. 73.

18. *The Arrow of Gold,* p. 256.

19. In his *Joseph Conrad: The Three Lives, A Biography* (New York, 1979) Frederick R. Karl does not provide additional information about the duel; nor does he identify the "Rita" of *The Arrow,* merely observing that Baines "fails to see how purely literary the conception of Rita was" (170). Karl finds no documentary evidence supporting Rita's existence, but he points out that there *were* a John Young Mason Key Blunt and a Mrs. Ellen Blunt, whose exploits, however, did not coincide with those narrated in the novel. Similarly, Karl contends that there is no record of the *Tremolino* and the whole sequence of events could be invention on Conrad's part. But, of course, the absence of legal entries does not necessarily mean that the *Tremolino* did not exist under a different name.

C. T. Watts suggests another possible source of the *Tremolino* affair: Conrad's mention of the boat "Tourmaline" which was a gun-smuggling yacht with a cargo of guns and ammunition; his expedition proved disastrous. See letter to Cunninghame Graham of February 4, 1898, in C. T. Watts, ed., *Joseph Conrad's Letters to Cunninghame Graham* (Cambridge, England, 1969), pp. 75–81.

20. *The Arrow of Gold,* p. 351.

21. *Notes on Life and Letters,* pp. 150–51.

22. *A Personal Record,* Author's Note, p. viii. While Conrad protests that he was chosen and adopted by the genius of the English language, it was

otherwise with his seamanship: "I had thought to myself that if I was to be a seaman then it would be a British seaman and no other. It was a matter of *deliberate choice.*" Ibid., p. 119.

23. In an article in *Kraj* [Home] 6 (April 16–28, 1899).

24. "Sir, I hold our beautiful Polish literature in too high esteem, to introduce it to my poor writings. But for the English my abilities are sufficient and secure my daile bread." Joseph Ujejski, *O Konradzie Korzeniowskim* [About Conrad Korzeniowski] (Warsaw, 1936), p. 18.

25. Quoted by Ludwik Krzyżanowski in "Some Polish Documents," *Polish Review* (Winter–Spring 1958):60.

Chapter Two

1. *The Nigger of the "Narcissus,"* Preface, p. xii.
2. *An Outcast of the Islands,* pp. 333–334.
3. Ibid., p. 276, also p. 275.
4. *The Nigger,* p. xii.
5. *Notes on Life and Letters,* "Well Done," p. 185.
6. Ibid., pp. 188–89.
7. Ibid., p. 185.
8. *The Sisters* has no literary value but it offers an interesting example of an unsuccessful autobiographical novel—a very minor portrait of an artist without Joyce's psychological insights or linguistic virtuosity. Zdzisław Najder found, however, that in Poland *The Sisters* "was greatly prized. To a large extent this was due to translation, not only because it was a very good one, but primarily because *The Sisters* simply reads better in Polish than in English. The syntax, loose and contrived, becomes natural and even limpid in a word-by-word rendering." Joseph Conrad, *Congo Diary and Other Uncollected Pieces,* Z. Najder, ed. (New York: Doubleday, 1978), p. 41.
9. Thomas Moser, *Joseph Conrad, Achievement and Decline* (Cambridge, Mass., 1957).
10. Bernard C. Meyer, *Joseph Conrad: A Psychoanalytic Biography* (Princeton, 1967), p. 18.
11. Ibid., p. 43.
12. Jeffrey Berman, *Joseph Conrad: Writing as Rescue* (New York, 1977).
13. Meyer, p. 83.
14. Ibid., p. 117. It is ironic that the cinematic adaption of the novel in 1952 (with Trevor Howard as Willems, Robert Morley as Almayer, Wendy Hiller as Mrs. Almayer, and a young Arab girl, Kerima, as Aïssa) focused rather heavily on the "sex appeal" of the tale. The May 1952 issue of *Life*

featured Kerima on its cover page, lifting her skirts while standing in
shallow water and flashing a smile at (presumably) the admiring white man,
Howard (Willems). The caption beneath read: "Kerima. Her marathon kiss
is a movie sensation." Indeed, that prolonged kiss in the film (not much
described anywhere in the novel) does have cannibalistic overtones: the two
lovers are practically eating each other. Aïssa's appetite is apparently more
voracious than Willems's.

15. *Life and Letters,* 1:184. Letter to Edward Noble.

16. Karl, p. 349.

17. *Tales of Unrest,* Author's Note. p. ix. A half-hour cinematic adaptation of "An Outpost of Progress" is currently sponsored by the American
Film Institute's Conservatory Program, to be released in 1981or 1982; the
film is directed by Dorian Walker and produced by Kathleen Cromley.

18. Jocelyn Baines, *Joseph Conrad* (New York, 1960), p. 178.

19. *Life and Letters,* 1:202; letter dated March 14, 1897.

20. See my "Shakespearean and Polish Tonalities in Conrad's 'Lagoon,'"
Conradiana 8:2 (1976):127–36; also my *Conrad and Shakespeare and Other
Essays* (New York, 1976).

21. *The Rescue,* pp. 444–45. Further examples illustrating Conrad's
emphasis on the dreamlike aspect of reality are on pp. 217, 218, 339, 431.

22. Zdzisław Najder, *Conrad's Polish Background: Letters to and from Polish
Friends* (London, 1964), p. 234.

23. Manuscript dated September 24, 1897; letter to Edward Garnett,
same day. Quoted in Baines, p. 191.

Chapter Three

1. Robert Kimbrough, ed., *The Nigger of the "Narcissus,"* A Norton
Critical Edition (New York, 1979), pp. 359–60.

2. Guerard, Ibid., p. 228; Vernon Young, "Trial by Water: Joseph
Conrad's *The Nigger of the "Narcissus,"* in John A. Palmer, *Twentieth Century
Interpretations of the Nigger of the "Narcissus"* (Englewood Cliffs, N.J.:
Prentice-Hall, Inc. 1969), p. 31.

3. Ian Watt, "Conrad's Preface to *The Nigger of the Narcissus'"* and
"Conrad's Criticism and *The Nigger of the 'Narcissus'"* in Kimbrough, pp.
151–166 and 239–257.

4. In *Criticism* 10 (1968):54–64; also a chapter in David Goldknopf's
The Life of the Novel (Chicago: University of Chicago Press 1971).

5. Goldknopf, p. 83.

6. Watt, pp. 162–63.

7. Ibid., p. 163.

8. Ibid., p. 165.

9. Ibid., p. 167.

10. Gerald Morgan, "Narcissus Afloat," in Kimbrough, p. 262. Another essay by Morgan, also in Kimbrough, "The Book of the Ship *Narcissus,*" offers a most informative account of the real ship that served as Conrad's model, the real men who served on her and Conrad's departure from fact in his novel.

11. Morgan, "Narcissus Afloat," p. 273.

12. Ibid., p. 275.

Chapter Four

1. Completed in January 1901 and published in London by Heinemann in 1903 in a collection, *Typhoon, and Other Stories.* It also includes "Amy Foster" (1901), "To-Morrow" (1902), and "Falk" (1903).

2. "His heart, corrupted by the storm that breeds a craving for peace, rebelled against the tyranny of training and command" (*Typhoon,* 52). Conrad knew well this tyranny of command from his own experience. "MacWhirr," he writes, "is not an acquaintance of a few hours, or a few weeks, or a few months. He is the product of twenty years of life—my own life." Ibid., "Author's Note," p. viii.

3. Letter to Henry S. Canby, April 7, 1924. *Life and Letters,* 2:342.

4. "Amy Foster," *Typhoon, and Other Stories,* p. 132; first published in *Illustrated London News,* December 1901, pp. 14, 21, 28.

5. In "After Bread" Sienkiewicz relates the story of Wawrzon Toporek and his young daughter, Marysia, impoverished Polish peasants who emigrated to America. Toporek dies of fever, and his daughter commits suicide by drowning. Other Polish writers wrote about the problem of emigration, notably two whose work Conrad might have read: Adolf Dygasiński (whose novel *Head Over Heels* tells the sad story of Polish peasants in Brazil) and Maria Konopnicka (her epic poem *Mr. Balcer in Brazil* is also a story of Polish peasants in Brazil). The first canto of Konopnicka's work, titled "At Sea," and part of the second canto, "In the Emigrant Home" (begun in 1891 and completed in 1909), were published before Conrad wrote "Amy Foster" in 1901. Ford Madox Hueffer (Ford) suggested that he gave Conrad the idea for the story, but since the claim was made after Conrad's death, and the topic was so familiar in Polish literature, it is hardly to be taken seriously.

6. Jessie Conrad, *Joseph Conrad as I Knew Him* (London, 1926), p. 35. Also in Jean-Aubry's *The Sea Dreamer* (New York, 1957), p. 218.

7. Guerard, pp. 14, 49.

8. *Life and Letters,* 2:150.

9. The play was suggested by Sidney Colvin. Frederick Karl writes that the one-act *One Day More* was dictated by Conrad to Ford: ". . . forty-three

pages of the manuscript of *One Day More* are in his [Ford's] hand, and there is some reason to believe the play was a collaboration. Ford, indeed, wrote to Pinker of the work as being by 'self & Conrad.'" Karl, p. 559n. However, in his letter to J. B. Pinker, dated 7.8. '79, Conrad writes about a proposal by some obscure lady to dramatize this story: "I hope I am a modest person, but having dramatized *the story itself* and it having been performed in three English towns, in Paris and also (for a week) in Chicago, and Bessie Carvill being absolutely the first conscious woman-creation in the whole body of my work, I can't find enough humility in me to proclaim my belief in it by letting an obscure writer . . . attempt the same thing." Aubry, *Life and Letters,* 2:225.

10. Tony Tanner, "'Gnawed Bones' and 'Artless Tales'—Eating and Narrative in Conrad," in *Joseph Conrad—A Commemoration,* ed. Norman Sherry (London, 1976), pp. 17–37.

11. Karl, p. 513.

12. Joel R. Kehler, "The Centrality of the Narrator in Conrad's 'Falk,'" *Conradiana* 6:1 (1974):19–30.

Chapter Five

1. William Blackwood, Conrad's editor and publisher at the time. The letter is dated December 31, 1898. *Joseph Conrad: Letters to William Blackwood and David Meldrum,* ed. William Blackburn (Durham, N.C., 1958), p. 37. David S. Meldrum was literary advisor at the publishing house of William Blackwood and Sons of Edinburgh. He considered *Youth: A Narrative and Other Stories* (*Heart of Darkness* and "End of the Tether") an outstanding book.

2. "Geography and Some Explorers," *Last Essays* (Garden City, N.Y., 1926), pp. 12, 161.

3. Ibid., p. 16.

4. Ibid., p. 17.

5. "Edward Garnett . . . told me that Conrad once said to him: 'Before the Congo, I was a mere animal,' meaning that for the first fifteen years at sea he had lived almost without being aware of it, carried along by the ardor of his temperament in response to an almost unconscious desire for adventure, without ever thinking the reasons for his or other people's actions. The illnesses he contracted in the Congo, by immobilizing him, cutting down his physical activity, and keeping him shut up for long months, forced him to look into himself, to think over the experiences of which his life was so extraordinarily full—though he was still only thirty-three." Gérard Jean-Aubry, *The Sea Dreamer,* trans. Helen Sebba (Garden City, N.Y., 1957), p. 175.

6. Conrad is fond of this word *unextinguishable* because of its symbolic value, its reference to the imagery of light and dark. Hence, when Marlow speaks to Kurtz's Intended, the room grows darker ". . . and only her forehead, smooth and *white,* remained *illumined* by the *unextinguishable light* of *belief* and *love*" (158). Throughout this scene Conrad describes the light effects. The woman's forehead collects "all the *sad light* of the *cloudy* evening." Her head is surrounded by "an *ashy halo* from which the *dark* eyes looked out. . . ." The room in which the scene is set has three long windows ". . . like three *luminous* and bedraped columns. The gilt legs *shone. . . .* The fall marble fireplace had a cold and monumental *whiteness.* A grand piano . . . with dark gleams on the flat surfaces like a sombre and polished sarcophagus" (p. 156).

7. In a recent article, "Lying as Dying in *Heart of Darkness,*" *PMLA* 95 (May 1980):319–31, Garrett Stewart argues that Kurtz's death is modeled on fictional expectations in order to establish its symbolic darkness, which Marlow ultimately betrays by his lie to the Intended. Thus, Marlow the interpreter of Kurtz's tragic destiny turns into Marlow, the false author of a euphemizing lie.

8. John Hicks, ed., *Massachusetts Review* 18 (Winter 1967), a special number devoted to Afro-American art, scholarship and writing. Another, somewhat more enlightened, approach to Conrad's racial attitudes can be found in *Developing Countries in British Fiction* by D. C. R. A. Goonetilleke (Totowa, N.J.: Rowman and Littlefield, 1977). The author states this about *Heart of Darkness:* "Conrad is not able to render well the entanglements of Western civilization and primitive culture in its deepest reaches; he is not quite equal to the deepest issues which he raises. But what he achieves in the tale is substantial enough to make it a masterpiece whose relevance extends beyond the Belgian Congolese involvements at a particular period in history of today's imperial entanglements and cross-cultural problems." Quoted by Jeffrey Berman in his review of the book in *Conradiana* 10:2 (1978):187.

The universal appeal of this novella is attested to by the recent publication (among many new editions of the text and critical studies) of the following: a reissue of the Swahili version, *Kiini cha Giza* (Dar es Salaam: The Tanzania Publishing House, 1975), translated by W. T. Kisanji; a bilingual Italian-English edition (*Heart of Darkness*) *Cuore di Tenebre* (Milano: Mursia, 1978), ed. and trans. by Ugo Mursia, with the contribution of Renato Prinzhofer. It includes *The Congo Diary,* a collection of critical essays and bibliographies; a Hebrew version, *Lev Ha'm'afliya,* 2nd ed. (Tel Aviv: Sifriyat Poalim, 1978), trans. by M. Avi-Shaul.

9. For example, the two editorials in the *New York Times* (November 21 and 26, 1978); the *Time* essay "The Lure of Doomsday" (December 4, 1978). To wit: "The Jonestown story, like some Joseph Conrad drama of fanaticism

and moral emptiness, has gone directly into popular myth," *Time* (December 4, 1978). "But 'this' will eventually mean the bush, which always creeps back, perhaps to cover up the blood. The 'Heart of Darkness' isn't so much Africa as it is history." John Leonard's review of V. S. Naipaul's *A Bend in the River (New York Times,* May 14, 1979).

10. "Marlow's Descent into Hell," *Nineteenth-Century Fiction* 9 (March 1955): 280–92.

11. "A Further Comment on 'Heart of Darkness,' " *Modern Fiction Studies* 3 (Winter 1957–59):358–60.

12. Paul Wiley, *Conrad's Measure of Man* (Madison, Wis., 1954).

13. Zdzisław Nadjer, *ed., Joseph Conrad. Congo Diary and Other Uncollected Pieces* (Garden City, N.Y.: Doubleday & Co., 1978), p. 6

14. Cedric Watts, *Conrad's "Heart of Darkness": A Critical and Contextual Discussion* (Milan, Italy: Mursia, 1977).

15. Juliet McLauchlan, Review of Watt's Conrad's *Heart of Darkness* in *Joseph Conrad Today* 4 (April 1979):116.

16. See Norman Sherry, *Conrad's Eastern World* (Cambridge, England, 1966), Chapter 8, pp. 173–94.

17. Ludwik Krzyżanowski, "Joseph Conrad's 'Prince Roman: Fact and Fiction,' " *Joseph Conrad: Centennial Essays,* ed. Ludwik Krzyżanowski (New York, 1960), pp. 27–72.

Professor Krzyżanowski points out some direct borrowings from Mickiewicz's *Pan Tadeusz.* Jessie Conrad suggests in *Joseph Conrad as I Knew Him* (New York, 1926), pp. 138–39, that originally Conrad might have wanted to use the material for the story as a continuation of *A Personal Record.* The story appeared in *Oxford and Cambridge Review* (October 1911); it was then included in the posthumously published *Tales of Hearsay* (London: T. Fisher Unwin 1925). The quotations from "Prince Roman" in this chapter come from this edition.

Chapter Six

1. These notes for the story were jotted down in a partly filled family album which belonged to Conrad's grandmother, Teofila Bobrowska, and which contained popular Polish poems of the early 19th century, some rather patriotic in character. See Alexander Janta, "A Conrad Family Heirloom at Harvard," *Joseph Conrad: Centennial Essays,* ed. L. Krzyżanowski (New York, 1960), pp. 86–109.

2. Norman Sherry, *Conrad's Eastern World* (Cambridge, England, 1966).

3. More on this subject in my "Conrad as Painter," *Conradiana* 10:3 (1978):253–66. The pictorial and dramatic potential of *Lord Jim* was

brought to the screen by Richard Brooks, who wrote and directed the film adaptation of the novel in 1964, released by Columbia Pictures, with Peter O'Toole as Jim. In the program for the film, the director wrote: "Movies—like music, painting . . . are (or ought to be) an arrangement of images. In a film, words are secondary to the *visual* expression of feeling and ideas. . . . Hence, the necessity for translating the profound, intricate prose style of Joseph Conrad's 'Lord Jim' to the more elemental medium of images" (Brook's italics). Although Brooks felt that he was faithful to the mood and intent of Conrad's novel and theme "in the main," the production turned out to be mostly an adventure and action story, with very little of Jim's moral predicament or Marlow's quest and commentary reflected. But the film had some splendid shots of Patusan and the *Patna,* capturing some elements of Conrad's Eastern atmosphere.

4. There is more than a passing familiarity with *Hamlet* in the repeated use of such phrases as "I am hoist with my petard . . ." (G. Jean Aubry, 1, letter to Edward Garnett, dated September 29, 1897); "It is tomorrow already and high time for me to go to bed,—to dream, perchance to sleep" (ibid., letter to R. B. Cunninghame Graham, dated December 6, 1897). After the novel was finished, Conrad referred to it on a note of disparagement, lapsing into Shakespearean idiom: *"The Outcast* is a heap of sand, the *Nigger* a splash of water, *Jim* a lump of clay" (ibid., p. 299). "Yet are these feet, whose strengthless stay is numb / Unable to support this *lump of clay"* (I, *Henry VI,* II, v, 14). A few more illustrations of the Hamletian streak in Conrad: "I myself . . . have been ambitious to make it clear and have failed in that, as Willems fails in his effort *to throw off the trammels* of earth and of heaven" (ibid., p. 181, letter to Edward Garnett, dated September 24, 1895). In a long letter to Garnett (of January 20, 1900) Conrad tells his friend about his Polish heritage and his father's translations from Shakespeare, once more referring to Hamlet: "I have always intended to write something of the kind for Borys, so as to save all this from the abyss a few years longer. And probably he wouldn't care. *What's Hecuba to him or he to Hecuba?"* For more references to *Hamlet,* see my *Conrad and Shakespeare,* pp. 53–69.

5. Gustav Morf, *The Polish Heritage of Joseph Conrad* (London, 1930).

6. Ibid., p. 166.

7. Jim can be related to the Polish Romantic hero who is usually possessed by the ideal of saving his people but who is also a "superb egoist" trusting only his own efforts and heroism, and thinking little of the people themselves. The Romantic hero is a titanic figure who holds himself responsible for the fate of his country, as Jim alone of the crew considers himself responsible for the desertion of the *Patna,* and once again takes the blame for Brown's criminal actions upon himself. Elsewhere, I have written of a certain spiritual and moral atmosphere in Conrad's work, which brings him close to

some Polish masters of literature. See Adam Gillon, *The Eternal Solitary: A Study of Joseph Conrad* (New York, 1964).

8. *A Personal Record,* p. 28.

9. Tadeusz Bobrowski, *Pamiętniki* [Memoirs], 2 vols.' (Lwów, 1900), letter dated 28 October/9 November 1891.

10. Zdzisław Najder, *Conrad's Polish Background* (London, 1964), p. 26.

11. *Life and Letters,* 1:315.

12. Jerry Allen, *The Sea Years of Joseph Conrad* (Garden City, N.Y., 1965).

13. Ibid., p. 32.

14. Frederick Benton Williams (pseudonym of Herbert Elliot Hamblen), *On Many Seas: The Life and Exploits of a Yankee Sailor,* ed. William Stone Booth (1897).

15. *Life and Letters,* 2:296.

16. Ford Madox Ford, *Joseph Conrad, A Personal Reminiscence* (London, 1924), p. 58.

17. E. M. W. Tillyard, *The Epic Strain in the English Novel* (London, 1967), p. 166.

18. Ibid., p. 132.

19. *Life and Letters*, 2:296; March 1, 1923.

20. Ibid., 1:338; October 31, 1904.

21. Tillyard, p. 164.

22. For a more detailed discussion of this problem, see my essay "The Merchant of Esmeralda: Conrad's Archetypal Jew," *Polish Review* 9 (1964).

23. Morf, *The Polish Heritage,* p. 144. Also Morf, *The Polish Shades and Ghosts of Joseph Conrad* (New York, 1976).

24. Tillyard, p. 163.

25. Conrad wrote an essay about Poland's plight: "The Crime of Partition," *Fortnightly Review* 1 (May 19); it appeared also in *Collier's Weekly,* June 14, 1919, and was included in *Notes on Life and Letters,* 1921.

26. Introduction to *Nostromo* (New York: Modern Library, 1951), p. xxxix.

Chapter Seven

1. Conrad uses a similar construction involving Archimedes' lever, which he scorns for he had no use for engines: "Give me the right word and the right accent and I will move the world!" "A Familiar Preface," *A Personal Record* (xiv).

2. Conrad's italics.

3. John Hagan, Jr., in "The Design of Conrad's *The Secret Agent," ELH* 22 (June 1955), speaks of "a series of interviews—not merely 'scenes' in

James's general sense of the term, but of more or less official interviews. . . . There are seventeen interviews."

4. There are two dramatizations of Conrad's *The Secret Agent,* one in four acts, privately printed in 1921, and another in three acts which was produced at the Ambassadors' Theatre on November 2, 1922. The play ran only to November 11 and was not well received by the critics. Though it was closely based on the novel, the sardonic irony of the narrator is missing from it. The play's ending differs from the novel. Having received Verloc's money, Ossipon panics in shock at the discovery of Verloc's corpse and at Winnie's advances. He flees and is arrested. As he is being led to prison, charged with the murder of Verloc, we see the mad Winnie lying on the floor.

Conrad showed some interest in the cinema and has written a film scenario of "Gaspar Ruiz" in collaboration with his agent, Eric Pinker. Alfred Hitchcock's film adaptation of *The Secret Agent* was made in 1936, under the title *Sabotage,* with Oscar Homolka in the role of Verloc and Sylvia Sydney as Winnie. The film differs considerably from the novel. Verloc is the manager of a small movie theater. Winnie is courted by an attractive young detective (John Loder) working for Inspector Heat. The Professor carries his bomb into the movie house and is blown up, destroying all evidence against Winnie, who is then rewarded by the detective's embrace.

5. Guerard, p. 231.

6. Feodor Dostoevsky, *Crime and Punishment,* trans. by David Magarshack (Baltimore: Penguin Books, 1960), p. 433.

7. Ibid., p. 62.

8. For more details of this comparison, see my "The Russian Literary Elements in Joseph Conrad," *Conrad and Shakespeare,* p. 190, and Chapter 6.

9. For a more thorough discussion of this subject, see *Conrad and Shakespeare,* Chapter 2, Part 3, pp. 69–77.

10. A sample of Conrad's anti-Russian sentiments: "Italians are not Russians who (nobody would believe me in 1914) are born rotten." Letter to Sir Sidney Colvin, November 12, 1917. *Life and Letters,* 2:198.

11. Hugh Walpole's Journal, January 23, 1918. Quoted in Frederick R. Karl's "Conrad, Wells, and the Two Voices," *PMLA* 88 (October 1973): 1065.

12. Gerald Morgan, "Conrad's Unfaithful Ship." *Joseph Conrad Today* 3 (July 1978):93.

13. Letter to Sir Algernon Methuen, January 26, 1908. *Life and Letters,* 2:66.

14. Juliet McLauchlan, " 'The Duel' and 'The Duelists'—A Rejoinder," *Joseph Conrad Today* 4 (July 1979); 121, 123. See also Roderick Davis, "New Adaptations of Conrad," ibid. 3 (July 1978):91–92; William V. Costanzo,

" 'The Duellists': Transposing Conrad's Fiction Into Film," ibid. 4 (April 1979):117–18.

15. Baines, p. 340.

16. Frederick R. Karl, *A Reader's Guide to Joseph Conrad* (New York, 1960), pp. 206–207.

17. Douglas A. Hughes, "Conrad's 'Il Conde': 'A Deucedly Queer Story,'" *Conradiana* 7:1 (1975):17–25.

18. Of course, Heyst, too, can be regarded as a latent homosexual. See note 9, Chapter 8.

Chapter Eight

1. Baines, p. 381.

2. The manuscript title of *Chance* was "Explosives," for Conrad originally planned it as a short story, "something like 'Youth'—but not at all like it" (May 8, 1899). "This early beginning of *Chance,* definitely in mind in some version before *The Secret Agent* . . . places the novel well back in the 'Youth' and *Lord Jim* period." Karl, *J.C.: The Three Lives,* p. 581. This explains the distinct emphasis on the narrator's craft, which appeared more important to the author than the subsequent part dealing with Anthony's "Dynamite ship."

3. Camille R. La Bossière, *Joseph Conrad and the Science of Unknowing* (Fredericton, N.B., Canada, 1979), p. 100. Pedro Calderón de la Barca (1600–1681) was a Spanish poet and playwright.

4. Alice Raphael suggests in her book *Goethe the Challenger* (New York: 1932) that *Victory* is the *Faust* of our century. Heyst, Jones, and Lena are, respectively, Faust, Mephistopheles, and Margaret.

5. A close study of the Shakespearean texture of the novel is given in my *Conrad and Shakespeare,* Part 4; pp. 85–122.

6. I believe that *Victory* served as one of the sources of Vladimir Nabokov's *Lolita.* A full treatment of this analogy is given in my paper "Conrad's *Victory* and Nabokov's *Lolita*: Imitations of Imitations," *Conradiana* 12 (January 1980), pp. 51–71. The abstract of this paper appeared in *Joseph Conrad Today* 4 (April 1979):115, in Jeffrey Berman's report, "MLA 1978, Conrad and the Russians."

7. Meyer, p. 275.

8. For other examples of fetishism in *Victory,* see the paper cited in note 6.

9. Jeffrey Meyers, *Homosexuality and Literature* (Montreal: McGill-Queens University Press, 1977), p. 76. Note Davidson's comment at the end of the novel: "He was a *queer* chap. I doubt if he himself knew how *queer* he

was" (408). The subject is discussed at length in Robert R. Hodges's "Deep Fellowship: Homosexuality and Male Bonding in the Life and Fiction of Joseph Conrad," *Journal of Homosexuality* 4 (Summer 1979):379–93.

10. The dramatization of the novel by Basil Mac Donald Hastings, which opened on March 26, 1916, significantly at the Globe Theatre, was fairly successful; like Lena's victory, it was an ironic success for the novelist played a very negligible role in the production which emphasized the purely melodramatic aspects of the novel, leaving out any symbolic or tragic elements.

Chapter Nine

1. A number of critics regard the relationship between the Captain and Leggatt as homosexual. See Bruce Harkness, "The Secret of 'The Secret Sharer' Bared," *College English* 27 (October 1965):55–61. Also J. Meyers and Robert R. Hodges, note 9, Chapter 8 above.

2. See my *Conrad and Shakespeare*, pp. 46–51. "The Secret Sharer" was also adapted for film by Aeneas MacKenzie; it was produced by Huntington Hartford, directed by John Brahm, and first screened in Trans-Lux Theatres in New York City in 1953. The film starred James Mason as the Captain, Michael Pate as "The Swimmer," and Gene Lockhart as Captain Archbold. On the whole, it was a fine performance, capturing both the dramatic moments and the comic aspects, the latter brilliantly done by Lockhart.

3. Sherry, pp. 211, 249.

4. The story's dramatic potential was tested in the 1976 film version, directed by Andrzej Wajda, and produced jointly by Polish Films and Thames Television. In the cinematization the narrator is Conrad himself, played by Marek Kondrat, and the scenario is padded with documentary materials pertaining to Conrad's Polish background—thus significantly altering the story's universality. Although the film captures the supernatural atmosphere of the becalmed ship, and there is some spectacular photography of the ship (the English barkentine *Regina Maris*) and of Bangkok, it fails to convey the moral aspects of the Captain's initiation. Nor does it succeed in intimating the central symbolic descent into darkness and the return to light, or the story's chief metaphor—that of the human heart. See Andrzej Markowski, "'The Shadow-Line' on the Screen," *Joseph Conrad Today* 1 (July 1976); Jean Szczypien, "The ML Program on *The Shadow-Line*," ibid., 4 (January 1979); John Conrad's letter on "J.C. in Academe and 'The Shadow-Line' Film Version," ibid.; Bolesław Sulik, *A Change of Tack: Making the Shadow-Line* (London: British Film Institute, 1976), reviewed in *JCT* 3 (April 1978):86.

5. Baines, p. 29.

Chapter Ten

1. *Life and Letters,* 2:168; January 1915, letter to Lady Wedgwood.
2. Letter to Cunninghame Graham, December 6, 1897. Conrad's italics. ALS, Dartmouth (quoted by Karl, *J. C.: The Three Lives,* p. 560).
3. Joseph Conrad, *Tales of Hearsay.* With a Preface by R. R. Cunninghame Graham (London, 1925).
4. Meyer, p. 243.
5. Letter to Blackwood, dated June 5, 1902. ALS. Karl, p. 534.
6. Guerard, p. 93.
7. Karl, P. 609. Zdzisław Najder feels, however, that "possibly Conrad had more to do with the content of *The Nature of a Crime* than composing only one short passage" because "he found a whole batch of manuscripts and typescripts relating to Edmund Burden (one of the characters), some of these written in his own hand." Z. Nadjer, ed., *Joseph Conrad, Congo Diary and Other Uncollected Pieces* (Garden City, N.Y.: Doubleday & Co., 1978), p. 115.

Chapter Eleven

1. Virginia Woolf, *The Common Reader,* First Series, "How It Strikes a Contemporary" (New York: Harcourt Brace and World 1925), p. 239.
2. Arthur Symons, *Notes on Joseph Conrad* (London: Myers & Co., 1925), p. 29.
3. Ibid., p. 28.
4. *Life and Letters* (Garden City, N.Y., 1927), 1:268.
5. Letter to William Blackwood, June 5, 1902, *Joseph Conrad, Letters to William Blackwood and David S. Meldrum,* ed. William Blackburn (Durham, N.C., 1958), p. 155. Conrad's italics.
6. *Life and Letters,* 2:16.
7. Preface to *The Nigger of the "Narcissus,"* p. xiv.
8. See my "Conrad as Painter," *Conradiana* 10:3 (1978).
9. Preface to *The Nigger of the "Narcissus,"* p. xiii.
10. *Letters from Joseph Conrad, 1895–1924,* ed. with Introduction and Notes by Edward Garnett (Indianapolis: Bobbs-Merrill, 1928); letter of May 2, 1912.
11. "A Note on Mr. Conrad," *Latitudes* (New York: Huebsch, 1924), p. 50. Quoted by D. C. Yelton in *Mimesis and Metaphor,* p. 27.
12. Preface to *The Nigger of the "Narcissus,"* p. xvi.
13. Letter to R. B. Cunninghame Graham, dated August 5, 1897. *Life and Letters,* 1:208.
14. Preface to *The Nigger of the "Narcissus,"* p. xii.
15. Letter to E. L. Noble, *Life and Letters,* 1:184. Letter dated March 18, 1917.

Selected Bibliography

PRIMARY SOURCES

1. Conrad's Works (The dates of publication of short stories in magazines are given in parentheses.)

Almayer's Folly. London: T. Fisher Unwin, 1895.

An Outcast of the Islands. London: T. Fisher Unwin, 1896.

The Children of the Sea: A Tale of the Forecastle. New York: Dodd, Mead & Co., 1897. (Subsequently published under the title *The Nigger of the "Narcissus": A Tale of the Sea.* London: W. Heinemann, 1898.)

Tales of Unrest. ("The Idiots," 1896; "Karain," 1897; "The Lagoon," 1897; "An Outpost of Progress," 1897; "The Return," 1898.) London: T. Fisher Unwin, 1898.

Lord Jim, a Tale. Edinburgh;London: W. Blackwood & Sons, 1900.

The Inheritors, an Extravagant Story, with Ford Madox Hueffer (Ford). New York: McLure, Phillips & Co., 1901.

Youth: A Narrative and Two Other Stories. ("Youth," 1898; *Heart of Darkness,* 1899; "The End of the Tether," 1902.) Edinburgh-London: W. Blackwood & Sons, 1902.

Typhoon. New York: G. P. Putnam's Sons, 1902.

Typhoon, and Other Stories. ("Amy Foster," 1901; "Typhoon," 1902; "To-Morrow," 1902; "Falk," 1903.) London: W. Heinemann, 1903.

Romance: A Novel, with Ford Madox Heuffer (Ford). London: Smith, Elder & Co., 1903.

Nostromo. A Tale of the Seabord. London: Harper & Brothers, 1904.

The Mirror of the Sea, Memories and Impressions. London: Methuen & Co., 1906.

The Secret Agent: A Simple Tale. London: Methuen & Co., 1907.

A Set of Six. ("An Anarchist," 1906; "The Brute," 1906; "Gaspar Ruiz," 1906; "The Informer," 1906; "The Duel," 1908; "Il Conde," 1908.) London: Methuen & Co., 1908.

Under Western Eyes, A Novel. London: Methuen & Co., 1911.

A Personal Record. New York: Harper & Brothers, 1912. In England as *Some Reminiscences.* London: Eveleigh Nash, 1912.

'Twixt Land and Sea, Tales. ("The Secret Sharer," 1910; "A Smile of Fortune,"

1911; "Freya of the Seven Isles," 1912.) London: J. M. Dent & Sons, 1912.

Chance: A Tale in Two Parts. London: Methuen & Co., 1913.

One Day More, A Play in One Act. (Adaptation of "To-Morrow," 1913) London: Clement Shorter, 1917; London: John Castle, 1924.

Victory, An Island Tale. Garden City, N.Y.: Doubleday, Page & Co., 1915.

Within the Tides. ("The Partner," 1911; "The Inn of the Two Witches," 1913; "Because of the Dollars," 1914; "The Planter of Malata," 1914.) London: J. M. Dent & Sons, 1915.

The Shadow-Line, A Confession. London: J. M. Dent & Sons, 1917.

The Arrow of Gold, A Story Between Two Notes. Garden City, N.Y.: Doubleday, Page & Co., 1919.

The Rescue: A Romance of the Shallows. Garden City, N.Y.: Doubleday, Page & Co., 1920.

Notes on Life and Letters. London: J. M. Dent & Sons, 1921.

The Secret Agent, A Drama in Four Acts. (Adaptation of the novel.) Canterbury: H. J. Goulden, 1921.

The Rover. Garden City, N.Y.: Doubleday, Page & Co., 1923.

Laughing Anne, A Play. (Adaptation of "Because of the Dollars.") London: The Morland Press, 1923.

The Nature of a Crime, with Ford Madox Hueffer (Ford); written in 1906–1908. London: Duckworth & Co., 1924.

Suspense, A Napoleonic Novel (incomplete). Garden City, N.Y.: Doubleday, Page & Co., 1925.

Tales of Hearsay. ("The Black Mate," 1908; "Prince Roman," 1911; "The Tale," 1917; "The Warrior's Soul," 1917.) London: T. Fisher Unwin, 1925.

Last Essays. Garden City, N.Y.: Doubleday, Page & Co., 1926; London: J. M. Dent & Sons, 1926.

The Sisters. (Written in 1896; incomplete.) New York: Crosby Gaige, 1928; Milan, Italy: V. Mursia & Co. (with intro. by F. M. Ford), 1968.

Joseph Conrad's Diary of his Journey up the Valley of the Congo in 1890. London: Strangeways, 1926.

Three Plays—The Secret Agent, Laughing Anne and One Day More. London: Methuen, 1934.

2. Conrad's Letters

JEAN-AUBRY, G. *Joseph Conrad: Life and Letters.* London: W. Heinemann, 1927; Garden City, N.Y.: Doubleday, Page & Co., 1927

Joseph Conrad's Letters to His Wife. London: The Bookman's Journal, 1927.

Letters from Joseph Conrad, 1895 to 1924. Edited by Edward Garnett. Bloomsbury: The Nonesuch Press, 1928; Indianapolis: Bobbs-Merrill, 1928.

Conrad to a Friend, 150 Selected Letters from Joseph Conrad to Richard Curle. Edited by Richard Curle. London: Sampson Low, Marston & Co., 1928; New York: Crosby Gaige (under the title *Letters of J.C. to Richard Curle*), 1928.

Lettres Françaises. Edited by G. Jean-Aubry. Paris: Gallimard, 1919.

Letters of Joseph Conrad to Marguerite Poradowska, 1890–1920. Edited by John A. Gee and Paul J. Sturm. New Haven: Yale University Press, 1940.

Joseph Conrad: Letters to William Blackwood and David S. Meldrum. Edited by William Blackburn. Durham, N.C.: Duke University Press, 1958.

Conrad's Polish Background: Letters to and from Polish Friends. Edited by Zdzisław Najder. London: Oxford University Press, 1964.

Joseph Conrad and Warrington Dawson: The Record of a Friendship. Edited by Dale B. J. Randall. Durham, N.C.: Duke University Press, 1968.

Joseph Conrad's Letters to Cunninghame Graham. Edited by C. T. Watts. Cambridge, England: Cambridge University Press, 1969.

A complete edition of Conrad's letters is in preparation, to be edited by Frederick R. Karl.

SECONDARY SOURCES

1. Bibliographical Materials

BABB, J. T. "Check List of Additions to *A Conrad Memorial Library*." *Yale University Library Gazette,* 1938.

CHAPPLE, J. A. V. "Conrad." In *The English Novel.* Select Bibliographical Guides. Edited by A. E. Dyson. London: Oxford University Press, 1974.

Conradiana. Edited by David Leon Higdon. (Texas Tech University, Lubbock, Tex. publishes "Conrad Bibliography: A Continuing Checklist.")

EHRSAM, T. G. *A Bibliography of Joseph Conrad.* Metuchen, N.J.: The Scarecrow Press, 1969.

Joseph Conrad Today. Edited by Adam Gillon. (A Newsletter of the Joseph Conrad Society of America, SUNY, New Paltz, N.Y. Publishes bibliographical entries pertaining to Conrad.)

KEATING, G. T. *A Conrad Memorial Library.* Garden City, N.Y.: Double-day, Page & Co., 1929.

LOHF, K. A., and SHEEHY, E. P. *Joseph Conrad at Mid-Century: Editions and Studies, 1895–1955.* Minneapolis: University of Minnesota Press, 1957.

NOVAK, J. *The Joseph Conrad Collection in the Polish Library in London.* London: The Polish Library, 1970.

TEETS, G. and GERBER, H. E. *Joseph Conrad: An Annotated Bibliography of Writings About Him.* De Kalb: Northern Illinois University Press, 1971.

WALKER, W. S. "Joseph Conrad." In *Twentieth-Century Short Story Explication—Interpretations 1900–1975 of Short Fiction since 1800.* Hamden, Conn.: The Shoe String Press; London: Clive Bingley, 1977, pp. 123–43.

WISE, T. J. *A Bibliography of the Writings of J.C., 1895–1921.* London: R. Clay & Sons, 1921; (Dawson of Pall Mall, 1964).

The following concordances to Conrad's works have appeared to date:

BENDER, TODD K., ed. *A Concordance to Conrad's "The Secret Agent."* New York and London: Garland Publishing, 1979.

———. *Concordances to Conrad's "The Shadow-Line" and "Youth."* New York and London: Garland Publishing, 1980.

———. *A Concordance to Conrad's "Heart of Darkness,"* New York and London: Garland Publishing, 1979.

———. *A Concordance to Conrad's "A Set of Six."* New York and London: Garland Publishing, 1981.

GASTON, PAUL L., and BENDER, TODD K., eds. *A Concordance to Conrad's "The Arrow of Gold."* New York and London: Garland Publishing, 1981.

GRIGGUM, SUE M., and BENDER, TODD K., eds. *A Concordance to Conrad's "Almayer's Folly."* New York and London: Garland Publishing, 1978.

JACOBSON, S. C.; DILLIGAN, R. J.; and BENDER, T. K., eds. *A Concordance to J. C.'s Heart of Darkness, A Pilot Study.* Carbondale: Southern Illinois University Press, 1973.

PARINS, JAMES W.; DILLIGAN, ROBERT J.; and BENDER, TODD K., eds. *A Concordance to Conrad's "Lord Jim."* New York and London: Garland Publishing, Inc., 1976.

———. *A Concordance to Conrad's "Victory."* New York and London: Garland Publishing, 1979.

PARIS, JAMES W.; and BENDER, TODD K., eds. *A Concordance to Conrad's "The Nigger of the Narcissus."* New York and London: Garland Publishing, 1981.

These concordances are indispensable to any serious scholar of Conrad's language. So is the Teets and Gerber *Annotated Bibliography,* whose range is quite extensive; it is being updated. The Ehrsam volume is quite valuable, too; it contains many important elements, e.g., translations of Conrad's works, some with reviews, a list of photographs, portraits, caricatures, and motion-picture films based on Conrad's works.

2. Biographies

ALLEN, JERRY. *The Sea Years of Joseph Conrad.* Garden City, N.Y.: Double-day & Co., 1965. Good investigation of Conrad's maritime years marred by some unproven hypotheses.

————. *The Thunder and the Sunshine: A Biography of Joseph Conrad.* New York: G. P. Putnam's Sons, 1958. Flawed, popular account of Conrad's early years, mainly in Marseilles; identifies the Rita of *The Arrow of Gold* as Paula de Somoggy without final evidence.

BAINES, JOCELYN. *Joseph Conrad: A Critical Biography.* London: Weidenfeld & Nicolson, 1960. The best though not the most exhaustive biography until F. Karl's arrived on the scene. Some criticism of the works tend to be too literal, but no student of Conrad can ignore this book.

CONRAD, BORYS. *My Father, Joseph Conrad.* London: Calder & Boyars, 1970; New York: Coward-McCann, 1970. Intimate recollections of Conrad's elder son, at times entertaining, with vivid glimpses of the Conrad residences.

CONRAD, JESSIE. *Joseph Conrad and His Circle.* London: Jarrolds, 1935 New York: Dutton, 1935. Many interesting photographs, anecdotes, and a wife's point of view.

————. *Joseph Conrad As I Knew Him.* London: W. Heinemann, 1926; Garden City, N.Y.: Doubleday, Page & Co., 1926. Intimate views of Conrad as father and husband and troubled artist.

CURLE, RICHARD. *The Last Twelve Years of Joseph Conrad.* London: Sampson Low, Marston & Co., 1928; Garden City, N.Y.: Doubleday, 1928. A friend's admiring portrait; a moving description of Conrad's death.

FORD, F. M. *Joseph Conrad: A Personal Remembrance.* London: Duckworth, 1924; Boston: Little, Brown & Co., 1924. Interesting but not always accurate.

JEAN-AUBRY, GERARD. *Joseph Conrad: Life and Letters.* London: W. Heinemann, 1927. In addition to the letters the two volumes contain many valuable details of Conrad's life and relationships with prominent writers.

————. *Vie de Conrad.* Paris: Gallimard, 1947.

KARL, FREDERICK R. *Joseph Conrad: The Three Lives.* New York: Farrar, Strauss, Giroux, 1979. This 1,000 page biography supersedes all others. Despite its circuitous narrative method, this is a vast collection of biographical data drawing on past research and the perusal of some 4,000 letters. Impressive coverage of the Polish heritage is followed by the painstaking presentation of Conrad's three separate yet interlocked existences. It is the standard life, indispensable to any student of Conrad.

MEYER, BERNARD C. *Joseph Conrad: A Psychoanalytic Biography.* Princeton, N.J.: Princeton University Press, 1967. A fascinating Freudian interpretation of hitherto undiscussed aspects of Conrad's personality, such as mother worship and fetishism; ingenious readings of his fiction, occasionally a bit too farfetched.

MORF, GUSTAV. *The Polish Shades and Ghosts of Joseph Conrad.* New York: Astra Books; distr. Boston: Twayne Publishers, 1976. Important discussion of Conrad's Polish background and Conrad as a "duplex" man, with some keen critical insights.

RETINGER, J. H. *Conrad and His Contemporaries, Souvenirs.* London: Minerva, 1947; New York: Roy, 1947; Miami: The American Institute of Polish Culture, 1981. Good reading, at times of questionable veracity. Beautiful illustrations by Feliks Topolski.

SHERRY, NORMAN. *Conrad and His World.* London: Thames & Hudson, 1972. A delightful, crisp mini-biography with 142 illustrations. Essential for the beginner, refreshing for the scholar.

————. *Conrad's Eastern World.* London: Cambridge University Press, 1966. Excellent investigation of sources of Conrad's early writing years, thoroughly documented.

————. *Conrad's Western World.* London: Cambridge University Press, 1970. Some brilliant discoveries of the sources of Conrad's masterpieces like *Heart of Darkness, Nostromo, The Secret Agent,* and other books.

TENNANT, ROGER. *Joseph Conrad: A Biography.* New York: Atheneum, 1981. A readable, non-scholarly life, largely derived from older biographies and Conrad's fiction; often superficial, e.g., in its skimpy account of the Polish background.

The English translation of a new and important biography by the Polish critic Zdzislaw Najder is in press. It will be published by Rutgers University Press.

3. Critical Studies
Given the vast number of books and articles about Conrad, the following list

must needs be fragmentary, with no pretense of infallibility. The biographical materials cited above can readily supplement it.

A. Collections of General Critical Essays

DARRAS, J., and LOMBARD, F. *L'Epoche Conradienne,* May 1979. Papers (first part) from the 1978 Amiens Joseph Conrad International Conference, in English. Important essays on a variety of topics by well known Conradians.

GILLON, ADAM, and KRZYŻANOWSKI, LUDWIK, eds. *Joseph Conrad: Commemorative Essays.* New York: Astra Books, 1975; distr. Boston: Twayne Publishers. A catholic representation of essays delivered at the International Conference of Conrad Scholars at the University of California in San Diego, dealing with comparative views of Conrad, his text and life.

HIGDON, DAVID LEON, ed. *Conradiana* 10:3 (1978). Papers from the 1977 Second International Conference of Conrad Scholars, Miami University. An interesting collection of essays on biography, Impressionism and Conrad's painterly and philosophical aspects.

KRZYŻANOWSKI, LUDWIK, ed. *Joseph Conrad: Centennial Essays.* New York: The Polish Institute of Arts and Sciences in America, 1960. Important Polish background documents, including corrective bibliographical note by ed. Pioneering essays by leading Polish critics.

MUDRICK, MARVIN. *Conrad: A Collection of Critical Essays.* Englewood Cliffs, N.J.: Prentice-Hall, 1966. Good essays by practiced hands on the major works.

SHERRY, NORMAN, ed. *The Critical Heritage.* London: Routledge and Kegan Paul, 1973. An illuminating collection of reviews by Conrad's contemporaries.

————. *Joseph Conrad: A Commemoration.* London: Macmillan, 1976; New York: Harper & Row, 1977. A valuable anthology of papers from the 1974 International Conference on Conrad, University of Kent, England. Truly international and representative of Conrad's immense range.

STALLMAN, R.W., ed. With an Introduction. *The Art of Joseph Conrad.* East Lansing: Michigan State University Press, 1960. A solid anthology of studies covering biographical and critical aspects of Conrad.

TARNAWSKI, WIT, ed. *Conrad Żywy* [The Living Conrad]. London: Świderski, 1957. Except for John Conrad's reminiscences about his father, a collection of critical essays and poems by émigré writers and a few living in Poland—in Polish; however, an English-language summary is provided.

ZABEL, MORTON DAUWEN. *Craft and Character in Modern Fiction.* New York: The Viking Press, 1957. The four essays on Conrad are valuable.

ZYLA, W. T., and AYCOCK, W. M. *Joseph Conrad: Theory and World Fiction.* Lubbock: Texas Tech University, 1974. An important collection of papers delivered at the Seventh Annual Comparative Literature Symposium, held at the Texas Tech University.

B. Literary Journals Devoted to Conrad's Writings

The leading publication is *Conradiana,* an international journal devoted to all aspects and periods of the life and works of Joseph Conrad, published thrice yearly at Lubbock, Texas Tech University, edited by David Leon Higdon. Founding editor was Edmund A. Bojarski; Donald W. Rude was co-editor for several years. This journal is a mine of important new critical approaches and textual studies; it is indispensable to any student of Conrad. The other journals and newsletters devoted to Conradian studies are:

Conrad News. Polish Conradian Club, Society of Friends of the Polish Maritime Museum, Gdańsk, Poland. Edited by Andrzej Braun, Joanna Konopacka, Stefan Zabierowski and Andrzej Zgorzelski. In English. Irregular publication devoted mostly to good surveys of Polish Conradiana.

Journal of the Joseph Conrad Society, United Kingdom. Edited by John Crompton of the University of Newcastle Upon Tyne; as of vol. V, no. 1, the editor is Alan Heywood Kenny (Kelantan, Main St., Scothern, Lincoln, England).

Joseph Conrad Today. The Newsletter of the Joseph Conrad Society of America. Edited by Adam Gillon, SUNY, New Paltz, N.Y.

L'Epoche Conradienne (mostly in English), edited by François Lombard, the journal of Société Conradienne Française, published by the Départment d' Anglais, U. E. R. des Lettres et Sciences Humaines, University of Limoges, France.

Newsletter of the Joseph Conrad Society (Italy). Edited by Mario Curreli, Instituto di Inglese, Università di Pisa, Italy. In Italian.

Polish Review, New York, edited by Ludwik Krzyżanowski and Krystyna M. Olszer; often publishes one or more articles about Conrad.

C. Collections of Critical Essays and Books about Individual Works

Conrad: Lord Jim. By Tony Tanner. Studies in English Literature, No. 12. David Daiches, General Editor. Great Neck, N.Y.: Barron's Educational Series, 1963. A readable introduction and evaluation for the beginner.

Conrad: Nostromo. By Juliet McLauchlan. London: Edward Arnold, 1969. (Studies in English Literature No. 40.) A most effective introductory study for beginners.

Conrad's "Heart of Darkness": A Critical and Contextual Discussion. By Cedric Watts. Milan, Italy: Mursia International, 1977. An excellent, stimulating book, reviewing early criticism and offering new insights.

Conrad's "Heart of Darkness" and Other Stories. Introduction by B. Harkness, commentary by G. Veidemanis. Boston: Houghton Mifflin, 1971. A useful volume.

Conrad's "Heart of Darkness" and the Critics. Edited by Bruce Harkness. Belmont, Calif.: Wadsworth, 1960. Good textual criticism, broad spectrum of views mark this text and collection.

Heart of Darkness. The Nineteenth Century Novel and Its Legacy, Unit 17, The Open University Press. Prepared by Cicely Havely. Walton Hall: Milton Keynes, 1973. An interesting guide for the beginner.

Heart of Darkness and The Secret Sharer. Edited by F. Walker, New York: Bantam Books, 1969. Suitable for beginners.

Joseph Conrad's "Heart of Darkness"—Backgrounds and Criticisms. Edited by L. F. Dean. Englewood Cliffs, N.J.: Prentice-Hall, 1960. A very slight critical selection with teaching apparatus geared to high school students.

Nostromo (Joseph Conrad). By C. B. Fox. Oxford: Basil Blackwell, 1964. A good introduction for the general reader.

The Secret Agent. A Selection of Critical Essays edited by Ian Watt. London: Macmillan, 1973. Of interest to serious students, this collection offers a critical survey with some critical essays by noted scholars.

The Stone Horse: A Study of the Function of the Minor Characters in Conrad's "Nostromo"; "Patna" and Patusan Perspectives. Both books are by Jan Verleun. Groningen, The Netherlands: Bouma's Boekhuis B.V., 1978 and 1979, respectively. A serious student of *Nostromo* and *Lord Jim* will find much of interest in these volumes.

Twentieth Century Interpretations of The Nigger of the "Narcissus," edited by John A. Palmer. Englewood Cliffs, N.J.: Prentice-Hall, 1969. A significant collection of critical essays.

The following critical editions (text with background materials and critical essays) have been issued by W. W. Norton & Co., New York: *Heart of Darkness* (revised edition), edited by Robert Kimbrough; *Lord Jim,* edited by Thomas C. Moser; *The Nigger of the "Narcissus,"* edited by Robert Kimbrough. Generally good for beginning students.

D. Selected Books about Conrad

BERMAN, JEFFREY. *Joseph Conrad: Writing As Rescue.* New York: Astra
     Books, 1977; Boston: Twayne Publishers, G. K. Hall. An illuminating
     study, analyzing Conrad's complex imagination as it derives from his
     suicide attempt.

BUSZA, ANDRZEJ. *Conrad's Polish Literary Background and Some Illus-
     trations of the Influence of Polish Literature on His Work.* In *Antemurale* 10.
     Rome: Institutum Historicum Polonicum, 1966. A valuable contribu-
     tion to the Polish aspects of Conrad.

CRANKSHAW, EDWARD. *Joseph Conrad: Some Aspects of the Art of the
     Novel.* London: John Lane, 1936. One of the best discussions of Conrad's
     style.

DALESKI, H. M. *Joseph Conrad: The Way of Dispossession.* London: Faber &
     Faber, 1977. An interesting study of variations in Conrad's depictions
     of loss of self.

FLEISHMAN, AVROM. *Conrad's Politics: Community and Anarchy in the
     Fiction of Joseph Conrad.* Baltimore: John Hopkins Press, 1967. Conrad
     is seen in the English tradition of Burke and Mill.

FORD, FORD MADOX. *Joseph Conrad: A Personal Remembrance.* Boston:
     Little, Brown, 1924. Weak on biographical aspects despite close associ-
     ation with Conrad, but revealing in his discussion of fictional technique
     in Conrad.

GILLON, ADAM. *Conrad and Shakespeare and Other Essays.* New York: Astra
     Books, 1976; Boston: Twayne Publishers, G. K. Hall. Shakespearean
     influence on Conrad, comparative approaches, Conrad's Polish aspects
     and his reception in Poland.

————. *The Eternal Solitary: A Study of Joseph Conrad.* New York: Bookman,
     1960; New York and Boston: Twayne, 1966. A discussion of the themes
     of isolation in Conrad's work and life.

GORDAN, JOHN DOZIER. *Joseph Conrad: The Making of a Novelist.*
     Cambridge, Mass.: Harvard University Press, 1941. One of the most
     serious, masterful critical assessments of Conrad's work, with an em-
     phasis on the early novels.

GRAVER, LAWRENCE. *Conrad's Short Fiction.* Berkeley: University of
     California Press, 1969. Conrad presented basically as a short-story
     writer.

GUERARD, ALBERT. *Conrad the Novelist.* Cambridge, Mass.: Harvard
     University Press, 1958. One of the best critical discussions of Conrad's
     major works.

HAY, ELOISE KNAPP. *The Political Novels of Joseph Conrad.* Chicago:
     University of Chicago Press, 1963. A valuable analysis of political
     themes in the major novels of Conrad.

HEWITT, DOUGLAS. *Conrad: A Reassessment.* Cambridge, England: Bowes and Bowes, 1952. An important discussion of Conrad's alleged decline during his last fifteen years.

KARL, FREDERICK R. *A Reader's Guide to Joseph Conrad.* New York: Farrar, Straus & Giroux (Noonday Press), 1960; revised edition, 1969. An important discussion of all Conrad's novels and stories.

LA BOSSIÈRE, CAMILLE R. *Joseph Conrad and the Science of Unknowing.* Fredericton, N. B., Canada: York Press, 1979. Examines the principle of *coincidentia oppositorum* as it underlies Conrad's fiction.

LEAVIS, F. R. *The Great Tradition.* London: Chatto and Windus, 1948. An important study which examines Conrad as a major figure in the tradition of English fiction.

MÉGROZ, R. L. *Joseph Conrad's Mind and Method: A Study of Personality in Art.* London: Faber and Faber, 1931. Conrad's Polish background is shown to have affected his thought and novelistic method.

MORF, GUSTAV. *The Polish Heritage of Joseph Conrad.* London: Sampson, Low, Marston, 1930. One of the first serious studies of Conrad's Polish background and its impact on his work and life.

MOSER, THOMAS. *Joseph Conrad: Achievement and Decline.* Cambridge, Mass.: Harvard University Press, 1957. An important if somewhat controversial study of Conrad's decline after *Under Western Eyes* and of love as Conrad's "uncongenial" subject.

NETTELS, ELSA. *James and Conrad.* Athens: University of Georgia Press, 1977. An excellent and readable comparative study of the personal and literary relationships of the two men.

PALMER, JOHN A. *Joseph Conrad's Fiction: A Study in Literary Growth.* Ithaca, N.Y.: Cornell University Press, 1968. An interesting book; especially important is the chapter, " 'Achievement and Decline:' A Bibliographical Note."

ROSENFIELD, CLAIRE. *Paradise of Snakes: An Archetypal Analysis of Conrad's Political Novels.* Chicago: University of Chicago Press, 1967. Analyses of *Nostromo, The Secret Agent,* and *Under Western Eyes* from the Jungian vantage point.

SYMONS, ARTHUR. *Notes on Joseph Conrad.* London: Myers & Co., 1925. A brief but elegant and often touching commentary on Conrad as a universal artist.

THORBURN, DAVID. *Conrad's Romanticism.* New Haven, Conn.: Yale University Press, 1974. Though it ignores the Polish Romantics, these discussions of Conrad's affinities with nineteenth-century romantic adventure fiction are interesting.

WILEY, PAUL. *Conrad's Measure of Man.* Madison: University of Wisconsin Press, 1954. An influential study of Conrad's achievement.

Index